Researching Online

KT-514-206

www.skills4study.com – the leading study skills website

Palgrave Study Skills

Authoring a PhD
Business Degree Success
Career Skills
Critical Thinking Skills (2nd edn)
Cite them Right (8th edn)
e-Learning Skills (2nd edn)
Effective Communication for
  Arts and Humanities Students
Effective Communication for
  Science and Technology
The Exam Skills Handbook
The Foundations of Research (2nd edn)
The Good Supervisor
Great Ways to Learn Anatomy and
  Physiology
How to Manage your Arts, Humanities and
  Social Science Degree
How to Manage your Distance and
  Open Learning Course
How to Manage your Postgraduate Course
How to Manage your Science and
  Technology Degree
How to Study Foreign Languages
How to Study Linguistics (2nd edn)
How to Use your Reading in your Essays
How to Write Better Essays (2nd edn)
How to Write your Undergraduate
  Dissertation
Information Skills
IT Skills for Successful Study
Making Sense of Statistics
The International Student Handbook
The Mature Student's Guide to Writing (2nd edn)
The Mature Student's Handbook
The Palgrave Student Planner
The Personal Tutor's Handbook
The Postgraduate Research Handbook (2nd edn)

Presentation Skills for Students (2nd edn)
The Principles of Writing in Psychology
Professional Writing (2nd edn)
Researching Online
Research Using IT
Skills for Success (2nd edn)
The Study Abroad Handbook
The Student's Guide to Writing (2nd edn)
The Student Life Handbook
The Study Skills Handbook (3rd edn)
Study Skills for International Postgraduates
Study Skills for Speakers of English as
  a Second Language
Studying Arts and Humanities
Studying the Built Environment
Studying Business at MBA and Masters Level
Studying Economics
Studying History (3rd edn)
Studying Law (3rd edn)
Studying Mathematics and its Applications
Studying Modern Drama (2nd edn)
Studying Physics
Studying Programming
Studying Psychology (2nd edn)
Teaching Study Skills and Supporting Learning
The Undergraduate Research Handbook
The Work-Based Learning Student Handbook
Work Placements – A Survival Guide for Students
Writing for Law
Writing for Nursing and Midwifery Students (2nd edn)
Write it Right
Writing for Engineers (3rd edn)

Pocket Study Skills
Series Editor: Kate Williams

14 Days to Exam Success
Blogs, Wikis, Podcasts and More
Brilliant Writing Tips for Students
Completing Your PhD
Doing Research
Getting Critical
Planning Your Essay

Planning Your PhD
Reading and Making Notes
Referencing and Understanding Plagiarism
Science Study Skills
Success in Groupwork
Time Management
Writing for University

Researching Online

David Dolowitz, Steve Buckler and
Fionnghuala Sweeney

palgrave
macmillan

First published 2008 by
PALGRAVE MACMILLAN

Palgrave Macmillan in the UK is an imprint of Macmillan Publishers Limited, registered in England, company number 785998, of Houndmills, Basingstoke, Hampshire RG21 6XS.

Palgrave Macmillan in the US is a division of St Martin's Press LLC, 175 Fifth Avenue, New York, NY 10010.

Palgrave Macmillan is the global academic imprint of the above companies and has companies and representatives throughout the world.

Palgrave® and Macmillan® are registered trademarks in the United States, the United Kingdom, Europe and other countries.

ISBN-13: 978-1-4039-9722-7
ISBN-10: 1-4039-9722-5

This book is printed on paper suitable for recycling and made from fully managed and sustained forest sources. Logging, pulping and manufacturing processes are expected to conform to the environmental regulations of the country of origin.

A catalogue record for this book is available from the British Library.

A catalog record for this book is available from the Library of Congress.

10   9   8   7   6   5   4
17   16   15   14   13   12   11

Printed in China

To David, Anne, Donald, Deirdre, Malcolm and Dilys

Thank you for your never-ending love and support

Contents

List of Tables

List of Figures

Acknowledgements

While we take full responsibility for the contents of this text, the people who have helped us to produce it are just too numerous to mention them all by name. We would, however, like to thank the team at Palgrave Macmillan whose patience we tried many times and who did such a wonderful production job. We are particularly indebted to the advice and suggestions of the anonymous reviewers – thank you. In addition, we would like to extend our sincere thanks to Suzannah Burywood, without whom we would never have been able to produce this text. Last, but not least, we would like to thank all the students we practised on and drew advice from during the production of this work. Finally, we would like to apologise to anyone we may have forgotten to mention: know your help was not forgotten.

Introduction: Why Bother with this Book?

> As access to information becomes easier and less expensive, the skills and competencies relating to the selection and efficient use of information become more crucial . . . capabilities for selecting relevant and discarding irrelevant information, recognising patterns in information, interpreting and decoding information . . .
>
> (*Oxford English Concise Dictionary*, 1996)

Not long ago, anyone interested in conducting research had to spend long hours in the library searching card catalogues and stacks for relevant material. Those involved in advanced research had to spend just as many hours interviewing and administering questionnaires to people over the phone, by post or face-to-face (FTF) and subsequently transforming this data into a format usable for analysis.

With the advent, growth and increasing penetration of the internet, this is changing. Every day more information is placed on the Web and new technologies constantly extend the internet's potential as a tool for conducting both primary and secondary research.

Given the apparent ease with which information may be accessed, anyone who has ever searched online may wonder why they should bother with a book like this. Surfing the Web is as simple as point-and-click. What could be easier? But, as John Renesch notes, 'If we are on a path of getting nowhere fast, technology is allowing us to get nowhere faster and faster' (http://www.quoteland.com). Nothing could be truer of the **internet**. While the **Web** is a useful finding-tool for day-to-day information, its use in academic research is more complex, requiring greater forethought and structure.

Research involves trying to solve problems by systematically investigating a range of primary and secondary sources in order to establish facts, develop arguments and draw conclusions. Researching online requires the adaptation of traditional research skills and knowledge of a new technological research tool, the internet. It is our hope that by the end of this book we will have provided help with the range of skills necessary to successfully conduct research through the internet.

One of those skills involves the ability critically to appraise the internet and its uses in research and academic environments. As internet usage grows, students increasingly turn to it for information. A growing body of evidence is emerging that suggests that this has not, however, led to an improvement in the intellectual content of coursework. Nor does it appear that the ease with which individuals and groups may be identified and contacted through the internet is helping students develop research methods and methodologies appropriate to the internet age. Rather, technology results in the use of 'lowest common denominator' information and, as we will discuss in Chapter 11, leads to ever-increasing levels of overt and covert plagiarism in essays and coursework.

As a result, some have begun to argue that the internet is causing more harm than good to the undergraduate learning process. Rothenberg (1998) has gone so far as to argue that, as the internet expands and more undergraduates turn to it, students tend to develop less creative arguments, engage in less reflective practices, and undertake less independent thinking. Jaeger (2001) agrees with Rothenberg, noting that electronic resources appear to reduce students' ability to engage in rigorous thinking, to encourage 'academic laziness' and to inhibit the ability to engage actively in the higher forms of analysis that a university education typically fosters (http://www.uu.edu/centers/faculty/articles/article.cfm?ID=17). Even academics who support the use and expansion of online technologies in the enhancement of student learning have begun to argue that without considerable effort by teaching academics, the online environment will lead students to lose their 'ability to see the links between information' and 'to think laterally' (Hewitson, 2001, p. 49).

Despite these valid concerns, with appropriate forethought and critical awareness, the internet can still be an immensely useful resource. While there are drawbacks to the use of the internet, particularly the Web, in the learning process, full **information literacy** is both possible and an increasingly essential skill for students and academic researchers. The purpose of this book is to help you develop this sort of literacy and to master the use of the internet so as to enhance rather than inhibit effective research.

Most people are by now used to employing internet technology to help their studies in particular ways: as a supplement to traditional methods, looking up online library catalogues, finding an article that your reading suggests to you might be useful and so forth. However, here we are concerned with how this technology may be more than an occasional supplement, with how the working online may actually become one of the central aspects of the research process. It can contribute to all stages of that process, including selecting and refining a topic, research design, data collection and analysis, conducting interactive research, right through to the final production and presentation of the work. Online technology can be of significant use in all these aspects of research. Of course, if it is to play this important role, it is vital that a thoughtful approach is taken and full awareness is maintained of how the technology can be used fruitfully, such that it remains the servant and not the master of the research process.

● The Research Process

The **research process** is often depicted as following a linear progression. It begins with an interest in a particular topic, which leads to the development of a specific research question, continues through the research process and culminates in the submission of an essay, report or dissertation. In reality, research rarely progresses in an orderly manner from one clearly defined stage to another, and frequently involves constant circling between and within phases of the process until the work is finally complete. Nevertheless, it is useful to think of the research process as if one stage followed automatically from another. This is because a staged process is a useful (but not prescriptive) model for understanding the different types of tasks and resources that are required effectively to conduct online research.

Step 1: Finding a topic

The first step in the research process begins when you find something interesting enough that you actively decide to learn more about it. This interest can reflect any number of motivations: a desire to investigate a particular aspect of a text you were assigned to read, a specific aspect of a question you were required to answer by your professor, or even an observation made while sitting in class. Now, in addition to these traditional sources of interest, the internet provides an information gateway to a multitude of interesting topics. Often students and other researchers settle on a research topic while surfing the Web, rather than after conducting a directed search using search engines or subject directories.

> **Glossary**
> **Surfing** the Web is a process of going from website to website using hypertext links in an almost blind attempt to find 'something'. **Searching** the Web is when you have a dedicated strategy for finding specific information.

Step 2: Establishing a proposition

No matter how or why you find yourself interested in a particular topic, once you have found an area of interest (even if you are basing this decision on a belief that the topic is the 'least-worst topic' from a list of pre-assigned essay questions), the second stage in your research process should be to develop a series of propositions. These are statements that clarify what you believe the relationship between your topic and the broader context to be. For example, as a student you might be interested in how students get good marks at university, and develop the question: 'How do good students go about getting good marks?' From here you would develop a set of statements based on your own understanding and initial readings around the topic as to how students get good marks. So, you might propose that: 'the way to get better marks is to study more'. You might propose that: 'good students get better marks, not by studying more, but by asking instructors what they are looking for in a good answer'. You might even propose that: 'the reason good students get the marks they do is because they study together'.

The process of moving from a topic to a proposition need not be based on reading – it may be based on an observation. For example, you might observe that students from rich families appear to do better than those from poor families. Using this observation, you might become interested in the topic or question: 'what is the relationship between socioeconomic status and student grades?' From here you might develop the proposition that 'students from higher socioeconomic backgrounds do better because they went to private instead of state schools'. Or you might propose that: 'children raised in economically advantaged families have been given the emotional and intellectual support necessary to do well in school'.

Developing propositions before you actively begin your research is useful because, among other things, it helps motivate your research and provides it with a direction. Basically, the process of developing propositions helps you narrow down the types of literature you will need to consult before finalising your research question and conducting your literature review.

For those who are not familiar with their chosen research topic, the internet offers a whole new way to begin systematically working through the logic underpinning the propositions. This will be clear to anyone who has used a subject catalogue to burrow down through a particular subject area to a specific article or angle on the topic. Based on the nature of the propositions you establish and the questions they lead to, you will find that the types of online resources most appropriate for your project will naturally suggest themselves.

Stage 3: The research question

Stages 1 and 2 of the research process allow you to narrow your general topic to a specific research question or problem to investigate. This question will allow you to focus on the most appropriate online resources. These will enable you to take your research project beyond a 'so-what?' undertaking, towards a project capable of supporting a specific claim based on the findings of your research. For instance, in the above example, based on your propositions (and initial readings about income and educational achievement), you might want to investigate whether an individual's income determines their ability to achieve high academic marks.

TIP When narrowing your topic area to a research question consider some of the following:

- Is your question still too general for the time you can allot to the study?
- Is your question more appropriate for an undergraduate dissertation or a course essay?
- Is your question more complex than it appears?
- Is your question likely to require you to engage in unrealistic or time-consuming activities?
- Will there be hidden costs associated with your research? If so, will you be able to bear the burden of these?
- Will you need special permission to conduct your study – e.g. by an ethics committee?

Adapted from Davies (2007), p. 21.

Another approach is to problematise your proposition. For instance, it might be that, while your initial interest is in the relationship between income and educational achievement, you decide after looking though a subject directory that you want to narrow your focus to an investigation into whether the educational system has been specifically designed to test the skills that children from upper SES (socioeconomic status) households tend to gain, at the expense of those from lower SES households.

Step 4: The literature review

In order to develop realistic propositions and research questions, you should have been reading about your topic since you first became interested in it. Although this initial foray into the literature should have familiarised you with the basics of the topic, once you have formulated your question, and until the day you hand in your completed project, you will need to delve deeply and critically into the literature surrounding your research question. The literature review needs to be directed at ensuring that you understand what has already been said about your topic, the different approaches that have been used, and the key debates involved.

While the need to conduct a literature review once limited your research topic to the resources available through your university, local library or school, the internet has transformed this. Researchers are no longer limited to hard-copy resources available through their home library. Through the 'online resources' subscribed to by your university or provided for free on the internet, it is now possible to access an almost limitless range of academic literature. Not only does online technology allow you to access the holdings of other libraries connected to the internet, it includes an ever-growing range of electronic books, journals, magazines, newspapers and other online material.

> **Hint:** As you proceed with your literature review, use it to help develop a list of key words and phrases that you can use in a search engine to find more information.

In fact, the key issue most researchers now face when conducting their literature review is not a lack of information but rather the problem of deciding what material to include in the review, and what to exclude. And, because of the extent of any literature review undertaken using internet and online resources, it is extremely important to record accurate citation details for every site you may use in the final project (regardless of whether they are used in the final project or not). Not only will this allow you to recover the information at a later date, it will provide a basic working bibliography.

Finally, you should remember that, due to the eclectic, arguably democratic nature of the internet, it is important when conducting your literature review to evaluate critically any sources and resources you locate. This is vital because, broadly speaking, anyone can publish pretty much anything online. There are no guaranteed editorial conventions, peer-review procedures, or any means of ensuring the accuracy or truthfulness of what is placed online. So, while much of the traditional literature – in books, journals, reputable newspapers and magazines – will have gone through an extensive review and vetting process, you will have to gain the skills necessary to judge the quality of online material yourself and to assess whether or not it is likely to have been academically evaluated.

Step 5: The selection of your research method

Once you have analysed enough of the literature associated with your research question to understand what has been said about your problem and how different scholars have collected the data used to reach their conclusions, you can begin to formulate your own data collection needs and analytical methods. You should keep this in mind while conducting your literature review, for one of the primary tasks your review will help you complete is the next step of the research process: deciding on how you approach your research.

> **Note**: If you have the freedom to select your own research question, both the question and methodology that you employ to answer it are going to be directly drawn from your ontological and epistemological positions. As such, it is worth taking time to think about these concepts and how they shape your research.

We will discuss ontological and epistemological positions in more detail later on, as they can play an important part in shaping the methodological basis of your research. In brief, an ontological position refers to a view of what exists and therefore what constitutes an appropriate object for study. An epistemological position refers to a view about the nature and scope of the knowledge we can acquire, and will be related to one's ontological position. Positions vary and research methods are likely to vary with them. For example, if you are disposed to see the world as made up of objective facts and/or processes, the kinds of knowledge claims you are likely to want to make, and the methods you use to go about substantiating them, will differ from those claims and methods adopted by someone who is disposed to see the world and its meaning as dependent upon the concepts and presuppositions that people bring to it. Some reflection on the approach you wish to adopt in your research, and which approach will best answer your question, will help you clarify your method. It is also worth noting that the kind of question you are disposed to set yourself will probably say something about the kind of ontological and epistemological position you hold, even if implicitly. We will return to these issues in Chapter 2.

Step 6: Data collection

Once you have determined the best approach to your study, the next step is to collect the data needed to answer your question. The internet provides a range of different resources for this process. Some of the most important are the tools that have been designed to find and communicate with real people, also known as computer-mediated-communication (CMC). The internet provides numerous new ways for you to find individuals from whom you can collect data or who may participate in your project. This is as true for those interested in conducting observations of online communities as for those who need to administer questionnaires or conduct interviews.

In addition to providing new ways of finding and interacting with individuals from across the globe, the internet also provides you with the ability to locate, access and use a range of databases and resource archives that were once beyond the reach of most researchers. You can use databases and archives to collect written, oral and visual information and, if you are careful, you can use them to help you structure your own interviews and questionnaires.

> **Hint:** Accessing databases and archives tends to require you to delve into the hidden or invisible Web. To do this you will have either to know a site's Web address, or to become familiar with search tools dedicated to finding resources contained in the hidden Web, such as Usenet and listserv sites.

Just as offline surveys and questionnaires can be administered to compile quantitative data, so too can online surveys and questionnaires. Additionally, if you are not in a position to administer your own survey or questionnaire, a range of quality (primary and secondary) quantitative data sources exist in the archives and databases of the invisible Web.

Step 7: Data analysis

Once you have compiled and organised your data into usable formats, you will need to begin analysing it. The key to this process is the use of appropriate analytical techniques to discover what your data reveals about your research question. It will also be at this stage that you discover what new data you might need to collect in order to fill in any holes remaining, and provide a complete and convincing answer your question.

Not long ago, this involved many hours of manual data entry, calculations and contextual analysis. However, with the advent and advance of the internet and information technology (IT) this is becoming less necessary. It is possible to download data directly into database, spreadsheet and statistical packages, which can analyse and display graphical data without any manual counting or time-consuming mathematical calculations. Similarly, a range of software programs is available to help in the analysis of qualitative data.

These expand the range of analytical tests that can be done with qualitative data and the different uses that it can be put to in the attempt to answer your research question.

Step 8: Write-up

The final stage in the research process is when you put pen to paper – or, more accurately, fingers to keyboard. This is where you present claims based on your research data and analysis, and provide final answers to your research question. To do this you must find ways that help structure your answer and that maximise the impact of your answer on your intended audience.

Most projects require a series of set elements. Traditionally for social sciences, the most important sections to include in your write-up are: the introduction; a detailed review of the literature; a methodology section; another section presenting your findings; how you interpret them; and your conclusion. Research in the humanities typically includes an introduction, a substantive discussion of primary sources, incorporating, where relevant, the critical literature, theoretical approaches, your own interpretation, and a conclusion. Of course, these are general templates and you may need to adapt the structure of your work to suit the particular question you are addressing. But in any case, each of the sections of your project should contribute to guiding the reader through it. You need to explain not only why they should be interested in what you have done, but how and why you did it. Once this has been established it is also incumbent on you to demonstrate that your research techniques and the data used were appropriate in addressing the problem. Once you have presented the data and your answers to the research questions, you need to develop a conclusion. This should convince your reader that your answers are both valid and reliable, and that they are significant enough to validate the effort that went into the research.

● Chapter Outlines

We hope this introduction has provided you with a general sense of the themes that are to follow. We will conclude with a brief outline of the remaining chapters to help you navigate your way through this text.

Chapter 1 provides you with a brief review of the internet and its key components. It discusses the difference between the Web and the internet, and the different uses to which researchers can put them. The chapter goes on to explain internet protocols, domain names and URL addresses. It provides information and explanation of the tools of communication and research the internet provides, including E-mail, Telnet, File Transfer Protocols, Discussion Groups, Usesnet Groups, Weblogs, and Chat and **Instant Messaging** (IM). It concludes with a discussion of the viability of the internet as a research tool and the possible uses of its various components.

Chapter 2 looks at key stages in the preparation of a piece of research work, and at ways in which the internet might be an effective and helpful ally in this process. The chapter begins by suggesting the usefulness of the internet in gaining an initial overview of the research topic. It looks at how you might decide on project aims and objectives, then integrate these to an appropriate project design. Some of the methods you may wish to use in conducting your research are discussed, including: the uses of theory; how to explain, evaluate, categorise and describe your material; and some techniques of online data collection. Lastly, the chapter weighs some of the ethical considerations that may arise in the course of conducting your research, and emphasises the importance of methodological reflection.

Chapter 3 builds on the previous discussion of methods by addressing differences between, and respective uses of, qualitative and quantitative methods. It continues with a discussion of online data collection techniques, including documentary searches, surveys, questionnaires, interviews and observations. The chapter emphasises the importance of experimental techniques in the design and conduct of internet research, and provides details of the ways in which experimentation on the internet provides an important opportunity for research innovation.

Chapter 4 looks at how you may use the internet to develop a research strategy. It provides information on the search tools available online, including the range of directories and search engines, and on how to conduct basic and advanced searches. It also deals with the 'people-finding' services provided on the Web, from the freely available to professional searches for which a charge is levied.

Chapter 5 addresses the important but all-too-often overlooked aspect of internet research and communication: the ethical questions that arise when conducting online research. The chapter emphasises the importance of an awareness of ethical issues for the researcher, dealing specifically with two major issues: firstly, how you use and present findings; and secondly, how findings are acquired. It deals with aspects of copyright and provides tips on how to avoid infringement, as well as highlighting the importance of online etiquette, accompanied by a set of rules to help keep you on the straight and narrow.

Chapter 6 addresses the challenge of finding the right sources. We introduce the three kinds of sources: primary, secondary and tertiary, and provide an overview of their uses. This is followed by a discussion of the kinds of online sources available, and the means by which they may be accessed. There is discussion of the uses of information gateways, databases, index, full-text catalogues and subject-specific databases. The next section deals with ways of finding primary sources – particularly archival material – online, and is followed by a discussion of how the researcher may evaluate Websites as sources of data, information and commentary.

Chapters 7 and 8 should be read together. These chapters discuss the use of the internet as a means of generating and accessing primary data, how to decide on the kind of data you need, and how best to acquire it. Together, they provide a guide on how best to use the internet to conduct online interviews and questionnaires, and address some of the key issues you are going to face when attempting to structure your surveys and questions. In conjunction with each other, they also help you understand when and how you might go about using the internet to conduct online observations. In both chapters, information and advice is provided on how to engage in different types of sampling, how you might go about making contact with participants, and the range of techniques that are available to you for conducting these primary data-gathering activities.

Chapter 9 deals with the ways in which you can move your research project forward by transforming raw data into findings and conclusions. It stresses the importance of appropriate analysis and analytical techniques, covering the process from the formatting of the initial data, through discussion of the differences between qualitative and quantitative data analysis, some of the analytical techniques used, to, finally, how to draw inferences from the material you have considered.

Chapter 10 is intended to help you with the final stage of the research project: writing-up. It suggests ways in which you can systematically approach your write-up by staging your approach to the process. It provides suggestions as to how you might deal with structuring your work, and looks at the importance of your introduction and how to go about writing it. It also focuses on paragraphing and ways in which you can improve your writing style through emphasis on clarity and concision. The use of peer review as a way of improving your own work and helping you to learn from and provide oral and written feedback is detailed, as are the uses of graphs and diagrams. Lastly, the chapter provides tips on how to proofread and present your work to best effect.

In Chapter 11 we will discuss the increasing prevalence of plagiarism and how it may be avoided. Both standard plagiarism and the pitfalls and temptations provided by internet plagiarism are addressed. The importance of correct and comprehensive methods of citation and reference is emphasised, with information provided on the correct ways of citing and referencing internet sites.

References and Resources

Ackermann, E. (2006), *Using the World Wide Web for Research*, http://www.webliminal.com/search/search-web03.html, accessed 02/07/2007.

Booth, W., Colomb, G. and Williams, J. (2003), *The Craft of Research*, 2nd edn (Chicago: Chicago University Press). This text offers practical advice on the research process that is expected of most college and university students. It does this through an easily followed staged approach. It starts with issues of how to find a topic and ends with a very good discussion of how to go about writing everything up. This text should help any student involved in writing everything from a simple class essay all the way to a final-year dissertation.

Corbetta, P. (2003), *Social Research* (Thousand Oaks, CA: Sage). This book offers a holistic approach to the research process. It provides its reader with an appreciation of the foundations and methods of the research process and of how the philosophy of science can help shape your decision to undertake either qualitative or quantitative techniques.

Davies, B. (2007), *Doing a Successful Research Project* (Basingstoke: Palgrave Macmillan). This book is an excellent introductory manual to carrying out research. It takes students though the research processes of both qualitative and quantitative research.

Gomm, R. (2003), *Social Research Methodology* (Basingstoke: Palgrave Macmillan). This has been written to help the reader select appropriate research strategies and determine the credibility of others' research. The text itself offers examples and explores the suppositions contained within research methods.

Grix, J. (2004), *The Foundations of Research* (Basingstoke: Palgrave Macmillan). This offers students an accessible introduction to the social research process. It does this by covering the tools, terminology and perspectives that students will need to know in order to successfully complete their research assignment, whether the assignment involves a 500-word essay or a final-year dissertation.

Hewitson, A. (2001), 'Use and Awareness of Electronic Information Services by Academic Staff at Leeds Metropolitan University', *Journal of Librarianship and Information Science*, 34(1): 43–52.

Jaeger, J. (2001), 'Do Online Resources Destroy Student Research Papers?' *The Compass*, http://www.uu.edu/centers/faculty/articles/article.cfm?ID=17, accessed 5/5/2005.

Kumar, R. (1996), *Research Methodology: A Step-by-Step Guide for Beginners* (London: Sage). This text offers a good introduction to the research process, which divides into eight successive stages. What makes this text particularly useful is that each step is followed by a set of user-friendly exercises to help the reader learn about the issues and ideas involved in that particular stage of the research process.

Monash University Library (2004), *Library Online Tutorials: How to Do Research on the Internet*, http://www.lib.monash.edu.au/vl/www/wwwcon.htm, accessed 05/07/2007.

Nicholson, M. (2002), *Conducting Internet Research: Strategies, Tools, Techniques*, http://www.deerford.com/research, accessed 06/07/2007

OECD (1996), *The Knowledge Based Economy* (Paris: OECD).

Quote Land, http://www.quoteland.com, accessed 26/02/2007.

Rothenberg, D. (1998), 'How the Web Destroys Student Research Papers', *Education Digest*, 63: 60.

Sarantakos, S. (2004), *Social Research*, 3rd edn (Basingstoke: Palgrave Macmillan). This is a well-written introduction to research methods, suitable for a range of undergraduate courses. It is compact, orderly and balanced in its discussion of different methods.

1 What is the Internet and What are its Most Useful Research Tools?

All research projects go through similar processes of questioning, gathering and analysing information, and arriving at findings and conclusions. The internet is one of the newest, and perhaps the most powerful, research tool to emerge in recent history, and as such its uses and abuses are manifold. Before addressing the research process and the opportunities that conducting your research online provides, we would like to review the **internet** (Net) and its key components. In doing so, we hope to demonstrate that the Net can be more productively used for research when thought of as a tool comprising not just the **World Wide Web** (WWW) but a range of online resources that may be integrated to the research process in any given study.

What, then, do we think of when we use the terms 'WWW' (Web) and 'internet'? Many people use the two interchangeably, despite the fact that the Web is only a small part of the internet as a whole. Equally, many people believe that the internet has been around since the early days of the computer. This, too, is incorrect. Rather, the embryonic internet did not emerge until the late 1960s with the launch of ARPANET (Advanced Research Projects Agency Network), which succeeded in linking (or networking) a grand total of four host computers (at Stanford, UCLA, UC Santa Barbara and the University of Utah). During the next decade, the number of networked computers grew by another 107, with the first international connection being made in 1973 when the University College London (UK) connected to ARPANET (via a link established in Norway). In fact, even as late as the early 1980s the internet, as we know it today, had not yet come into being. At that time, the internet consisted of little more than a couple of hundred networked computers, with access limited to the academic community, who tended to use it as a means of communication via basic e-mail programs.

What we now consider the internet began to emerge in the mid-1980s. This emergence was the result of two advances in the design and use of computer technology. The first advance involved the development and standardisation of the internet's underlying protocols: the rules governing how computers connect and communicate with each other. This was itself based on the creation of two interlinked protocols. The first is known as the **Internet Protocol** (IP), which is responsible for regulating the 'data packets' sent from one computer to another through phone lines, optical cables and satellites. This protocol works in conjunction with a second or **Transmission Control Protocol** (TCP), which is responsible for managing the flow of information packets along the superhighway, and ensuring that the packets arrive at their destination computers without errors.

Together, these protocols are referred to as the internet **TCP/IP protocol**. With the standardisation of the TCP/IP protocol the number of host computers jumped from a couple of hundred in the early 1980s to over 60,000 by 1988. By 2006 the number of host computers had grown to over 373,284,187. The importance of TCP/IP development is not that it led to the astronomical growth in the size of the internet, but rather that it allows your personal computer (or the one you are using) to access a remote host computer though an **internet service provider** (ISP), and download internet files and pages through an internet Web browser.

For a detailed history of the internet see: *Hobbes' Internet Timeline*, (http://www.zakon.org/robert/internet/timeline), or *A Brief History of the Internet* (http://www.isoc.org/internet-history).

Key Components of the Internet

World Wide Web (WWW)

While the implementation of TCP/IP allowed the internet to increase dramatically in size and ease of use, the development that transformed the internet from a domain used almost exclusively by researchers to the free-for-all we see today was the development by Tim Berners-Lee, a computer programmer at the European Council for Nuclear Research (CERN), of what has become known as the World Wide Web (WWW). Berners-Lee did this by developing a graphic interface which allowed both host and user computers to transmit and receive not only text files but also photos, graphics, sounds and video files. All of this was made possible by Berner's use of the pre-existing **Hypertext Markup Language** (HTML). Equally as important in the development of the WWW was the fact that HTML allowed users to develop embedded **links**. It was this development that led to the current 'point-and-click' navigation system used to navigate from one Web page to the next or from one Web-based file to the next.

In brief, HTML itself is nothing more than a set of codes (or tags) which

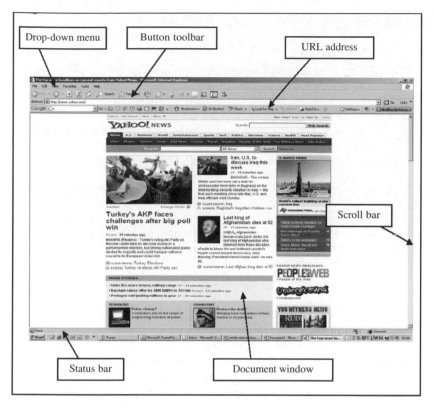

Figure 1.1 Basic features of a browser interface.

Reproduced 2008 by Yahoo! Inc. YAHOO! and the YAHOO! logo © with permission of Yahoo! Inc. are trakemarks of Yahoo! Inc.

tell a Web browser how to display a document. The advantage is that hypertext is universally readable, making it possible to access HTML documents from variety of different **Web browsers** (programs capable of reading and displaying Web pages) operating on a range of different computer platforms (see Figure 1.1). Because of this, it does not matter if you are using a common Web browser, such as Netscape Navigator or Internet Explorer, or a less common browser like Firefox. More importantly, because hypertext can be read across different computer platforms, the Web can be accessed by most linked computers, regardless of whether they are UNIX-based machines, or operating on Macintosh or Windows systems.

Prior to the advent of the TCP/IP protocol and the use of embedded HTML tags, researchers had to be conversant with all of the protocols and

TIP   How to maximise the use of your Web browser

1 If the browser stalls, do not wait forever. Click *stop* and then the
   refresh/reload button.
2 If the browser is slow you might be able to speed it up by turning off
   'image loading': go to 'Settings' in 'Preferences" (internet option).
3 If your browser cannot find an address, try retyping it.
4 To retrace your steps you can use the *history* function – this will allow
   you to view the URL addresses of the Websites you have visited on any
   given day.
5 To find a specific passage within a Web page you can use the *Find*
   function command within the *Edit* drop-down menu.
6 If you are stuck it is worth using the *Related Links* function in the *Tool*
   drop-down menu.
7 If you have the memory capacity (and your internet connection is fast
   enough) you can open more than one browser window. This will allow
   you to study one site while you download another.
8 Find and use browser overlay programs.

programs that make up the underlying framework of the internet (or at least
those they wanted to use).

These protocols included governing programs such as: **E-mail**, **File
Transfer Protocol** (FTP; the protocol governing the transfer of text or
binary files between computers), **Usenet** (a program that has been developed to distribute information between newsgroups) and **Telnet** (which
allows the user to login and utilise a 'foreign' or offsite host computer).
However, with the advent of the underlying framework of the WWW, many
of the formerly independent protocols have become accessible through a
common Web browser. Because of this, it is no longer necessary to be
conversant in all internet protocols. All any user needs to understand are the
basics of their Web browser, which provides a single, user-friendly interface
for finding the material available though different protocols.

Complementing the ease of use that the advent of the Web introduced
into the use of the internet is the fact that each Web page is assigned a
unique location or address. This resting place is known as the page's
Universal Resource Locator address (URL). The address tends to be
displayed as a unique mixture of letters, numbers and symbols that identify
the host computer, directory, folder and file that you have directed your Web
browser to retrieve. The reason for mentioning the URL is that any
researcher (that includes you) who understands the basic make-up of the
URL address can make an educated guess at where the information they are
looking for can be found and go directly to the site.

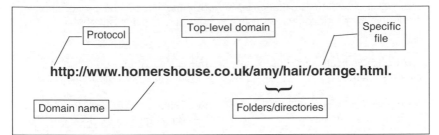

Figure 1.2   The internet address.

Figure 1.2 provides a general example of the core components of a typical URL. The first thing to note about Figure 1.2 is that it is composed of four key components. First, everything appearing before the :// indicates the protocol. The protocol provides your computer with the information it needs to achieve compatibility with the resource you are trying to access. The protocol governing all Web documents is known as the **Hypertext Transfer Protocol** (http), due to its foundation in HTML.

> **Hint:** Most Web browsers will automatically insert http://. This allows you to shorten your direct entry and reduces the likelihood of mistyping the overall address.

While http is the most common protocol you will access through your browser, most are able to access a range of other protocols including: ftp://, **gopher**://, and telnet://. Note that while it is a necessary component of a Web address, the symbol :// serves no purpose other than to separate the protocol from the rest of the address. The second core element of a URL falls immediately following the internet protocol (in Figure 1.2 it is the phrase: www.homershouse.co.uk) where you will find the site's domain name. This is composed of three crucial elements.[1] Reading from right to left, the first component of the domain name (uk) is known as the top-level domain. This simply indicates the country where the server is registered: in this example the United Kingdom. The second element of the domain name (homershouse.co) indicates the name and type of organisation housing the server. In this example the company is called homershouse and is a commercial

---

[1] The domain name can appear as numbers. This provides the same information, which takes the form of the computer housing the information's IP address.

.com (.co) indicates a commercial site (most for-profit companies use this extension)	**.org** indicates a non-profit or non-commercial organisation
.edu (.ac) indicates an educational establishment	**.int** is reserved for organisations established by international treaties
.gov indicates a government agency, institution, organisation	**.net** refers to a network (most of these belong to internet service providers – ISPs)
.mil indicates a site operated by the US military	**.pro** is reserved for accredited professionals and related entities

Table 1.1   Common organisational codes in the top-level domain[2]

organisation. The final element of the domain name (www) indicates the server housing the information. While most Websites operate www addresses, there are also other servers. For example, http://sun3.lib.uci.edu indicates that the information is hosted on a sun3 server, rather than a www server. Similarly, many European Union sites operate on the europa server and can thus be accessed though the homepage, http://europa.eu.int

For anyone interested in Web-based research, the most important element contained in a Web address is its top-level domain. It is this element of the address that contains the information you will need to guess at the actual address of an organisation's homepage – the opening page of a Website, designed to welcome the visitor and providing a map of the site's remaining pages and links. The first element of the Webpage address indicates the type of organisation housing the information. While there are now over 17 types of accepted post-dot (.) organisational codes, for your research proposes we believe the eight listed in Table 1.1 will be the most useful. (For a full listing see Appendix B.)

Once you have come to terms with the first part of the top-level domain, you will need to begin considering its second element. This consists of a unique two-letter country code. While all of the existing codes are listed in Appendix A, some of the codes you are more likely to see within your research can be found in Table 1.2. You might notice that the United States is not listed; this is because as a general rule institutions and organisations

---

[2] For more information on the assignment of internet codes and addresses it is worth visiting the Website: Internet Assigned Numbers Authority, http://www.iana.org/gtld/gtld.htm

Austria	.at	Ireland	.ie
Australia	.au	Italy	.it
Brazil	.br	Mexico	.mx
China	.cn	Russia	.ru
France	.fr	Switzerland	.ch
Germany	.de	United Kingdom	.uk

Table 1.2 Common country codes

operating in the United States do not use the US country code (.us). However, while few organisations operating (or housing their files) on US-based servers use their US country code, individual states within the United States do have a unique state code that their governmental agencies and institutions use, which will help you know that the site you are accessing is being maintained by the state's government (see Appendix C).

Knowing the protocol and the site's domain name should provide you with enough information to make an educated guess at the homepage address of almost any organisation with a Web presence. However, it is important to realise that the symbols following the domain name refer to the actual trail leading to the file you are looking for (each folder is separated by a forward slash / until the final file). While the path for some files is quite complicated, once you realise that what the path indicates is the string of folder/s leading to a file, it is sometimes possible to figure out how to go directly to many detailed sites.[3] In our example, the amy/hair/orange.html is telling the computer to open the file 'amy', then look in the sub-folder called 'hair' and finally open up the file called 'orange.html'.

When trying to guess an address, it is equally important to realise that if you do not enter a specific file name in the address window, the browser will look for an index page for the folder you end the address with (if no folder exists it will go back to the previous folder, and so on). Because of this, it is possible to begin guessing not only at precise file locations, but, if you have been directed to a site, to truncate the address to access a specific folder's index. At a minimum it should allow you to discover the site's

---

[3] Note: most Web addresses end in a forward slash (/). While it is not necessary to include this when entering an address, if you do so it potentially reduces the page's download time.

homepage, which should provide links that help you find the information you are looking for.

E-mail

In addition to the Web, there is a range of resources that can be accessed though a typical Web browser (or directly on the Web through a dedicated software package) that you will find useful in your research. Of these, the most used is electronic mail, or e-mail. This is a program that allows computer users to exchange information and files almost instantaneously. There are three fundamental aspects of e-mail as far as your research is concerned.

> **Hint:** An e-mail address takes a similar form to that presented in Figure 1.2. The user's name appears before the @, the host computer (where the mailbox resides) appears immediately after the @, and before the domain name (indicating the type of institution housing the mailbox). For example, lookatyougo@aol.com is the mailbox for the person lookatyougo whose e-mail resides on AOL's server, which is a for-profit commercial organisation.

First, unlike regular mail, e-mail messages generally arrive within seconds and are placed in an electronic mailbox where they will remain until deleted. Second, e-mail provides the option of attaching electronic files to the message. Any non-ASCII or **Multipurpose Internet Mail Extensions** (MIME) files can be attached to an e-mail message. For instance, if you are interested in implementing a questionnaire, you can create one in Microsoft Word and subsequently attach it to an e-mail message which can be easily opened by the recipient, as long as they have the correct version of Microsoft Word installed on their computer. In fact, not only can sound, graphic and video files be attached and opened by recipients, most non-Web-based e-mail programs now also have the ability to read files written in HTML.

Third, in conjunction with the Web, e-mail provides you with the opportunity to find and contact individuals who were once beyond the reach of most undergraduate and graduate researchers. Not only can e-mail be used to contact your friends and grandparents, it has the potential to expand your research context and environment. Electronic mail can save you research time, it tends to be easy to use, and e-mail can greatly reduce the costs associated with other forms of contact, particularly the travel costs involved in face-to-face interactions, long-distance telephone contacts, or the postage and delay associated with conventional mail.

Telnet

While the Web and e-mail are the elements of the internet familiar to many, there are a range of other, less familiar protocols available to researchers wishing to access information. Of these, Telnet is the primary protocol for accessing host computers outside the Web. Telnet allows you to log into host computers on the internet from your local workstation and use the online databases, catalogues and other programs available on the host computer. The key drawback to the Telnet protocol is that it is a non-graphic interface. It relies on command codes and only displays text. Furthermore, unlike the Web, which uses hypertext links to take you from site to site, accessing a host computer using Telnet requires you to know a specific address. In fact, some host computers require you to connect to a specific port. This is done by typing the port number after the server's address. For example, if you want to access a telnet site requiring you to go to port 100, you would have to type: Telnet somplace.com 100.

One reason the Web is such a good research resource is that most Web browsers are able to access protocols other than http. One of these is Telnet. Because Telnet can be accessed directly from your Web browser by typing Telnet into the protocol, it is easy to use Telnet resources in your research. One point worth noting in relation to the Telnet protocol is that with the growth of the Web and the number of resources being made available to Web browsers, Telnet is slowly becoming obsolete. However, it is still a valuable internet research tool because there are resources that are still available only through Telnet protocol, including some major library catalogues and databases (for more information visit http://www.telnet.org).

File Transfer Protocol (FTP)

While Telnet is gradually being replaced by Web-based information, File Transfer Protocol (FTP) is still one of the key protocols of the internet. As a researcher, it is important to realise that FTP is both a program and the method used to transfer files between different computers. As a researcher, you should become familiar with FTP sites because they allow you to download resources ranging from books, articles, images and sounds, all the way to complete software programs, multimedia presentations and an almost limitless array of datasets. (See Table 1.3 for a guide to the different types of files available through the internet.)

It is also useful to note that a range of programs have been developed to conduct file transfers, even though most of the time you will use the Web to perform transfers. As Figure 1.3 illustrates, until very recently, the most common way to engage in the transfer of files from one computer to another

.aiff	Sound file for Mac
.avi	Video files for Windows
.bmp	bitmap graphics
.cgi	CGI script or common gateway interface
.doc	Microsoft Word file
.dot	Windows Word Pad
.exe	A program file or self-extracting archive file
.gif	Graphic files: most often used for photographs
.hlp	Windows Help file
.html, .htm	Hypertext Markup Language – language of the Web document
.jpg, .jpeg, .jpe	Graphics files
.mid	Music files for creating your own music
.mpeg, .mpg, .mpe, .m1v	Video files – often used for movies and short clips
.mpe, .mp3	The most common Web format for distributing music online
.mov, .qu	Quicktime movie file
.pdf	Portable Document Format – this is a common way of saving and distributing electronic documents coded into Adobe Acrobat hypertext
.ppt	PowerPoint presentation
.ram, .ra	Real Audio sound file – this is a format that allows for real-time music downloads
.rtf	Rich Text Format – word-processed file that can be read by most word-processing programs
.sea	Mac self-extracting file
.sit	Stuffit file – primary compression format for the Mac
.tiff, .tif	Graphics files – generally reserved for large images
.txt, .text	A text or ASCII file which can be opened by most word-processing programs
.uu	UUencoding – this file format allows for the conversion of binary data into text which can subsequently be sent as an e-mail
.wav	Windows sound file format
.wpd	Word Perfect document
.xls	Excel spreadsheet file
.zip, .tar	A compressed file

Table 1.3   Guide to common file formats

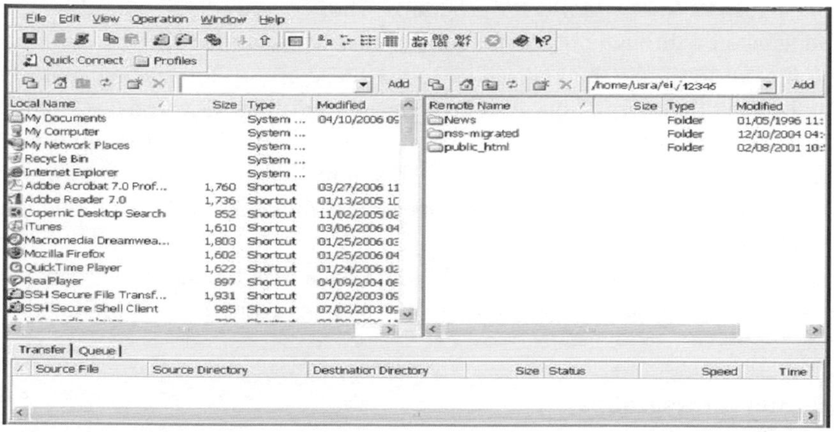

Figure 1.3   A typical FTP window.

was through a dedicated FTP program. For Windows-based computers, the most common of these is the WS_FTP program, while for Mac, Yummy FTP is a widely used program.

> **Hint:** While it is important to know how to utilise an FTP program for research, you should keep in mind that most modern Web browsers can be used as FTP platforms, eliminating the need to purchase and use a dedicated software package.

Listserv (mailing lists)

Knowing how to access a range of file types and databases is an important research skill. This, however, is only one aspect of the research process. You will also need to communicate with others interested in your area of research. This may involve little more than contacting your supervisor though your university's e-mail system, or it may involve communicating with a broader internet population. This is where the internet can truly enhance your research, as it hosts a large number of communities carrying out active e-mail discussions relating to almost every topic under the sun. Probably the most widely known of these are the e-mail discussion groups. These are often referred to as listservs or mailing lists – though in truth listservs are only one type of mailing list, so named due to the name of the underlying software. Rather, a range of e-mail distribution lists exist but are run by lesser-known software programs. Thus, e-mail distribution lists are administered through programs such as Majordomo and Listproc.

In your research, the key will be to use these groups for making contacts and collecting information. At a basic level, to do this all you have to do is subscribe to a list. Once you have done this, messages from other subscribers (or the list's moderator) will automatically be forwarded to your e-mail in-mailbox. Keep in mind that to use the most recent information available through a discussion group, you will have to subscribe and have an active e-mail account, though it is possible to access the archives (recorded history of the group) through a range of resources without having to join the list.

Usenet (newsgroups)

While listserv groups are a good way to follow the most up-to-date discussions on a range of issues, they tend to be a rather one-way process, as all messages are sent to a moderator who then posts them to the e-mail list. A more active way of participating with the online population is through Usenet, often referred to as newsgroups. Usenet comprises a series of virtual bulletin boards encompassing millions of computer users. Usenet groups may be useful for your research not simply because of the information they distribute and contain but because they use the bulletin board technology to exchange information on a vast range of topics.

Hint: In the research process the most important difference between Usenet and discussion groups is that Usenet messages are not posted to your mailbox. To access Usenet messages you must have a news reader program that subscribes to the group and then use it to connect to the computer housing the messages. In short, Usenet requires you to actively access messages on a host computer while discussion lists allow you to be a passive recipient of messages sent directly to your mailbox.

From a research perspective it is important to remember that the thousands of existing newsgroups range in quality from those engaged in high-quality academic debate, to those doing little more than spreading lies, rumours or propaganda. It will be up to you to decide not only on which topic best suits your needs but also on what level of debate you are interested in engaging, for there are a lot of options out there. To help you limit your searches, however, Usenet groups are placed into categories that can

alt.	discussions of alternative topics and subjects
biz.	discussions covering business-related topics
misc.	discussions of topics that do not really fit any other category
news.	announcement relating to newsgroups updates – not current events
sci.	relates to scientific discussions
soc.	social and cultural discussion groups
talk.	opinion-based discussions

Table 1.4   Major newsgroup categories

be deciphered based on their designated call letters. At present, while there are over 17 different categories, chances are you are most likely to be interested in one of the groups listed in Table 1.4.

Wikis: the democratic future?

OK, we know: the first thing to come to your mind is Wikipedia, the online encyclopaedia compiled by you and anyone else who wants to dazzle the world with their knowledge, or lack thereof. However, Wikipedia is not the only, or necessarily the most appropriate **Wiki** for your research needs. This is because the Wiki movement is more than Wikipedia: it is a developing online community whose backbone consists of a compilation of the 'simplest online database that could possibly work', allowing any user of the site to act as an editor to anyone else's text (http://www.wiki.org/wiki.cgi? WhatIsWiki, accessed 12/06/2007). What makes the Wiki movement interesting is not only that the content of a Wiki site can be edited by any number of individuals, but also that a range of Wikis have emerged that are dedicated to very specific subjects, including how to establish your own Wiki (see: Wetpaint   http://www.wetpaint.com   or   WikiMatrix   http://www. wikimatrix.org).

The Wiki movement is clearly a potential subject of interest to researchers investigating contemporary developments in the production of collaborative knowledge. As a reseach tool, however, Wikis, like blogs, have a range of possible disadvantages. Trustworthiness is probably the most critical of the issues you are going to face when using Wikis. Although it is tempting to turn to Wikipedia, for example, the problem is that you have no way of knowing who has written the entry you are reading, or how knowledgeable they are about the area they are writing about. This problem is compounded by the fact that Wikis allow for, and often have, links to outside resources and materials. You have no way of knowing whether these materials have been checked for accuracy, currency or even non-partisanship. Because of this, it will often be difficult for you to know for sure whether what you are reading contains misinformation, or is anything more than a clever form of propaganda.

● Is the Internet a Viable Research Tool?

As you can see, the range of protocol resources available on the internet is vast and growing. As a researcher, what you need to understand is how different online resources relate to the research process. One of the first questions this should bring to mind is whether the internet offers a viable research platform or whether it complicates the existing range of offline resources and techniques. We believe the answer is straightforward: Yes, the internet does provide valuable and powerful research tools.

> **Glossary**
> **Research** is the process of systematically gathering information in an attempt to answer a specific question in order to solve a problem. **Internet research** is the systematic use of online resources to answer a specific question in order to solve a problem that is amenable to investigation via internet protocols and resources.

However, if you lack the requisite online skills, you are likely to become frustrated and confused when trying to integrate online research tools into the traditional research process. That said, the information we provide in this text is intended to act as a guide, rather than an instruction manual to be followed to the letter. If you follow that guide, however, you should be able to find your way through the challenge of internet research.

Exercise 1: Advanced browser features

Once you have familiarised yourself with the basic features of your preferred browser and search engines, access and examine the advanced search features offered by your browser and each of the engines. Based on these explorations, compare and contrast your preferred engines (e.g., how are returns ordered, how many ways can you search, what are the key advanced features that you can use in your browser, etc.). Once you have discussed these issues, reconsider which engine you intend to use as your primary engine and explain why you intend to use it.

Exercise 2: Listservs – why use them?

Develop a list of organisations with Websites that deal with your subject area, both by using your chosen search engine and by 'guessing' URLs. Check which of these run associated listservs, and sign up to one or two that you think may be relevant to you. Write down why you have chosen these listservs, and how you intend to use them. How useful do you find these listservs?

Exercise 3: Wikipedia – what is it good for?

We all know what Wikipeda is but how many of us know how good it is? Let's find out! Go to Wikipedia and find three entries associated with your topic. Provide a brief summary of each entry. Next, go to a traditional research resource (basic textbook, journal article, bound encyclopaedia, etc.) and find the same or similar information. Based on the information contained in these more traditional sources of information, critically assess your Wikipedia information for accuracy, reliability and relevance.

Now, choose a topic in your area for which there is no Wikipedia entry, and write that entry up, using whatever resources are necessary. When you have finished, consider the quality of your entry. How much do you really know about this topic? Did you learn more about the topic researching it than you might have by reading what you have written? What sources did you use? Do you think your entry could be legitimately quoted by another researcher on the same topic?

● References and Resources

'A Brief History of the Internet', http://www.isoc.org/internet-history, accessed 10/09/2006.

Basch, R. and Bates, M. (2000), *Researching Online for Dummies*, 2nd edn (New York: IDG Books). This book provides a good introductory guide for conducting effective online searches. It does this by pulling together into a single source much of the existing wisdom about searching while offering a range of sources that might be of use to a range of different research areas.

Europa, http://europa.eu.int, accessed 24/02/2007.

Google Blog Search, http://www.google.co.uk/blogsearch?hl=en, 24/02/2007.

Google Groups, http://groups.google.com, 24/02/2007.

Hobbes' Internet Timeline, http://www.zakon.org/robert/internet/timeline, accessed 01/09/2005.

http://sun3.lib.uci.edu, accessed 4/05/2005.

Internet Assigned Numbers Authority, http://www.iana.org/gtld/gtld.htm, 24/02/2007.

Renesch, J., http://www.quoteland.com, accessed 16/10/2005.

Research, WordNet 1.7.1. Princeton University, 2001. *Answers.com* 5/08/2006. http://www.answers.com/topic/research-1

Stone, B. (2004), *Who Let the Blogs Out?* (New York: St Martins Griffin). This text helps the reader understand and follow the rise and use of online blogging. In doing this it also provides a fairly simple and accessible guide for individuals in starting their own blog.

Technorati: Who's saying what right now, http://www.technorati.com, 15/09/2006.

Telent, http://www.telnet.org, 24/02/2007.

Wing, K., Whitehead, P. and Maran, R. (1999), *Teach Yourself the Internet and the World Wide Web Visually*, 2nd edn (New York: IDG Books). For individuals who respond to graphical data better than written text, this book will be a wonderful additions. This is because not only does the text provide a fairly simple, yet concise, guide to using the internet, but it does this through high-quality step-by-step drawings.

2 Topic Development

● **Doing Research on the Web**

Any piece of research work that you produce, from a short essay, to a lengthy project, to a 15,000-word dissertation, will benefit from some initial thought and planning. Whilst it is easy to feel that until the words start appearing on the page you are not making any progress, in fact, thinking through the project at the outset will almost always prevent you wasting time and becoming frustrated later on. This chapter looks at some key elements in the effective preparation for a piece of research work, and at ways in which the internet can help you in this preliminary stage of the overall research process.

The first and most obvious planning task is to decide upon the area that you are going to research. Of course in many cases, this will have been decided for you by the set essay questions or predetermined research topics given to you as part of the assessment for a course or module. Where you have greater freedom to choose, it is advisable to put some thought into suitable areas of potential research. Having to change topic at a later point because you find that your initial proposal was not feasible, or that the topic simply does not interest you, will inevitably increase the time pressures towards the end of the project. This, in turn, may result in your being unable to produce as thorough or polished a piece of work as you might have done had you made a more considered choice of topic first time round.

It is always useful to reflect beforehand on the areas and themes, within the limits of relevance set by the remit of your course, that are likely to stimulate you intellectually. You may also have to live with the topic for some time, so consider how long it is likely to retain your interest. And, of course, as well as being interesting, the topic you choose needs to be feasible. You need to be sure, for example, that there is enough accessible source material to provide a sound basis for your research. If you find that there is a dearth of material relating to the topic you have in mind, perhaps because it concerns events too recent to have been properly addressed, or perhaps because the relevant material is not in the public domain, then you may have to think again.

The internet can be helpful here. It is likely during the early stages of considering a research topic that you will alternate between reflecting on the nature and scope of your project, and actually doing some initial research work, on the Net and through more traditional sources. Checking the feasibility of the topic you have in mind will probably be where you make your first foray into some actual research. Previously, checking feasibility was often a more onerous task, involving sifting through library catalogues, archives, back issues of journals and so forth. Using the internet can save you a lot of time at this stage. Any of the well-known search engines will give you a general idea as to the scope of material available on a given topic, and general searches of this kind can usefully be combined with the employment of more scholarly research tools, such as Google Scholar (http://scholar.google.co.uk/schhp?sourceid=navclient&hl=en-GB) or J-STOR (http://www.jstor.org), which will guide you more specifically towards academic work on the topic.

At this stage, it is important to remember that the Web contains a great deal of useful information, as well as slews of rubbish. Much of the information available, however, is more relevant to certain topics and areas than others. For example, the Web contains a lot more information relating to current affairs and current news than it does to events that took place between the turn of the century and 1993 (when the Web began to be widely used). Therefore, when considering your topic, if the Net is going to form a core tool, *you should consider exactly what it is good for and then maximise its potential within your research project.*

With this in mind, when starting to develop your topic, you will be primarily interested in getting a general overview of the material available. While doing this, it is a good idea to retain information about any sources that look especially useful. Typically this should include a description of the source, and a citation which will enable you to find your way back to it should you need to. In the case of major sources such as archives, databases or journals, you may be best advised to save the Web address on your browser's 'favourites' list, so that you can easily return to the site later. In the case of more specific documents that look as though they will prove relevant, you might consider developing a database in which you can save them (or if you have the resources, to simply print them off and retain them as hard copy). You might not utilise all these sources in the end, but retaining potentially useful material will generally save time and effort later.

Once you have a topic that is interesting and looks feasible, the next step is to focus the project. You may be clear, for example, that you want to research contemporary feminism, or the Victorian novel, or the United

Nations, but a topic left framed in such general terms will not provide you with a good basis for well-organised research and you may be in danger of digging up a large quantity of information without a clear idea as to what to do with it. So a general topic will need to be focused down into a clearly defined project with definite ends in mind. One way of doing this is to think about a title for your project that can be expressed in the form of a question: if you can produce a clearly formulated question that you can set out to answer, then you will be able to focus and direct your research more effectively. For the research topics mentioned above, greater focus can be achieved through formulating questions of the following sort:

- How effectively does contemporary feminism deal with multiculturalism?
- Was the Victorian novel a response to specific social conditions?
- To what extent is the United Nations subject to the influence of the most powerful states?
- To what extent does the United States dominate the lending practices of the International Monetary Fund (IMF)?

There are, of course, many other questions that one could formulate in respect of these broad research areas. Again, here some initial Web searches may help give you ideas as to what more particular themes might be addressed within your chosen research area. A little searching can provide you with a sense of what questions other people have found it important to pursue, and what seem to be the main topical themes and concerns in that area upon which an interesting question might be based.

Looking at the kinds of arguments and debates that have taken place in your research area will also be useful in the process of formulating propositions that can help you home-in on a particular question, and on the particular angle that you wish to take. Some initial investigation might tell you, for example, that some critics contend that the claims of modern feminism do not sit well with multiculturalism and with the need to respect different cultural standpoints on the issue of gender, whilst others would disagree. You might find differing claims being made as to how far cultural products such as novels are always reflections of socioeconomic circumstances and how far, on the other hand, they can be considered as 'autonomous'. And again, you might find contending views being taken concerning the neutrality of the United Nations. Reflection on varying claims of this kind will help you to thematise your research and focus in on the question.

● Project Rationale: Aims and Objectives

> Research planning and architectural planning have much in common. Each requires a conceptualisation of the overall organisation and a detailed plan before work on the project can begin. For successful completion, a building requires plans that are clearly conceived and accurately drawn. A research project should be no less totally visualised and precisely detailed.   (Leedy, 1989, p. 79).

Now that you have your research question, and possibly a hypothesis – an assumption that you will set out to prove or disprove – you are ready to start developing your project design. The purpose of the design, or strategy, is to guide you through the remaining research process. A well-constructed design will ensure you do not get lost during your online journey. The first and most important step in this will be to go back to your research question, problem or hypothesis, and specify the aims and objectives you wish to achieve.

> **TIP** When developing your strategy you should consider and justify: (a) what your research is about; (b) what you are trying to discover; (c) how you intend to discover the answers; and (d) the procedures you will use to collect data.

It is important to remind yourself why you are interested in your question, why someone else should be interested in your answers, and, as will be discussed in more detail in the following chapter, what means exist for collecting the data necessary to finding the answer to your question. In other words, just as most successful trips begin with a map, a good research project requires a good research strategy. And, like a map, the goal of this strategy should be to help you focus your attention on the overall direction your research will go, the obstacles you may encounter when conducting your research, and the best route or method for reaching your desired goal.

> **TIP** Use the internet to observe how others have framed similar research. This will allow you to place your research in context and review how other projects have developed their strategies.

The first step in developing your strategy should be to establish a clear statement of what you are attempting to do and why. By coming to terms with your desired outcomes, not only will you begin to understand the types of methodological issues you will face, you will also begin to understand the types of resources that will be required to assemble the data necessary to achieve your desired outcomes.

As discussed, when examining your objectives you also have to consider the logistics of conducting this research and consider any possible time, financial or other constraints you might face. As we will discuss in the following chapter, this will help you assess which online tools and resources will be most appropriate to your particular study.

Once you have established your initial statement relating to the aims and objectives that are particular to your research question, problem or hypothesis, it is vital that you step back and consider the general goals that are implied. The importance of this is that it forces you to consider the larger issues that you will be interacting with and addressing during your research.

> **Glossary**
> **Hypothesis**: a proposition as to why a particular phenomenon occurs or a statement as to how two or more variables relate one another.

A range of classificatory schemas have been developed to organise the general objectives that research projects can have. One of the better of these has been suggested by Grix, who argues that it is possible to place all research along a continuum ranging from projects interested in simple description of what is occurring or found, to those interested in detailed explanation (2004, pp. 18–19). While Grix's continuum (see Figure 2.1), running from theory to description, provides a good framework for assessing the types of studies that are available, when using the internet as a research platform (going beyond the resources it makes available for conducting a literature review) the range of meta-objectives your question may force you

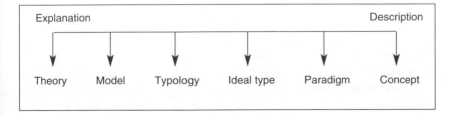

Figure 2.1   Continuum of research objectives.

Source: Adapted from Grix (2004, p. 19).

Theory building and testing	Using a study to test or develop an organised system of accepted knowledge. This system should be capable of being applied to a variety of circumstances and should be able to explain any specific set of the phenomena.
Hypothesis testing	Using a study to test whether a highly specific proposed explanation for a phenomenon is accurate. The test will itself draw data from observations, experiences, or a scientific reason.
Evaluation	Using a study to appraise or value. In policy terms this type of study is generally used to study the outcomes or outputs of a policy or programme.
Categorisation	Using a study to place the object under consideration into a category or categories; to classify.
Description (concept)	A statement which describes, sets forth, or portrays; a graphic or detailed account of a person, thing, scene, etc.

Table 2.1   Types of meta-objectives

to address can be divided up slightly differently. Although it is possible to pursue almost any objective when using the internet in your research process, we believe that you should consider how your project relates to five possible meta-objectives, bearing in mind that your particular project may involve more than one of these (see Table 2.1).

Theory building and testing

As discussed in Chapter 1, no matter what subject discipline you are coming from, your individual epistemology and ontology will underpin your attitudes towards what can be researched, how this shapes what you accept as being an appropriate methodological approach to your research, and the overall goals of your project. In addition to these underpinnings, your research question may direct your project towards theory. Research questions that revolve around theory generally try either to investigate or apply an existing theory to a new situation to elucidate the principles of something, or actively to develop a new theory though the formulation of abstract knowledge.

Although these goals may appear abstract, you should remember that if your research question is directed towards either of these, the internet offers a range of useful tools. For example, you may find that your question directs you towards looking at state theory. In this you may find yourself interested in testing the theory of elitism. Thus your question's goal could be to test whether 'elites' have used the internet to develop networks designed specifically to help embed their position on a global scale.

Not only can the internet be used to examine an existing theory (both by using the tools available online and by studying the internet itself) but the internet offers just as many opportunities to help you develop theory. For instance, your question might be concerned with how individuals communicate. This could lead you to focus on the development of a new theory of dialectical interaction embedded in the special nature of computer-mediated-communication (CMC).

Hypothesis testing

As a researcher you will be looking to find answers to something you (and the wider research community) do not understand. If your research question guides you towards engaging in hypothesis testing, what you are trying to do is discover whether a specific explanation that you devise can account (or partially account) for the circumstances or observation that you describe in the question itself. For example, you might find yourself interested in why students are increasingly relying on plagiarised material in their coursework. Here you might hypothesise that students are increasingly plagiarising not because there is more material online (as is often argued), but because of the ease with which online resources can be cut and pasted into computer word-processing programs. Similarly, you might hypothesise that there has not been an increase in plagiarism, but that, due to the increased use of computer software dedicated to the detection of plagiarism, more students are getting caught. What should be clear from these examples, if we have explained the process clearly enough, is that their fundamental meta-objective is an explanation of real or perceived use of plagiarised material in student coursework.

Evaluation

In addition to explanatory research, there are questions that require you to engage in evaluation. Evaluative questions involve more than explanatory questions because they require you to make a judgement about the object of your research. For example, your question might be concerned with how individuals communicate with each other. You might discover that you are further interested in using the internet in this process. As a result, you narrow your question to an examination of online communications. Your meta-objective might then be a quality evaluation of the online communications occurring in a specific chatroom. Similarly, your research question might involve the use of a specific online database, leading you to become involved in evaluating the quantity of data available in the database, or the ease with which it can be accessed and used in the research process.

The key to understanding evaluative questions is that they involve you in more than simple description or measurement. Rather, you must become actively involved in making judgements and establishing values in relation to the object of your study. We mention this because any question that requires you to become involved in an evaluation has, by its nature, the possibility of affecting the validity and reliability of your results.

Categorisation

When your research objective is the categorisation of a phenomenon, what you are really trying to do is to develop a typology or framework capable of explaining why and how the concepts or events you are researching fit together. To do this you will need to find ways to organise the data or examples you collect into groups or classes that represent similar kinds of data. One way to think about this is to go back over this chapter. In it we have been providing you with ways to think about the possible meta-objectives that can be embedded in your project. However, instead of stating the obvious – that almost anything can be considered a meta-objective – we have been categorising the different types of objectives to help you organise your own understanding of the topic. The value of this is not that it helps develop a theory or even explains why different objectives exist; rather, its value derives from how it helps you think about the possible objectives you may have when engaged in research and the way you might want to represent these objectives.

A more concrete example of how it is possible to develop a range of categories to organise information, rather than explain it or theorise from it, can be seen in Table 2.2. In this table Mason (2002) has attempted to categorise the range of sources that are available to researchers when gathering their data. As you can see, the core idea contained in the table is that six categories of data sources have been developed. There has been no attempt to theorise about these or provide a deeper explanation of how each of them operates. As such, all that can be said about the categories is that they have been developed in an attempt to organise an almost limitless set of resources into a manageable number of main categories, each having a range of sub-categories detailing who or what is involved when utilising the category.

Description

A final type of question you might develop is less concerned with theory building or evaluation than being able to develop quality descriptions of the

People	individuals, groups, collectives
Organisations, institutions and entities	
Texts	published, unpublished, virtual
Settings and environments	material, visual/sensory and virtual
Objects, artefacts, media products	material, visual/sensory and virtual
Events and happenings	material, visual/sensory and virtual
Source: Adapted from Mason (2002, p. 52).	

Table 2.2   Mason's categorisation of quantitative data sources

phenomena under consideration. Research questions that have description as their meta-objective require you to become familiar enough with your selected topic to be able to develop 'a picture of what happened, or of how things are proceeding, or of what a situation or person, or event is (or was) like, or means, or of how things are related to each other' (Punch, 2005, p. 34). Going back to our plagiarism example, it might be that your question is less interested in explaining why it appears that more students are plagiarising, than in describing the ways in which students are plagiarising and how this has changed with the advent and spread of the internet. Similarly, you might be interested in trying to describe where students are plagiarising from. For example, you might find that instead of plagiarising from the open Web students are turning to the hidden Web and its essay databanks.

What we want you to be clear about is that while all of these goals can be seen in isolation, any individual study might involve a combination of two or more of these objectives. In these cases it may be necessary for you to combine different research methods and data collection tools. Similarly, depending on which discipline you are coming from, it is likely that you will be more or less interested in any particular meta-objective. It will only be when you have come to terms with your objectives that you will be able properly to assess the most appropriate method for collecting your data. Regardless of the objectives implied within your research question, as will be discussed in Chapters 3–5, by understanding your goals you will be able to decide which internet resources will be most useful for your project and which of the online research tools available though the internet best suit your information-gathering needs.

● Consideration of Your Project Methods

Once you have a well-formulated question and some initial sense of what themes and arguments are relevant to it, you are in a position to start developing the project. At this point, some reflection is called for on the question of research methods. To a large extent, the research methods that you will find most appropriate will be determined by the question you are seeking to answer, and the discipline in which you are working. Different research methods also reflect deeper theoretical assumptions concerning the kinds of objects that we can study and the kind of knowledge that we can have of them, and it is as well to be aware of these deeper issues. Discussions of research methods often refer to the 'ontological' and 'epistemological' positions underlying them. These terms originally derive from branches of philosophy but have acquired a particular meaning in the context of methodological discussion. An ontological position is taken to refer to a particular view about what exists and therefore about what can form a suitable object of study. Social scientists, for example, are often aghast at the work produced by literary critics, on the grounds that the events, characters, actions or ideas analysed are 'not real'. Equally, historians might comment that the work of many political scientists is without academic substance because it is insufficiently historically informed. An epistemological position, on the other hand, is taken to refer to a view about the nature and scope of the knowledge that we can acquire. We might expect a psychologist, for example, listening to a story being told by a patient, to come to very different conclusions than, say, an historian or anthropologist taking a life history from the same subject. Clearly, however, these respective standpoints also tend to be related to what you consider an appropriate research method. A literary theorist might consider the views and personal history of the author as irrelevant to any discussion of the work, whereas this kind of information could be central to the work of a cultural historian.

As will be discussed in more detail in the following chapter, it is generally accepted here that a divide exists between two academic 'camps'. First, there are those of a positivist disposition, who generally frame the world in terms of objective phenomena, independent of our knowledge of them, that are describable in purely factual terms. The kind of knowledge sought in this context is empirical, based on observation and the testing of hypotheses. This model of research is a 'quantitative' one, seeking factual information and formulating causal hypotheses that might be shown to explain it. The model is akin to the form of research generally associated with the natural sciences or studies that attempt to apply scientific methods to the study of social phenomena. Second, and by contrast, there are those of a more 'interpretive' disposition, who see the world not as objective in the above sense, but rather as made up of phenomena that are, in part at least, 'constructed' by our own understanding. Correspondingly, they see true knowledge not in terms of objective fact but in terms of interpretations made available through the concepts and categories that we deploy in order to make sense of things. This view implies a central place for 'qualitative' research, where the aim is to unearth and examine the meanings attaching to the phenomena under investigation.

By way of example, in the area of social studies, those taking a quantitative approach are likely to look for statistical data concerning forms and patterns of human behaviour and to form empirically testable hypotheses concerning the relation between forms of behaviour and other explanatory factors. By contrast, those adopting a more qualitative approach are likely to seek out the symbolic meanings attaching to forms of behaviour and to see how they are 'read' and understood by participants. They will be more likely to look at documentary sources and interview material than at statistical information and the aim is less to explain than to understand.

Whilst the quantitative and qualitative approaches do tend to correspond most closely with, respectively, a more positivist and a more interpretivist standpoint, they should not be seen as exclusively tied to those particular standpoints. And indeed there are other theoretical standpoints available that are neither thoroughly positivist nor thoroughly interpretivist: 'realists', for example, generally support the claim that there is an objective world to be known which can be subject to causal explanation, but also recognise the implications of the way in which that world is constructed socially. Realists thus tend to find a role for both quantitative and qualitative research (Marsh and Furlong, 2002).

There is no reason to suppose, therefore, that quantitative and qualitative approaches cannot be used in combination and, in the end, the approach taken is best developed in the context of the research question posed. As Read and Marsh (2002, p. 231) put it: 'the quality of any piece of research is most likely to be affected by the appropriateness of the research design and the skill of the researcher; slavish adherence to particular methods carries few rewards'. It is also worth noting that only in mathematics can anything ever be formally 'proved'. In the sciences, axioms and hypotheses explaining phenomena hold only as long as they cannot be disproved, while in the humanities and social sciences, any piece of research, or conclusions based on that research, are open to revision, or derision, by subsequent researchers. What researchers must ensure, however, is that, within the ontological and epistemological limits in which they are working, research methods are rigorously derived and applied, that other scholarship on the topic is incorporated and addressed, and that conclusions are reasonable and upheld by the available evidence.

One advantage of being open to a research agenda that incorporates different methods is that it is likely to increase the opportunities for 'triangulation' in research. Triangulation involves checking one set of research results against another in order to prevent the drawing of false or partial conclusions based on limited results. Triangulation is something that can be undertaken within a particular methodological approach; but a combination of different approaches is likely to further increase your opportunities to ensure the validity of the conclusions drawn. For example, someone researching the relationship between voting behaviour and social class may approach the issue by looking for correlations in the relevant statistical data. The results of this could in turn be looked at in relation to further empirical data concerning, perhaps, governments' economic performance, welfare state policies and so forth. This could help determine whether the original findings were too simplistic. However, one might also want to introduce information of a more qualitative sort, such as interview data concerning prevailing conceptions of democracy and attitudes towards political identity and electoral politics. This might help provide a more sophisticated picture of people's voting behaviour than the earlier research could have produced on its own.

> **Glossary**
> **Triangulation**: the use of multiple data sources or techniques to check the accuracy and reliability of your findings.

There are advantages, then, to keeping an open mind as regards the research methods you may use; and, ultimately, the appropriate methods will ultimately depend upon the research question being addressed and upon the particular angle you decide to take upon it. Once you have decided on these parameters, your methodological strategy, if appropriate, can be incorporated into the next step in the research process.

Basic Data Collection Techniques

Once you have decided upon your method the next step in the project design will be to decide upon the techniques you will use to collect your data. While this is going to be the subject of the following chapter, we have compiled Table 2.3 to provide you with a brief introduction to these techniques. This is because once you have decided upon a research method (or combination of

Method	Overall purpose	Advantages	Challenges
Documentation	Used to collect information that has been published by an individual or organisation	• generates historical data • comprehensive • non-invasive • information exists	• takes time • info may be incomplete • need to be clear about data needs • data restricted to what exists
Survey	Used to get information from people in written or oral form	• can complete anonymously • inexpensive • can administer to many people at once • can generate a lot of data • can draw on existing sample questionnaires and question banks	• might not get carefully thought through feedback • wording and question order can bias responses • is impersonal • in surveys, may need sampling expert • often generates general rather than specific data
Questionnaire	Used to collect data on individual opinions and views	• get range and depth of information • can be flexible in administration and question presentation	• time-consuming • data can be hard to analyse and compare
Interviews	Used to collect data on individual (or group) opinions and views	• get range and depth of information • can develop a working relationship with interviewee • can be flexible in administration and question presentation	• time-consuming • data can be hard to analyse and compare • interviewer can bias responses

Table 2.3 Data collection tools – *continued overleaf*

Method	Overall purpose	Advantages	Challenges
Observation	Used to generate first-hand information about situation under examination	• generates data as interaction occurring • can adapt to events as they occur	• can be difficult to interpret and categorise observation data • act of observation can influence the behaviour of the observed
Experiment	Used when control over variables is necessary to reach a conclusion	• control enhances one's ability to infer cause–effect relationships • reduces problems associated with interpretation	• tends to be limited to small groups • can be expensive/difficult to set up experimental situation on the internet

Table 2.3   *continued*

methods) the next step in building your research design will be to establish the specific techniques you will use to collect your data.

As you can see from Table 2.3, when using the internet to collect data you have a choice of tools, ranging from document access all the way to online experiments. It will be incumbent upon you to decide which technique (or combination of techniques) best suits the data needs generated by your question, ontological beliefs and chosen research method.

⬤ Initial Ethical and Time Considerations

In order to complete your project design, you are going to have to consider both how much time may be involved in conducting your research and what type of ethical issues may emerge from the use of the internet in conducting your research. We will examine this in more detail in Chapter 5, but, for social scientists, it is worth stressing here that the key to this part of your design is a consideration of how you are going to treat your research subjects. This goes beyond considerations of whether you are going to harm them physically, as this is fairly unlikely if you are using the internet. Rather, as we will discuss in Chapter 11, it involves issues such as how you intend to store the data you collect in light of data protection legislation. It also concerns issues of subject confidentiality, particularly as most forms of online communication allow you to identify who is communicating with you and to store this information in ways that might be less than secure. Ethical issues even cover how you treat people. Thus, if you are observing the interactions occurring in a listserv or Usenet group, should you tell the participants or act as a fly on the wall? Moreover, if you are going to inform the group, who do you negotiate access with, and to what extent will this limit your ability to use the data you collect, particularly if you want to use it in ways that go beyond simple description and instead act as an academic judge of the activity or group in question.

Once you have taken all of these questions into account, a final issue worth considering in your project strategy is timing. This involves an evaluation of how long you think the project is going to take and how much time you might be able to devote to any given stage of the project. For example you might make a timeline that looks something like Table 2.4.

Overall your research strategy should include:

- A brief statement setting out your research question, problem or hypothesis.
- A statement of your aims and objectives (including a justification as to why you are conducting the research).

Literature search/reading	Initial (1 week) For literature review (3 weeks) Ongoing as required
Selection of data gathering technique and designing specific questionnaire/interview schedule etc.	2 weeks
Pilot study	1 week
Finalise data collection techniques	1 week
Data collection	4 weeks
Data analysis	2 weeks
Gathering missing information	1 week
Write-up	3 weeks

Table 2.4   Timetable of research process

- An overview of the research design you are going to adopt which should address the specific tools or techniques you are going to use to gather and analyse your data.
- A discussion of any ethical issues that might be involved in your project.
- A detailed timetable of the project and its various stages.

Once you are clear on the time you have at your disposal, have decided on your question aims and research design, and have considered and addressed to any ethical issues you can foresee, then you are ready to embark on the research proper. In this chapter, we hope we have outlined the things that are helpful for you to think about as you embark on your research. Some preliminary reflection and organisation before you begin the research proper can save a lot of time later, as well as contributing to the overall success of your research project. Because some or all of the work you are undertaking is to be done using the internet, consideration of the role the internet is playing and will play in your research is crucial. The following chapters provide a guide to the specific ways in which you can use the internet as part of the research process.

Exercise 1: Developing a research question

Assuming you are engaged in a piece of directed, independent study, write down the general topic area you are interested in. Next, write down a list of things about this topic area that are of specific interest; then generate a question based on each of the areas you identify. Consider the questions one by one. Which is the most clearly focused? Which is the most feasible given the time and resources at your disposal? Which involve ethical issues, and what are those issues? If there is one that interests you more than the others, but which presents problems in the area of resources, feasibility, scope and focus, or ethics, how might you adapt the question so that it better meets your research needs?

Exercise 2: Establishing the resources you will need

Having determined what your research question will be, make a list of the data, resources and other material you may need in order to answer it. Which of these are available online, or how might you make use of the internet in generating the information you need?

Exercise 3: Assessment of the data-gathering techniques in light of your project

Different projects will require you to take advantage of different data-collection techniques. To help you come to terms with this, consider, in light of your specific research area, the advantages and disadvantages of the various data-collection techniques that are discussed in this chapter. Consider the advantages and disadvantages of each of these techniques in light of your specific research assignment (e.g., 500-word essay, term paper, final-year dissertation, etc.).

● References and Resources

Blaikie, N. (2000), *Designing Social Research* (Buckingham: OUP). This book offers students a well-presented scheme for preparing research designs and research proposals. The book is concerned less with how to carry out a research project than it is with its planning and how this links to some of the core methodological issues you are going to face when conducting your project.

Davies, M. (2007), *Doing a Successful Research Project* (Basingstoke: Palgrave Macmillan). This text provides a user-friendly introduction to the entire research process. There is special emphasis on the importance of planning for the successful completion of a research project.

Google Scholar (UK), http://scholar.google.com/schhp?sourceid= navclient&hl=en-GB, accessed 01/07/2006.

Grix, J. (2004), *The Foundations of Research* (Basingstoke: Palgrave Macmillan).

Howard University Library, *Basic Steps in the Research Process*, http:// www.howard.edu/library/Assist/Guides/strategies/process.htm, accessed 06/07/2007.

JSTOR (Journal Storage: Scholarly Journal Archive), http://www.jstor.org, accessed 24/02/2007.

Leedy, P. D. (1989), *Practical Research: Planning and Design*, 5th edn (Basingstoke: Palgrave Macmillan).

Manuel, K. (2005), *The Five Steps of the Research Process*, http://lib.nmsu.edu/instruction/TheFiveStepsoftheResearchProcess.pdf, accessed. 02/07/2007.

Marsh, D. and Furlong, P. (2002), 'A Skin not a Jacket: Ontology and Epistemology in Political Science', in D. Marsh and G. Stoker (eds), *Theory and Methods in Political Science*, 2nd edn (New York: Palgrave Macmillan).

Mason, J. (2002), *Qualitative Researching* (London: Sage).

O'Dochartaigh, N. (2002), *The Internet Research Handbook* (London: Sage). This text provides a detailed guide to the key issues of online research. The key to the use of this text is that it treats the Net as a tool that can be used through the entire research process. This includes advice on how to use the Net to help formulate a basic research question, all the way through to how to use the Web to publish your research online.

Punch, K. (2005), *Introduction to Social Research: Qualitative and Quantitative Approaches*, 2nd edn (London: Sage).

Read, M. and Marsh, D. (2002), 'Combining Qualitative and Quantitative Methods', in D. Marsh and G. Stoker (eds), *Theory and Methods in Political Science*, 2nd edn (New York: Palgrave Macmillan).

Samuels, H. (2004), *Basic Steps in the Research Process*, http://www.crlsresearchguide.org, accessed 07/07/2007.

3 Research Methods

As we touched upon in the previous chapter, once you have established your objectives you will need to consider how you understand the world and thus what you consider to be legitimate answers to the questions you pose. At this point you are going to have to select a research method. This will inform the procedures you will subsequently use to collect and analyse your data. While this is intrinsically connected to your ontological and epistemological positions, at a general level your research will involve either a qualitative approach or a quantitative approach; or, where appropriate, a combination of both.

Chapters 5–7 will provide a detailed discussion of how to use the tools available online for collecting qualitative and quantitative data. Before that, however, we would like to address one of the final steps in the development of your research strategy, which is to reach beyond your objectives and see how they shape the tools most appropriate for conducting your research. Specific objectives, of course, call for specific types of data, and as such will suggest (if not dictate) the most appropriate methods for conducting your research. When considering your technique, it is worth remembering that both quantitative and qualitative techniques will require you to use a range of similar skills and that both are quite capable of producing meaningful results. The key to achieving these results is to realise that while the two approaches are different in their core techniques and the language used to express their results, the one you use will be in part determined by your research question (or the dictates of your individual course and teacher's preferences).

Qualitative Methods

As illustrated in Table 3.1, at the most general level methods tend to be discussed as either qualitative or quantitative in nature. When choosing to adopt one of these methods, you are in essence determining the types of data you will collect, and, as such, the core tools you will need to use when engaging with the internet during your research process. In light of the

Qualitative	Quantitative
Aim is discover the nature or essence of what is under investigation, often with little desire to use the finding to generalise or predict the future.	Aim is to classify, count and statistically analyse what is observed in order to make predictions or generalisations, or test a hypothesis.
Concepts tend to be expressed in terms of words, themes and patterns.	Concepts are converted into variables which are subsequently quantified.
Researcher generally enters the research situation with little more than a rough idea of what they are looking for.	Researcher enters the research situation knowing exactly what they are looking to find (e.g., Did A cause B?).
The details of the project (and its data needs) often develop and change as the project proceeds from stage to stage or as new data is generated.	All aspects of the study and its data needs are designed and understood before data is collected (often after a pilot project has been conducted to finalise any issues with the data collection techniques).
Tends to be concerned with discovering the specific details of a situation. As such they tend to be identified with studies of microissues.	Tends to be concerned with looking at general or large pictures. As such these studies tend to be associated with the study of macroissues.
Data tends to be collected and analysed in the form of words, pictures or objects.	Data is collected and converted into numbers.
Researcher tends to immerse himself or herself in the subject matter.	Researcher tends to remain separated from the subject matter.
Data tends to be collected in 'random', non-representative samples.	Data tends to be collected in non-random, representative samples.
Data tends to contain a great deal of detail but is less open to generalisation.	Data tends to have less detail and can lead to generalisations.
Tends to be described as a more subjective approach to research.	Tends to be discussed as being an objective approach to research.

Table 3.1   Qualitative and quantitative methods

discussion presented in the previous chapter, it can be argued that on a general level, qualitative methods are going to be more acceptable to those of you who believe in the importance of personal accounts and the overall context surrounding your research topic. For it is only though this detailed, holistic approach that you will develop enough of an understanding of your topic to begin formulating an answer to your question. This is because qualitative methods not only encourage the use of personal interpretation (though not an unbalanced account or interpretation of the subject of the study); they are also designed to study the situation from the perspective of that which is being studied. Or, in the words of Walliman, qualitative studies are designed to: 'construe the attitudes, beliefs and motivations within a subject . . . the researcher . . . will attempt to gain an inside view of the phenomenon, getting as close as possible to the subject of the research' (2005, p. 247).

> **Note**: While qualitative studies tend to rely on spoken or written words, numbers can also be used.

Because qualitative methods are designed to help you develop 'deep understandings' of the person, situation or literature being studied, there is a tendency to rely on words (spoken and written) rather than numbers. Similarly, due to the 'personal' nature of qualitative methods and analysis, qualitative studies tend to be conducted on a much smaller scale, and involve far fewer participants, than quantitative studies.

Quantitative Methods

On the other side of the divide are studies and questions that are more open to the use of quantitative methods. Quantitative studies tend to be most interested in questions that are amenable to the gathering of data that can be quantified and measured. Thus, quantitative methods tend to involve large-scale studies, where the researcher attempts to be as 'objective as possible'. They do this by converting data into numbers, which subsequently undergo statistical analysis. As such, many discuss the quantitative approach as most closely following the dictates of the scientific method of enquiry with its systems of control, measurement (the process of turning data into numbers), and use of statistical analysis to interpret the numeric data, so as to provide answers to research questions.

When using online (or offline) quantitative tools and resources, it is imperative to remember that numbers do not grow on trees. Rather, you will either have to rely upon the numbers someone else has produced and placed in an online database, or you will have to collect data through the use of online questionnaires or surveys, then convert the data into numbers yourself. If you go online to find numeric data that you have not compiled yourself for your project, it will be incumbent upon you to consider why any given numeric data was placed online, how the data was collected, what assumptions and methods were used in converting the data into numbers, and even who converted the data into numbers. The answers to these questions are needed if you are going to use secondary numeric data, because while quantitative methods are often portrayed as being objective, there is nothing natural about the structures that we develop and impose upon data when converting it into numeric form. What we are saying here is that there is no guarantee that data presented online in numeric or statistical fashion has not been developed or manipulated for particular or even nefarious purposes (see Huff, 1954).

Regardless of your personal preference, it is vital that you remember the following: 'It is the nature of the research problem that should dictate the appropriate research method . . . There is no intrinsic virtue to either style of method . . . There is a great deal wrong with [both]' (Ackroyd and Hughes, 1992, p. 30). For this reason, it is worth remembering that it is possible that your objectives will call on you to use both quantitative and qualitative methods. One way or the other, you must ensure that you justify your choice when establishing your research strategy, by indicating when each method will be used, how each will contribute to your answer, what gaps exist and how you intend to address them.

● Online Data Collection Techniques

Once you have settled on a research method, your next task is to select the most appropriate tools for the collection of the type of data that will best help you answer your research question. There are an almost limitless number of ways that the internet can be configured and used to collect qualitative and quantitative data, but the main categories of online information-gathering tools that you are likely to use in your own research are represented in Figure 3.1.

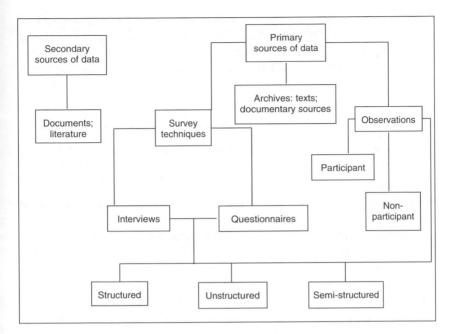

Figure 3.1 Primary techniques used to collect data

Documentation

Almost any project will benefit from the use of the internet if for no other reason than the internet has fundamentally altered the ability of the researcher (that is you) to find primary and secondary documentary material. A document is simply any written, printed, photographed, painted or recorded material that can be used to provide information or evidence. The Web has a massive and ever-increasing store of primary documents, ranging from scanned or digitised versions of historical documents, newspapers, paintings, photographs or literary texts held in digitised archives; to 'listen again' recordings from radio and television; to video clips available on YouTube, and the multimedia content of social networking sites. It is equally an important source of secondary information: commentary, critical studies, critical or popular reception.

Not only can the Web be used to find documentary material to help you narrow your topic into a specific research question, but the documents you collect online are likely to become the core of your literature review. While almost any reading list you develop to help direct your research will benefit from inclusion of the resources available online, many projects revolve around the analysis of documents themselves. For instance, you might be interested in discovering how an advertising company developed a particular advertising campaign. Or, you might want to investigate how a particular author understood the world they were writing about, or the difference between the publicly and privately expressed views of an important historical or public figure.

> **Glossary**
> **Invisible Web**: This is actually the largest component of the internet. It comprises sites that have not been – and often cannot be – catalogued by standard search engines and have not been added to a standard subject catalogue.

You may even want to investigate how a particular government policy was developed. Or you might want to use a range of documents to begin understanding the particular discourses surrounding an event or program. To do this, you will need to collect and analyse documents. As we have noted, the range of documents available online is considerable and increasing all the time. For instance, not only do most governments place reports, statements and proceedings online, but there is a range of databases and Websites that have been developed to help you access and obtain highly personal documents. These include sites that provide access to the personal letters and diaries of key historical, literary and political officials, or to out-of-print material or rare books. Moreover, it is often possible to use the internet to access restricted or confidential documents, such as internal company memos and e-mails – though you should always consider the ethical and legal implications of attempting to access or use these documents, even if you are a prosecutor involved in the investigation of individual or corporate activities.

The key to using the internet in a study requiring documentary evidence or analysis of primary texts is finding out what material is available online and learning how to locate the available relevant material. As Chapters 4 and 5 illustrate, this requires you to be proficient in the use of a range of online directories and engines that have been developed specifically to locate and retrieve information, much of which is hidden in the **Invisible Web**. This is true whether you are relying on the content of personal diaries you access through an online database, or whether the primary documents you are interested in analysing are developed and placed online by government or party Websites.

Surveys

Unlike documentary analysis which requires you to access a range of primary and secondary documents, including information compiled by past surveys and questionnaires, and placed in an online database (or documents created for your analysis, such as journals, diaries or even a Webblog), survey research requires you to collect information directly from individuals or groups in the form of **questionnaires** and **interviews**. This process is made both easier and more difficult by the internet. On the one hand, the internet can reduce the resources required to conduct more traditional survey research. On the other, it makes compiling many forms of representative (non-biased) samples difficult to outright impossible. This may not necessarily present a problem if you intend to conduct a qualitative study. But if you wish to engage in quantitative analysis, from which you intend to try and generalise beyond your particular study, not being able to compile a representative sample can be a serious (or even fatal) stumbling block to progress with the project.

Survey type 1: the questionnaire

The questionnaire is amongst the most common tools used in survey research. This is because all a questionnaire requires you to do is devise a form comprising a list of questions you believe will help generate the data you require, and then find a group of individuals willing to complete and return the questionnaire. While this may sound easy, in practice it is less so. This is because individuals are responsible not only for filling in and returning a questionnaire, but for reading and understanding the questions in front of them. As such, it is up to the participant to decide what information you are trying to elicit from a question. You will not be available, in person or online, to explain what information you are attempting to collect or how any given question should be understood.

> **Glossary**
> **Reliability** refers to how accurate your data gathering methods are. A reliable technique allows you to repeat the measurement using the same technique (in identical circumstances) and get the same results each time.
> **Validity** refers to whether your data collection tools are measuring what you think they are. A perfectly valid tool will have a one-to-one correlation between what you say it is measuring and what it measures. **Generalisability** is when (or not) the findings (or results) of an individual study can be applied to other studies or samples. In quantitative studies generalisability generally refers to whether the sample population was drawn in such a way as to ensure that the results of the study can be applied to the entire population from which the sample was drawn.

Because of this it is extremely important for you to design your questions (and questionnaire) to be as unambiguous and comprehensible as possible. Otherwise, the data that is generated may not indicate what you think it does, as different respondents have interpreted the questions differently – eliminating the **reliability** and **validity** of your study. As we will see throughout the remainder of the text, the internet has the potential to revolutionise how you can find subjects to participate in your questionnaire, who you can administer your questionnaires to, and even how you design and administer your questionnaire. All of these advantages present particular problems of validity, reliability and generalisability. Thus your study design needs to account for these potential problems in ways that previous researchers did not have to consider.

Survey type 2: the interview

Surveys employing questionnaires will require you to develop and then provide participants with the completed form via e-mail (or a dedicated Web page). In self-administered questionnaires, respondents fill in the answer independently and then return the whole form. Interviews, on the other hand, are administered by you (or your representative) directly to the participant. What the Web does in some cases is greatly expand not only who you can interview but also the way in which you can conduct an interview (obviously it reduces those whom you can survey and interview to those with internet access and literacy skills). For instance, there are a range of real-time word processing-based programs (such as instant messaging), non-synchronous programs (such as e-mail or listserv postings), and even non-word processing-based real-time programs (such as the video/audio links made possible through Skype) that can be employed.

Like questionnaires, interviews too are designed around a series of questions. However, instead of being developed so that they can be self-administered, interview questions are arranged into an interview schedule and formulated in such a way as to extract a range of information from participants. As such, the interview tends to be more time-consuming for the researcher to administer than the questionnaire, and in the past tended to require a range of interpersonal skills that could have a dramatic impact on the findings of those who did not possess them. The use of computer-mediated interview technology requires a whole new set of skills in addition to those traditionally necessary to conducting successful interviews. You need to become proficient in all of these in order to maximise the effectiveness of your interview and minimise any possible misunderstandings that may arise due to the lack of body language or face-to-face contact.

This will be explained in more detail later; however, at this stage it is useful to consider both the type of questions that can be included in an interview schedule (just as in questionnaires) and the kinds of schedules that can be devised, which range from completely structured to completely unstructured. The structured interview requires you to ask a predetermined set of questions that are arranged in a very structured order. When using structured interviews, you must ask each participant exactly the same question, using the same wording and ordering. In structured interviews, there is no room to change the interview schedule in any way. The key to structured interviews is that they allow you to collect the same information from each participant, a method which will subsequently allow for much simpler comparisons when analysing your data.

At the opposite end of the continuum are completely unstructured interviews. When conducting an unstructured (or in-depth) interview you will enter the interview situation with little more than a guide to remind you of the topics or categories you are interested in investigating. This guide will not have specific questions or a direction you want the interview to go. Rather, you will develop questions spontaneously. While this technique allows the interview to develop much more naturally, it can make the comparison of data across interviews difficult.

TIP Due to the nature of the technology associated with online interviewing, we suggest you develop a strategy somewhere between the structured and unstructured interview. This should allow you to maximise the advantages of online technology while minimising many of its possible disadvantages.

Regardless of the format you choose, one of the advantages of the internet is that it not only allows you to conduct individual interviews but it makes conducting group interviews (**focus groups**) considerably more practicable for the beginner. This is because with the internet you are no longer required to bring the group together in the same room at the same time. Nor are you required to conduct the group interview with all individuals interacting at the same time. For example, one way to use online technology to conduct a group interview is to adopt one of the many bulletin board software packages. This will allow you and your group members to continually interact. With this type of software not only can you conduct real-time synchronous interviews but you will also be able to conduct or direct ongoing interviews and interactions when individual members of the group can come together at their own convenience.

Observations

While surveys are conducted in order to collect the opinions of individuals and groups, **observations** consist of information gathered through your senses rather than through the practice of asking questions. In traditional research, an observation emerges not only from our visual senses but also through taste, hearing and touch. According to Kumar (1999), observations are a 'purposeful, systematic and selective way of watching and listening to an interaction or phenomenon as it takes place' (p. 105). To this we would add that observations can also involve the observation of pre-recorded visual or auditory data, for the purpose of developing an interpretation of the event or activity. The key here is to understand that not only are observational techniques good in their own right but at times they are the only way to gather data. For instance, in situations where an individual is motivated to provide less than truthful information on a questionnaire or in an interview, observations may be the best way to gather data. Similarly, if your research involves linguistic analysis, it may require you to listen to the spoken language rather than to implement a questionnaire or undertake a documentary analysis.

There are two primary observation techniques available to you when using the internet to collect data: participant observation and non-participant observation. Participant observation requires you to actively participate in the activity or event that you are investigating, with or without the knowledge of the other participants. When engaged in online participant observation, it is important to do your best to be as open-minded as possible. You should do as much as possible to limit the impact of any prior assumptions about what is important on your judgement and observations. Rather than going into an observatory situation with prior assumptions and beliefs, you should attempt to immerse yourself in the online interactions of the people or events you are attempting to analyse. While this might seem to limit the use of participant observation in the online research process, in reality the internet provides a wide range of opportunities for the utilisation of participant observation.

For example, you might be interested in investigating how groups interact in the absence of the visual clues that generally help govern human interaction. The internet is the perfect location for this study. Not only can you sign up for and actively participate in pre-existing Usenet groups, but it is just as possible for you to design an experiment using real-time technologies, such as Webcams or instant messaging, to create an experimental situation requiring you to actively immerse yourself in the project's interactions.

In non-participant observation, the observer prevents him- or herself from taking part or getting involved in the activities under investigation. Thus, if you engage in non-participant observation, you must remain passive, trying to act like a spectator. You should avoid interacting with the object of your study in any way. For example, if you are interested in the activities of online blogging you could develop a study in which you observe several blogs but do not ever post a listing or engage in blogging activities yourself.

In general, as with questionnaires and interviews, there are two ways to approach observations. On the one hand, you can go into an observatory situation with a set of categories you want to observe. In these instances you specifically look for occurrences of these events, words, phrases, ideas, situations, etc., and therefore you are engaging in fairly structured observations. On the other hand, you might be interested in seeing how events develop and subsequently attempt to organise the data into 'naturally' occurring categories. In research terminology, the latter study is known as an unstructured observation, while the former technique is referred to as a structured observation. In attempting to understand these techniques, it is generally useful to associate structured interviews with the participant observer and unstructured observations as the core of the non-participant observer technique.

No matter what technique you employ when using the internet as a platform for making research observations, you will need to consider a number of possible problems that can distort your data. The most important of these will be your own beliefs, needs, desires and position. If you allow any of these to affect the observation you are undertaking, that observation is likely to be distorted, or, if the effect is strong enough, lead to a predetermined outcome. If this occurs, it will be impossible to verify or even trust any inferences you might attempt to draw from the observation.

A related problem is the possibility of participant bias, particularly if the participant is, or becomes, aware that they are being observed. Individuals and groups often change their behaviours when they discover that they are being observed. When this happens it is referred to as the **Hawthorne effect**. Any study in which the Hawthorne effect is discovered will have a hard time unravelling whether the observed behaviour was a natural occurrence or the result of altered behaviour (whether that is positive or negative). A final problem with observations is that it is often possible to miss important details. This can occur because categories are assigned prior to the observations being undertaken, or because there is a lack of breadth in an observatory study in which specific categories are being developed. Either way, if important details or interactions are missed due to where you choose to focus your attention, the value of the data you collect will be compromised.

Experimentation

Before we turn to an examination of experimentation, we would like to emphasise that as a research tool, it is not in the same category as the other techniques listed. In fact, experimentation can include use of many of the techniques listed above. However, experimentation deploys these techniques under controlled conditions designed to ensure exogenous factors do not influence the results. This is to ensure that cause-and-effect relationships can be established. It is because experimentation uses the techniques listed above, but under controlled conditions, that we discuss it here.

While the techniques we have discussed in this chapter are all viable research tools, by themselves, they are generally considered non-experimental. This is because none of them have been specifically designed to test cause-and-effect relationships. This is where experimentation comes into the equation. When using the internet as a research platform, if you are interested in establishing relationships between your variables, you will need to use the experimental technique. This enables you to introduce a variable (the **independent variable**) and observe its impact on a situation (the **dependent variable**). For the purpose of developing experimental techniques using the internet, it is important to consider how and what you want from your independent variable.

It is especially important to define your independent variable when engaged in online research because when operating online a variable can be almost anything that exists in or can be expressed in electronic form. Thus, independent variables can range from naturally occurring phenomena (such as the development and spread of Weblogs) to something you introduce into a controlled situation (such as the insertion of an argument or photo into an ongoing Usenet discussion group to test whether a predicted response occurs). To use the experimental technique in online research, you will need to design your internet use so as to be able to 'manipulate' the independent variable in some fashion, and observe how this affects the dependent variable in a controlled situation, i.e., a situation in which you have control over any independent variables. You will know your question is amenable to the development of an online experiment if you are able to set out a viable hypothesis, or prediction, of a likely cause-and-effect relationship in which the outcome is dependent on the specific manipulations of one variable on another, within the online environment.

When conducting experiments using the internet as the primary medium for collecting your data, there are many potential study designs. However, the most viable are known as:

- the after-only design;
- the before-and-after design;
- the control design;
- the comparative design.

The easiest experimental technique to use when engaging the internet in your research is probably the after-only study design. In this model, you already know that your subjects have been exposed to an intervention. As such, all you have to do is measure or determine what impact this intervention had on the situation or group. Probably the most difficult aspect of this study design is that you are going to have to attempt to develop an understanding of the pre-intervention condition, or baseline. While it is possible to do this by asking participants to recall their impression of the situation, the responses you receive will inevitably be subject to recall and memory bias. Regardless of how you establish your baseline measurements, the aim is to collect accurate information about the condition or phenomenon you are interested in studying, as it existed before the intervention, so that you are able to reasonably determine the impact of that intervention.

The before-and-after design is used to address the problem of trying to establish a baseline found in the after-only study. In these studies you observe a condition, group or phenomenon occurring on the internet and then introduce an intervention. This will help you determine whether the intervention was responsible for any observed change and it helps ensure you have an accurate understanding of the condition before you introduced the intervention.

The control group design requires you to establish two rather than one test group or condition. Control group design requires that these groups are similar in their initial situations and/or characteristics. Once this has been established, you can then introduce the intervention to one group but not the other. Any measured change in the test group (receiving the intervention) not observed in the control group (not receiving the intervention) can be linked to the intervention.

Finally, while not the last type of research design, one of the more innovative ways of using the internet to conduct experiments is to consider whether your research question is amenable to the use of the internet to conduct a comparative research design. In this design you will need to select a population that you can divide into a number of smaller groupings. Each group will then undergo a different intervention. The idea is to test which intervention has the greatest, desired or negative impact on the test group. From this not only can you begin to examine the effects of the interventions, but you can compare their impact across the population.

Overall, the internet is highly adaptable to traditional research and data collection techniques. Learning how to use it effectively in this way can, providing you are rigorous in your methods, greatly improve the quality of your research data and outcomes. Research undertaken in the humanities and social sciences, whether qualitative or quantitative, can benefit from the incorporation of the internet as a research tool. For some projects, the internet is essential in ensuring that all relevant available material is accessed. This is particularly true of research dependent on documentary evidence, of which the internet is now one of the largest single repositories. Often, there is no other practical way of accessing the information or documentation you need. Equally, if correctly used, the internet can be used to extend the range of particular kinds of social research, and greatly reduce the time needed to carry it out. Although in this chapter we have tried to emphasise the uses of the internet in enabling research – in effect as a tool that particular techniques can be adapted to use – it is also worth remembering that the internet is itself a social as well as technological phenomenon. As such, it can just as easily be the object as the means of study.

Exercise 1: The online research experience

Take one of your past assignments in which you did not use the internet. Now consider how you could have improved it if you had utilised the internet. Be specific! Now consider a similar assignment that involved the use of the internet. Discuss how the internet hindered your research or led to a weaker analysis. Again, be specific!

Exercise 2: Designing your project

Consider the pros and cons of each of the research designs specifically as they might be used in your project. Be specific, noting in particular any shortcomings that would make a particular design untenable. Next, focus particularly on the problems or shortcomings of each design. To what extent are these shortcomings a feature of any of the online techniques you may use? How might you overcome these, using online strategies or otherwise?

Exercise 3: Double-checking your method

Consider your research design specifically in terms of the data, information, documents, texts or other material you need to carry it through. Be very specific. Is there any resource on your list that cannot be accessed or generated through the internet? Justify your response in the context of your initial research proposal. If there is material you may not be able to acquire using online techniques, how might you go about accessing it, or, alternatively, how can you tweak your research proposal so as to make that material unnecessary?

References and Resources

Ackroyd, S. and Hughes, J. (1992), *Data Collection in Context*, 2nd edn (London: Longman).

Grix, J. (2004), *Foundations of Research* (Basingstoke: Palgrave Macmillan).

Huff, D. (1954), *How to Lie with Statistics* (Harmondsworth: Penguin). The book provides students with an easily understood overview of how numbers can be used to trick you (either deliberately or due to unintentional misuse). Importantly, it also discusses how you can avoid being misled by numbers no matter what context they are provided in.

Kumar, R. (1999), *Research Methodology* (London: Sage).

Leedy, P. and Ormond, J. (2004), *Practical Research: Planning and Design*, 8th edn (New York: Prentice-Hall). This text is designed to help students understand and participate in the research process by illustrating the importance of the theoretical and methodical processes that must be followed in order to generate 'significant' results.

Mason, J. (2002), *Qualitative Researching* (London: Sage). This text addresses both the epistemological and theoretical issues associated with qualitative research and the core processes involved in the approach.

McQueen, R. and Knussen, C. (2002), *Research Methods for Social Science* (New York: Prentice-Hall). This text offers a comprehensive overview of the undergraduate social scientific research process, from the initial planning of a project through the implementation and presentation processes.

Oxford English Dictionary Online (OED), http://dictionary.oed.com, accessed 27/10/2006.

Punch, K. (2006), *Developing Effective Research Proposals* (London: Sage). This text is an accessible introductory guide to the development of research proposals. It does this through the examination of both qualitative and quantitative projects.

Salkind, N. (2004), *Statistics for People Who (Think They) Hate Statistics* (London: Sage). This text offers an introduction to statistics – in a friendly and often humorous manner. By the time the students have finished this book they should easily be able to understand when and why different statistical techniques should be used.

Walliman, N. (2005), *Your Research Project*, 2nd edn (London: Sage). This is an excellent text that presents a practical step-by-step guide to the academic research project. Employing a clear, structured approach to the research process and the theories behind it, this text is a good way to learn how to carry out research.

Wood, M. (2003), *Making Sense of Statistics* (Basingstoke: Palgrave Macmillan). This text provides an excellent guide to the study of both probability and statistics for the non-mathematician.

4 Search Strategies, Engines and Directories

One of the greatest ironies of the internet is that while it is possible to find, inquire about and generate data on almost any subject online, this wealth of information is also one of the internet's greatest weaknesses. With over two billion Web pages, tens of thousands of experts and millions of non-experts operating online, and millions of non-Web-based resources available though the internet, getting the correct information is a bit like 'trying to get a sip of water from a fire hydrant' (McGuire et al., 2000, p. 44).

The good news is that you are not alone. A range of online tools have been developed to help you direct your research towards the most appropriate information sources for your project and for the stage that your research project has reached. Thus, while the internet is like an ocean with many people using it to do little more than surf next to shore, this chapter will help you learn how to understand the ocean as a range of resources that can help you zero in on information that will be directly relevant to your information and data needs.

● Developing a Search Strategy

Chapter 1 briefly introduced you to a number of the tools available for conducting online research and generating project-specific data. In this chapter we want to build on this by examining two of the most important resources available to you for finding the literature and resources that will be most appropriate for your study. However, before you go online, it is imperative that you develop a search strategy. This is much like the project strategy in that it will help you focus your attention when employing the internet, and will help ensure that your online time is directed towards finding and using the literature and data-collecting resources that are most appropriate for your research.

While it might be true that a single search engine will get you thousands, if not millions of hits, it will probably take you longer to sift though the material in an effort to find useful information than if you slowed down and developed a good search strategy. When developing this strategy, the first thing to remember is to avoid many of your first instincts: do not head straight to your favourite search engine (i.e., the one you have been using since you first went online); do not type in the first word or phrase that comes to mind; and do not assume that everything you need can be accessed though one source or portal. The strategy we advise you to adopt is to ask three questions: What am I looking for? What are the most relevant search terms? What tool will be the most useful for helping me find it?

What am I looking for?

Once you have a research question or problem you think might benefit from online research, the first thing you should do is consider what you want to gain from going online. This will help you formulate what it is about your topic or assignment that is amenable to online research. One way to do this is to write out as precisely as you can what it is you are looking for, who you might be looking for, and what type of data you want to compile using online resources. For instance, you might be trying to confirm a fact, or you might want to find a specific person, or you may go online to find a particular statistic. Similarly, consider what you will need at different stages of your project. For example, during the early stages of your research you might be looking for literature; however, once you have collected this you might want to find numbers and statistics. You might even want to investigate the availability of software packages available online (on the open Web, the hidden Web, or through your campus intranet) that can be used to analyse and write up your data.

Regardless of what you are looking for, by considering these questions you should be better able to narrow your search to the information you are looking for (person, event, place, time etc.), the tools you will need to use (people finders, specialised search engines, topic-specific databases etc.), and some of the key words and phrases that might be associated with your topic.

What are the most relevant search terms?

Once you have considered the type of information you are looking for and when it is most appropriate to collect the data (i.e., for your literature review, for the collection of data, for the post-data analysis, etc.), you should be able to begin developing a list of concepts associated with your question. Do not limit yourself to the general: be sure to include any synonyms, specific words and even specific phrases that you think might be associated with your question.

In addition to the words and phrases you gather, bear in mind that you may also be looking for people. As such, it is worth noting down useful names, whether of authors or individuals you would like to contact in order to request information or data directly.

What's the best search tool for my enquiry?

Your next step is to use the search terms, phrases and other material you have developed effectively. Specifically, this information will influence which tools you use to conduct your searches and how you use those search tools. It will also help determine which facilities you use to supplement your search tools when gathering your data. For example, during the pre-project stage, when you are not likely to know much about your topic, you will probably find a general directory more useful than a specific directory or a search engine. If you are looking for a very specific resource, and you are fairly certain of how to organise your search parameters, you should probably use a search engine.

Because the information and tools available for accessing and retrieving online resources are not contained in a single computer-based catalogue, it can be difficult to find the information you are seeking. Because of this, search tools have become one of the Web's most popular items. However, it is important to understand how search tools operate and the differences between them. Depending on the tool you use, the same search parameters can return substantially different results. In fact, even different types of the same tool (e.g., Google and Alta Vista) will return considerably different results due to their internal program parameters. This noted, at a general level the two most common tools for finding information online are directories (or catalogues) and search engines.

● Directories

While we discussed the importance of understanding the Web address and its associated e-mail address in Chapter 1, it should go without saying that there will be times when you need to use more advanced tools in order to locate the information you are looking for. There is a tendency in this process to jump straight to a favourite search engine but this is probably not the most effective way to begin integrating the internet into your research. Rather, when first engaging with your research question online you are probably going to be better served by using a subject directory.

As their name implies, directories are Websites that provide a number of links arranged into a series of hierarchically organised topic areas. The key

> **TIP** Always place a site you find and want to refer to again into your book-marks/favourites file. This will allow you to re-access it easily in the future. If necessary, you can even export your bookmarks/favourites list to disk or data stick. This will allow you to take them with you wherever you access the internet.

advantage of this is that it allows you to begin searching for information on your topic before you know enough to direct your research at specific resources. Importantly, directories will allow you to see your topic in a broader context and then narrow it down to a specific category of information. Once you have this perspective not only will you be ready to take advantage of more advanced search tools and techniques but you will also have a much better idea as to what sources and tools are available in the later stages of your research.

Thus, unlike most types of search tools, directories have been designed to allow you to access a general topic and then follow clearly established and maintained hypertext links to sub-directories containing more specialised information, all the way to individual files relating to a specific aspect of the general topic area.

> **Hint:** Directories are developed, catalogued and maintained by human beings, often subject experts. This helps ensure the quality of the sites catalogued, making them a good starting place for individuals not knowing much about the topic or how to judge the quality of the information they are accessing online.

Figure 4.1 is Yahoo's main topic directory. As you can see, it has been organised into 14 top-level categories of arts and humanities RSS feeds. These are fairly general categories, so if you want to discover more about the arts and humanities you can click on the hypertext link and access the sub-menu (Figure 4.2) which consists of a range of specific sub-categories.

If you do not find the information that you are interested in at this level, you can keep drilling down through the directory. For instance, if you are interested in education, all you have to do is click on the link to access fairly specific educational resources (Figure 4.3). You can continue this process until you get to the specific subject you are interested in or the actual resource you need to carry out your research.

Before we discuss some of the more specific directories that may be of use to you, there are several characteristics you should know about directories

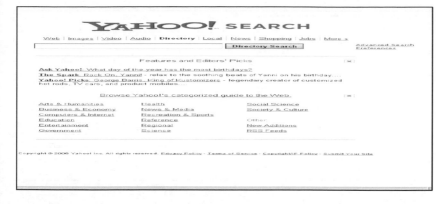

Figure 4.1   Yahoo's general subject directory.

Reproduced 2008 by Yahoo! Inc. YAHOO! and the YAHOO! logo © with permission of Yahoo! Inc. are trademarks of Yahoo! Inc.

Figure 4.2   Yahoo's arts and humanities sub-directory.

Reproduced 2008 by Yahoo! Inc. YAHOO! and the YAHOO! logo © with permission of Yahoo! Inc. are trademarks of Yahoo! Inc.

that will probably help when you use them for research. First, as you can see from Figures 4.1 and 4.2, most directories have their own integrated search engine. These can often be configured to allow you to limit what the engine will search for in its databanks. Thus, the Yahoo engine allows you to explore the topic area you are interested in, or the entire directory, or to expand your search to its database of Websites. In addition, looking back at Figures 4.2 and 4.3, you can see that most directories also indicate exactly how many sites they have within their directories dedicated to your topic of interest. For example, the Yahoo education sub-directory contains 226 links to information related to colleges and universities, and another 11 dedicated specifically to teaching.

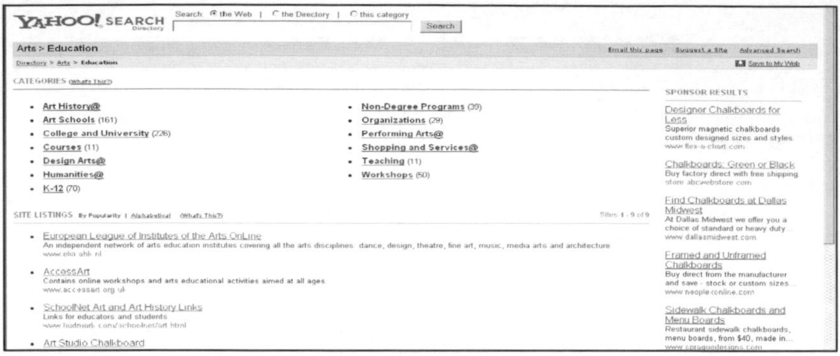

Figure 4.3   Yahoo's education sub-directory.

Reproduced 2008 by Yahoo! Inc. Yᴀʜᴏᴏ! and the Yᴀʜᴏᴏ! logo © with permission of Yahoo! Inc. are trademarks of Yahoo! Inc.

One drawback of these directories is that they have been designed to gather general information. So, when your research requires you to find and analyse specific data or arguments you are going to need to turn to a different resource, such as a subject-specific directory or search engine. Also, general directories are orientated towards the general population rather than towards subject specialists or professionals. Thus, while there are directories such as Librarians' Internet Index (http://www.lii.org), which is sponsored by the California State Library system and uses highly qualified professional subject specialists to develop and vet the information contained in the directory and its sub-directories, there are other directories which are more 'consumer' orientated, or even accept paid placements, such as LookSmart (http:looksmart.com).

> **TIP**   An often overlooked general directory is the Open Directory (http://dmoz.org). This uses volunteers to evaluate and catalogue its linking sites. As a general rule these are professionals in their field, making Open Directory a valuable research tool.

Regardless of which directory you turn to, most topics will benefit from a browse through its subject trees. But while the general directory can be useful during the early stages of your research, it is likely that you will need to move on to more specialist directories as your research progresses. This is particularly true as your project progresses to the point where the resources on the hidden (or invisible) Web are needed, or you need to access and utilise the expertise found in Usenet and listserv groups, which are best discovered using specialised search directories and engines.

Academic directories

While there are many general directories, there are an even larger number of smaller directories developed by academics for the specific purpose of helping students and professionals jumpstart research processes in specific disciplines and areas. Of these, Intute (http://www.intute.ac.uk) is amongst the best for helping to jumpstart the research process. This directory is maintained by a consortium of seven UK-based universities and consists of four indexes: Arts and Humanities; Science and Technology; Social Sciences; and Health and Life Sciences. All the sites contained in the directory are vetted for their academic content and appropriateness for university-level research. As such, Intute provides an excellent starting place for anyone interested in gaining a better perspective on a topic of interest and finding high-quality information housed on both the open and the hidden Web.

In addition to Intute, BUBL (http://bubl.ac.uk) offers another excellent academically orientated gateway into research. BUBL has been developed and is maintained by librarians and other subject specialists who actively search for and catalogue sites containing scholarly information. Not only does BUBL provide some of the most useful general resources, but its subject-specific directories contain sites that make it possible to undertake a quick and credible overview of almost any discipline or subject area (see Figure 4.4). However, it should be noted that like any subject directory, BUBL does not claim to be completely comprehensive. Rather, it aims to 'provide a quick, user-friendly lead into key resources in any major subject area' that can be trusted for its quality (http://bubl.ac.uk).

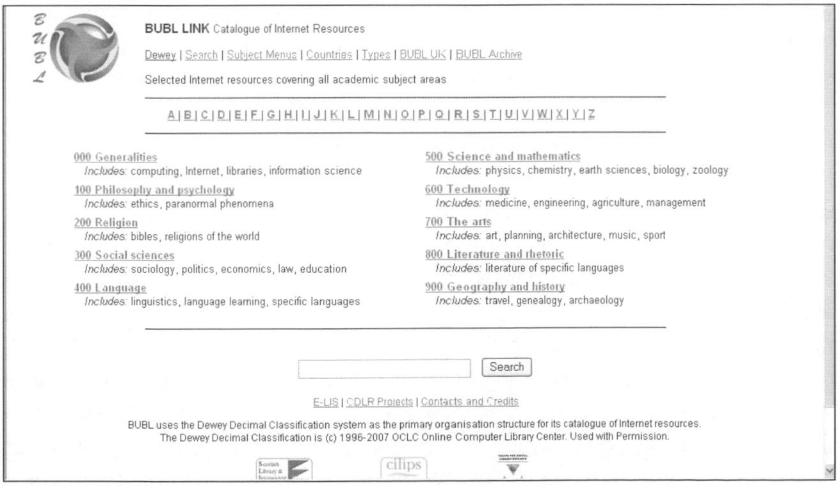

Figure 4.4 BUBL directory homepage

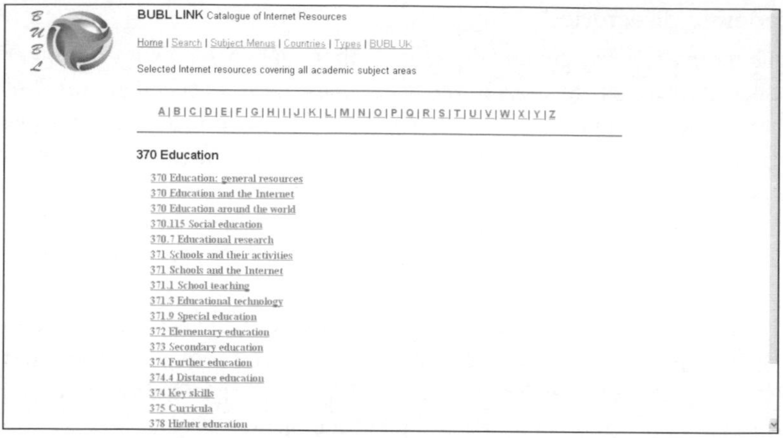

Figure 4.5   BUBL social science education sub-directory

To begin understanding the difference between general and dedicated directories, let us spend a moment comparing the education links available on Yahoo and BUBL. Figure 4.3 illustrates the education links that have been catalogued for Yahoo. As is shown by the categories displayed, these are general sites offering in many cases lowest common denominator sources and sites. Figure 4.5 illustrates the links available through BUBL's social science directory (other categories have their own education links). Not only are the types of categories more advanced in BUBL, but they are directed towards academic research, as becomes apparent if you burrow a little further. The next sub-directory includes links to general and specific social science educational resources sites and takes you to a range of country-specific resources for a range of international academic systems.

One other directory worth discussing here is illustrated in Figure 4.6. This is the homepage INFOMINE (http://infomine.ucr.edu). Like BUBL and Intute, INFOMINE is an academically orientated subject directory. It is maintained by the University of California and bills itself as a 'virtual library of Internet resources relevant to faculty, students, and research staff at the university level' (http://infomine.ucr.edu/about). What makes this site useful to the academic researcher is that it is compiled by experts from a range of top universities, and it catalogues a range of resources that are often not available to standard search engines or other directories. It includes a range of mailing lists and subject-specific academic databases such as CEOExpress (http://ceoexpress.com), which is dedicated to providing links to business news, and Governments on the WWW (http://www.gksoft.com/govt), which provides links to sites maintained by various governments around the globe.

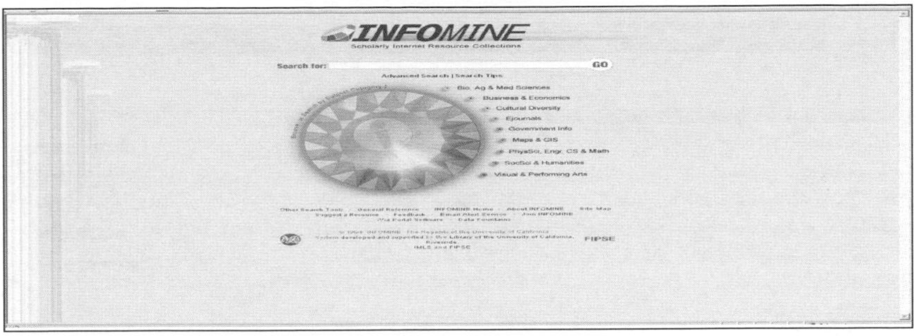

Figure 4.6   INFOMINE homepage

Subject-specific directories

As you might have gathered, while general directories are designed to point you towards sites containing information on almost any subject, there is a range of directories that have been designed to catalogue resources pertaining to a particular subject or resource. One of the best directories in social science is the University of Keele's Political Science Resource Page (http://www.psr.keele.ac.uk). As the name suggests, this site specialises in political science resources, allowing you to burrow though very targeted information relating to many aspects of British and international politics. A similar directory has been established by the University of British Columbia (http://www.library.ubc.ca/poli). We mention these two sites to illustrate the fact that, often, the best subject directories are compiled by, and found at, university libraries. Because of this, it is always worth considering using the library pages of any respected university to discover if they have compiled directories before jumping into the wider Web community.

Directories of resources

Going back to the discussion in Chapter 1, it is worth mentioning that many of the online resources available to the researcher can be (and often can only be) accessed though specialised directories. Of these, and as will be discussed in more detail in Chapters 6–8, the Hidden or Invisible Web provides some of the most relevant resources to an academic researcher. As such, it is always worth looking for directories dedicated to cataloguing the resources available on the Invisible Web. Of these, the Invisible Web Directory (http://www.invisible-Web.net) is a good example. This directory contains numerous sub-directories dedicated to government, social science, news site, and expert finders only available on the Invisible Web. Two other types of specialist directory you should be aware of are those dedicated to

Figure 4.7   Topica: full discussion list Website

finding and posting newsgroup listings, and those dedicated to finding and organising listservers into useful categories. As mentioned in Chapter 2, these are two of the best ways to interact with other individuals and experts interested in the same issues as you are. However, without the aid of a dedicated subject directory, finding newsgroups and listservers dedicated to your interests is not always easy. This said, without a doubt the largest directory of newsgroups and newsgroup postings is the Google Group directory (http://www.groups.google.com).

Specialised directories have also been developed that catalogue mailing lists. Of these Topica (http://www.topica.com) is amongst the best for general interest lists. Like Google, Topica organises its subject directories according to topic. However, as you can see from Figure 4.7, unlike Google, the directories tend to be more intuitively organised for students looking to utilise lists in their research process.

Figure 4.8 displays a standard entry (dedicated to history) from one of the best academic listservs available to the research, H-Net (http://www.h-net.org). Once you select a specific list you will be subsequently provided the name, description, contact, joining and archival information for the list.

One last directory we will mention here is List Gurus Page (http://lists.gurus.com), because Guru pages are another resource available for finding information on the internet, and particularly information hidden in the Invisible Web. Guru pages are sites that have been developed by an individual expert who wishes to help others find information on their topic by collecting relevant sites into a mini-directory or gateway. The best way to find a Guru page is through a subject directory.

Figure 4.8   Homepage for H-Teach

> **TIP** Guru pages are such rich sources of information that once you have found one it is well worth placing it into your favourite's folder – a Guru page is not easily replaced.

Clearinghouse subject directories

If you cannot find or directly access a useful subject directory by yourself, there are a range of directory 'clearinghouses' that may help. These have been specifically compiled to organise and catalogue online directories. While there are many useful clearinghouses for the academic researcher, we suggest that you begin with Argus Clearinghouse (http://www.clearinghouse.net). Argus 'provides a central access point for value-added topical guides which identify, describe, and evaluate Internet-based information resources' (http://www. clearinghouse.net/faq.html, accessed 13/11/2006). The key is that each guide has been put together by subject experts. This is important because it provides you with some assurance that the guides will only contain relevant directories and information. A further advantage of Argus lies in its site overviews. These allow you to make an initial judgement as to the useful-ness of your research.

● Search Engines

While subject directories can help you explore a topic and find online tools, once you have an understanding of your subject area you are likely to want to add search engines to your research arsenal. Unlike directories, which have been designed to help you burrow through a topic, search engines are designed to target a specific information request that you submit by searching its index and returning as many Web pages as it 'thinks' are relevant. A problem with using engines (particularly any single engine) as your sole tool for research is that in collecting Web pages for its index (or Web page database), search engines do not rely on human beings. Rather, each engine uses its own set of programs, known as spiders and crawlers, to move from Web page to Web page, based on their embedded hypertext links, and index the page according to the criteria established in its indexing program. Thus, while you burrow your way though a directory, organising your own search, when you use a search engine you enter keywords and phrases, and then let the engine decide what you want.

> **Glossary**
> **Keywords**: The words or phrases you enter into a search engine, which its search program attempts to match in the text (or other specified part of the Web page) of the documents in its index.

One of the problems with this is that when you use a search engine you are not searching the Web itself. Rather you are asking its retrieval program to look into its database or index. This index is itself only as comprehensive as the Websites its spiders have recently visited and catalogued. Because of this even the largest of search engines have only indexed a small portion of the total available information on the internet (for more information see: http://computer.howstuffworks.com/search-engine.htm, accessed 9/10/2006; http://www.infotoday.com/searcher/may01/liddy.htm, accessed 15/11/2006). Not only are search engines limited in their research potential to the pages that their spiders have actually visited and catalogued, but each engine uses a different set of parameters as to what should be catalogued. For example, some search engines catalogue only a small percentage of the total words or phrases available on a page. Other search engines only send their spiders to the first few levels of a Website, leaving the majority of its pages uncatalogued. Complicating this picture is the fact that although all the information you need might be indexed in your chosen search engine, because engines rank and display returns according to their own unique formula, it is possible that the information you are looking for will be displayed in the first few returns, but equally, it may not appear until entry 100,000 or even 1,000,000.

> **Glossary**
> **Relevance** refers to the way a search engine ranks and displays returns to an information request.

A further limiting factor in relation to search engines is the fact that much of the information available online is invisible to the current generation of spiders and crawlers. So there are a lot of pages unavailable to you if you rely solely upon search engines and, as we will discuss in the following chapter, these invisible pages are often the most useful parts of the internet for the research process. So, although a search engine is a useful tool, it will always be wise to use one in conjunction with other resources, as well as with other engines.

> **Glossary**
> **Hidden/Invisible Web**: this is the largest part of the internet but consists of Web pages that are not catalogued by conventional search engines.

Advanced features of the search engine

The variety of search engines available is matched by the different features they offer you for framing your keyword searches. Because of this, it is important when selecting engines to understand exactly what advanced features they provide, so that you can select a mix of engines that maximise the usefulness of your returns (see Table 4.1). The best initial strategy for limiting the number of returns you receive is to have developed a list of keywords that are as specific or distinctive as possible (although of course sometimes you may have to generalise them if you are not receiving enough returns). As part of this, many search engines are case sensitive. This means that if you are receiving a range of useless returns it might be possible to narrow the search by entering a case-sensitive search. For example, if you are looking for the residence of the President of the United States, instead of entering 'the white house' (which will give you entries on any white house that has been catalogued) you should enter 'White House'. Similarly, if you are interested in discovering the homepage of the International Monetary Fund (IMF) you could enter 'International Monetary Fund' or 'IMF' instead of 'international monetary fund'. Remember that case-sensitive searches go both ways: sometimes it may be useful *not* to use the upper case in your search. For instance, if looking for coffee you may choose to use the term 'java'. However, if you enter 'Java' you are likely to receive a range of sites related to the island or the computer language rather than coffee.

> **TIP**　Before using a search engine look at its Frequently Asked Question (FAQ) page. This will give you information on how it indexes the Web, how it ranks its returns, and which advanced search features it offers.

Search engines	Boolean	Default	Proximity	Case	Fields	Limits	Stop	Sorting
Google http://www.google.com	-, OR	and	Phrase	No	intitle, inurl, more	Language, filetype, date, more	Few, + searches	Relevance, site
AlltheWeb http://alltheWeb.com	and, or, and not, ( ), +, -, or with ( )	and	Phrase	No	title, URL, link, more	Language, filetype, date, more	No	Relevance, site
Live Search http://search.msn.com	AND, OR, NOT,( ), –	and	Phrase	Yes	title, link	Language, filetype, date, more	Varies, + searches	Relevance, site, sliders
Exalead http://www.exalead.com	AND, OR, NOT, ( ),-	and	Phrase, NEAR	No	No	language	Varies, + searches	Relevance, date
META-SEARCH ENGINES								
Engines that search multiple individual search engines at a time. Drawback is that their returns and functions are limited to the lowest common denominator search parameters of the engines searched.								
Excite Meta-Search http://www.excite.com	Searches a number of partner databases and has the ability to collect 30 results from each database.							

Dogpile http://www.dogpile.com	Allows you to choose different search tools and utilise Boolean operators.
Ask http://www.ask.com	Allows you to search with questions rather than precise terms. It is best to keep the questions simple.
MetaCrawler http://www.metacrawler.com	Searches a number of databases, eliminates duplicate results, has easy-to-use, understand and analyse return pages.
Search.Com http://www.search.com	Searches 1000 databases, categorises them based on the type of resource they were drawn from, and allows you to sort the results by date, source and relevance.

Source: Adapted from Search Engine Showdown (http://www.searchengine showdown.com). For more information see: Search Engine Watch, http://www.searchenginewatch.com

Table 4.1 Search engines in perspective

Most search engines look for each word, regardless of whether it is part of the phrase or not and no matter how far apart the words appear in the document (unless the engine allows you to provide it with a proximity feature – see below). Because of this, a second mechanism for increasing the relevance of your returns is to conduct an 'exact phrase search'. In general, there are two ways to perform this. First, many search engines recognise the use of quotation marks (" "). When you enclose your search terms in quotation marks in engines which recognise their use, you are telling the engine to find exactly what is contained in the quotation marks. A second way to do an exact phrase search is to access the advanced search section available in many search engines.

For example, Figure 4.9 is an illustration of Google's advanced search page. As you can see, Google allows you to enter exactly the phrase you want to find. If you do not use this feature, Google's default setting is to find each word individually, placing priority on the first term entered. In addition to phrase searching there are a range of techniques available to force search engines to alter their standard settings.

Of these, requiring and prohibiting operators are particularly useful. The most easily used are the plus (+) and minus (-) signs. By placing a + directly in front of a word you are telling your search engine to locate and return pages that contain the exact word or combination of words. Similarly, the minus sign – instructs your engine to exclude the term or phrase from the returns. For example, if you are interested in finding information on Star Wars, but not the movie, you could enter +"Star Wars" –movie. Similarly you

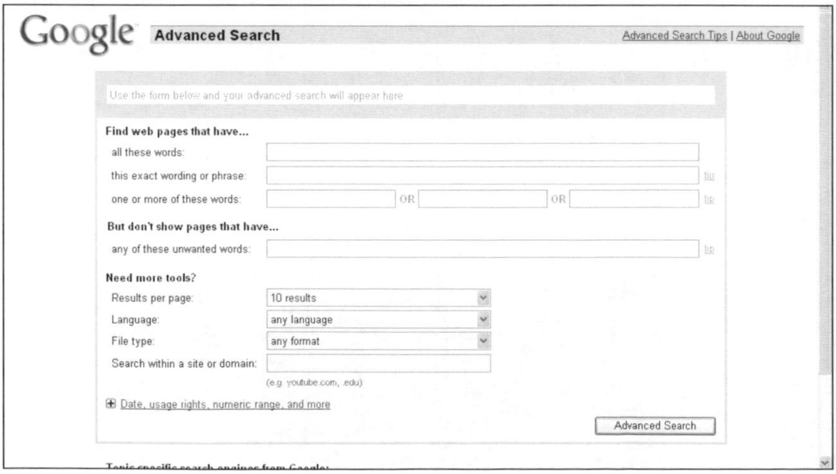

Figure 4.9 Google's advanced search options

might be interested in looking for information about President Lincoln but not the town of Lincoln. You could start narrowing your search like this: '"Abraham Lincoln" + president – England'.

Note: Many search engines use AND as a default search command. If you want to generate more rather than fewer results, use OR.

Closely related to the use of requiring and prohibiting operators are Boolean operators: AND, OR, NOT. As can be seen in Table 4.2, the AND functions between search terms to reduce the number of returns you receive by ensuring that all of the terms or phrases connected by AND are included in any hit. The OR function, on the other hand, does just the opposite, telling the engine to return items with either or both terms. In other words, it tells the engine to expand on the number of hits it returns to include 'everything'. NOT is used to exclude specific terms or phrases. It is worth remembering when using the NOT function in your searches that it is very easy to inadvertently tell the engine to exclude relevant items.

Let's look at a few examples. Say you would like information on the literary relationship between Herman Melville and Nathaniel Hawthorne. Looking at Table 4.3 you can see how the use of AND begins to narrow Google's returns. Notice that the more terms and phrases you combine in a search using AND, the fewer records are retrieved, increasing the likelihood that any given return will be of use in your research.

Operator	Example	Results	Venn diagram: Results shown are shaded
AND	Bush AND President	The search will return items containing 'Bush' and 'President'	
OR	Bush OR President	Engine will return items containing either 'Bush' or 'President' or both.	
NOT	Bush NOT President	Will return items with 'Bush' in them but not 'President'.	

Table 4.2   Boolean operators

Search terms	Results
Herman Melville	1,860,000
Nathaniel Hawthorne	1,460,000
Hawthorne AND Melville	453,000
Hawthorn AND Melville AND Gothic	54,000

Table 4.3   Boolean AND function

While AND narrows a search to returns including the terms and phrases linked together, searching using NOT will retrieve records in which only one of the terms is present. Take a look at Table 4.4. Here we want information on the Haitian Revolution, but want to avoid anything that discusses race. Using NOT we received the results shown in the table. No records are retrieved in which the word 'race' appears, even if 'Haitian Revolution' appears there too. NOT excludes records from your search results. Be careful when you use NOT, however: the term you want may be present in important documents that include the word you want to avoid.

TIP   When using the + and − operators you must eliminate any space between them and the word or phrase you want to require or prohibit, just as you will need to add a space between different words and phrases you want to include or prohibit in the overall search.

Note: A range of engines operate the NOT function in ways that require you to enter AND NOT or ANDNOT in place of NOT.

Search terms	Results
Haitian Revolution	618,000
Race	356,000,000
Haitian Revolution NOT race	353,000

Table 4.4   Boolean NOT function

While limiting and Boolean searches are very useful for expanding or narrowing the number of returns, there are a number of other search techniques that you should become acquainted with. Of these, field searching is amongst the most useful because it allows you to limit your search to a specific part of an address or document. To utilise a field search you will generally have to open the engine's advanced search features and tick the appropriate box. However, some engines allow you to enter the field you want to search followed by a colon (:) and then the keyword or phrase.

Each engine will have its own selection of fields that you will be able to search; the most common fields you will find are:

● TITLE: limits returns to documents whose title includes the search term;
● URL: limits the returns to URLs containing your search term;
● DOMAIN: limits your search to documents whose domain name ends with your search terms;
● LINK: limits returns to documents which are hypertext-linked to the site or phrase you enter.

These are probably the most common forms of advanced searching; however, we want to mention two further ways of limiting your search parameters. The first of these techniques is known as a proximity search. Engines that allow proximity searches generally allow you to specify one of three types of returns: WITH, NEAR, ADJACENT. When you use the WITH function you are telling your engine that two terms must be next to each other, and in the order you entered them, for a site to be returned. Using the NEAR function requires the engine to return pages containing the terms you enter to be either directly next to each other, in any order, or to be within a set number of words of each other. For example, if you are interested in finding sites referring to President and Bush you could enter 'President NEAR 5 Bush'. This tells the engine to return any pages where the terms President and Bush fall within five words of each other. Finally the ADJACENT operator acts much as the WITH operator in that it tells the engine to return pages with the terms entered to be adjacent to one another.

Finally, many search engines have a range of parameter limits. If an engine allows parameter limits they tend to be located in its advanced search sections and will allow some combination of limits on the dates searched, the languages of the page returned, and the type of file returned (i.e., ftp, html, Mp3). For example, Google allows you to limit your search not only by dates but also by language. Thus, if you are interested in only the most recent information relating to British modern art, you can limit your search to information relevant to this topic placed into Google's database in English within the past four months.

Specialised search engines

While search engines contain the largest databases, provide the most versatility, and return the largest number of hits, at times you will want to focus on a specific topic or resource. It is important, therefore, to acquaint yourself with some specialised search engines, keeping in mind that although specialised search engines appear to operate like subject directories, they are not the same. They are engines, and so display the advantages and disadvantages general engines offer, including the lack of human input in the compilation of Web pages.

People finders

Among the most useful types of specialised search engines are those dedicated to finding individuals operating on or available though the internet. Foremost amongst these are the engines dedicated to finding e-mail addresses, phone numbers and/or postal addresses. For example, if you need to find the office phone number of an academic you would like to contact in relation to your research question, there are a number of search engines dedicated to nothing but compiling lists of phone numbers and addresses. Although no online engine can access even a fraction of the phone numbers and addresses that exist, two of the best are the Worldwide Online Phonebook (http://members.lycos.nl/marc2001/) and World Pages Global Find (http://www.worldpages.com/global). An added advantage of these search engines is that they have multi-country and reverse look-up capabilities.

> **TIP** Reverse look-up allows you to go from a phone number (or e-mail address) to the name (and, if available, address) of the individual it is registered to.

Although e-mail information can go out of date rather quickly, as a general rule, e-mail finders are useful starting points when trying to locate a particular individual or expert. Two of the better engines are: ICQ (http://www.icq.com/search/E-mail.html) and WED (http://worldE-mail.com). The advantage that these two engines have over others is that their indexes include e-mail addresses outside the United States and both of them have incorporated reverse e-mail-finding capabilities.

We will look in more detail in Chapter 7 at the importance of being able to find and contact individuals interested in your topic. For now it is worth noting that as well as directories of newsgroups and Usenet groups, there are various tools available for finding individual experts. Of these, probably the most direct way of finding and contacting individual experts in your field is to access the homepages of universities and research institutions and then follow their links to the department or school dealing with your subject area. Once there, you can easily discover which member of staff is working in the area, what they have written, and how you can contact them. There are also specialist search engines that can help. Probably the most useful are those that have been developed to search the Net looking for university home-pages. Two engines stand out for the beginning researcher. First, there is the University of Texas's site (http://www.utexas.edu/world/univ). This site has the homepages of all US-based universities and community colleges listed by state or in alphabetical order. Second, Braintrack (http://www. braintrack.com) claims to be the world's largest index of universities. Technically, Braintrack is an index rather than a search engine; however, the more specialised an index and engine become, the more these two tools begin to merge.

In addition to dedicated engines, university experts can also be found through scholarly societies and non-profit organisations which maintain Websites containing expert-finding tools. For instance, most scholarly societies include indexes to associated departments. Some even maintain indexes of experts willing to answer questions placed to the society. For example, the United Kingdom's Political Studies Association operates a range of services for finding experts available to both members and non-members at (http://www.psa.ac.uk).

While you can take advantage of e-mail, university and other expert finding engines, another opportunity provided by search engines is the dedicated expert finder. There are hundreds of expert finders that can be used in academic research. Some of these are designed to enable you to find an expert working in the area you are studying, others allow you to submit a question that is then forwarded to a registered expert who will subsequently respond to your enquiry. Facsnet (http://facsnet.org), although primarily targeted at journalists, provides anyone with the resources necessary to improve their understanding of many academic areas. It provides an index of 'top experts and scholars on whom reporters can call for help' (http://www.facsnet.org/about/mission.php3). Similarly, Ask an Expert (http://www.askanexpert.com) provides the e-mail addresses of experts who have volunteered to answer your questions across a range of subject areas, greatly increasing the likelihood your query will meet with a response (although one drawback of this site is that it has a fairly limited range of categories relevant to the general research student). A final specialised engine worth mentioning is Reference Desk (http://www.refdesk.com/expert.html). We mention this engine because, unlike the other engines we have discussed, Reference Desk is dedicated to locating other expert finders, allowing you to maximise your search potential.

The professional services

A final set of tools you should consider when using search engine technology to access information is the range of professional services that is available on the Web. Although these services charge, they are some of the most valuable search tools you can use in your research. They are often able to provide information and sites that you will not be able to access in any other way, such as public records, legal decisions, conference papers, journal articles, scholarly papers etc. Not only do these services provide a range of valuable data but they scour thousands of data sources, so that a single search can turn up vast amounts of information, or can find a very specific record or document that you may be looking for. Moreover, as these are professional services, depending on paying customers for their survival, overall the information they produce tends to be more reliable than the material most students are able to find when left to their own devices. Of the numerous professional services available online, one of the most commonly subscribed to is Lexis-Nexis (http://www.lexis-nexis.com). Lexis-Nexis has a range of different search engines covering law, business, government and academic, and, whichever service you use, it offers one of the largest collections of academically relevant information available online.

In this chapter we hope we have shown you the ways in which carrying out an academic research project requires you to approach the internet in a particular way. Specifically, it helps if you place what you are doing into what is essentially a professional context: you are an academic researcher using the search and find functions available on the Web to source particular kinds of information and material to be used in your project. You are also using these functions to select academically useful information and filter out detritus. In deciding which search engines, gateways or databases to use, you are in many ways determining the shape and the quality of your research. For this reason, we urge you to plan carefully, using your academic judgement to decide what you want to find and how best you might do so. A focused search strategy, targeting the specific resources you need, will save you time in the long run, and provide considerable added value to your project as a whole.

Exercise 1: Develop and discuss your specific online search strategy

Attempt to develop a preliminary research strategy. In doing this, you should tell your reader exactly how you intend to go about conducting your online information hunt! As part of this you should discuss why you intend to follow a given search strategy. You should explain how you intend to get around any stumbling blocks during the online search and you must do all of this in such a way as to link it back into your research proposal/design. You should be able to demonstrate that you understand how your online strategy will be used at different stages of the research process, so as to guide your online time and the relevant online activities at each stage of the research process.

Exercise 2: Search terms and Boolean operators

With your research question in mind, make out a set of preliminary search terms to be used in one of the major search engines, and to search one of the electronic databases available through your university library, JSTOR for example. Plug these into each respectively, and note the number of returns you generate. Is it feasible for you to wade through all of these? Are they all relevant to what you are interested in studying?

Now, consider specifically what you want to know, and write out a search request using the Boolean operators AND and NOT. How are the number and relevance of returns affected? Is there a way you can reduce the number of returns to a manageable number of relevant documents using a combination of Boolean operators?

Remember to print out or save the returns you generate from targeted searches for future reading and reference.

Exercise 3: The Invisible Web

Explore and review no fewer than three hidden Websites *directly related* to your chosen research problem. When reviewing these sites you must discuss, amongst other things, what was contained on the site and how it relates to your topic (background material, tangentially related material, core information, etc.). You must also discuss:

1. How you found the Websites.
2. If you used a search engine embedded in the site:
   (a) Was it useful?
   (b) If not, why not? And what could you have done to improve the usefulness of the data it returned?
3. How useful the data on the Websites was for your project, including a discussion of how the information you found on the hidden site compared to information that you have been accessing on the 'open Web'.

● References and Resources

Argus Clearinghouse, http://www.clearinghouse.net, accessed 02/05/2006.

Ask an Expert, http://www.askanexpert.com, accessed 27/02/2007.

BUBL Information Service, http://bubl.ac.uk, accessed 01/01/06.

Braintrack University Index, http://www.braintrack.com, accessed 27/02/2007.

CEO Express: The Executives Internet, http://ceoexpress.com, accessed 27/02/2007.

DMOZ Open Directory Project, http://dmoz.org, accessed 27/02/2007.

Facsnet: Better Journalism through Education, http://facsnet.org, accessed 27/02/2007.

Google Groups, http://www.groups.google.com, accessed 27/02/07.

Governments on the WWW, http://www.gksoft.com/govt, accessed 27/02/2007.

How Stuff Works, http://computer.howstuffworks.com/search-engine.htm, accessed 27/02/2007.

http://www.clearinghouse.net/faq.html, accessed 13/11/2006.

http://www.icq.com/search/E-mail.html, accessed 02/12/2005.

INFOMINE: Scholarly Internet Resource Collection, http://infomine.ucr.edu, accessed 25/07/2006.

Intute, http://www.intute.ac.uk, accessed 15/10/2006.

Lexis-Nexis, http://www.lexis-nexis.com, accessed 27/02/2007.

Librarians' Internet Index, http://www.lii.org, accessed 27/02/2007.

Liddy, E. (2001), 'How a Search Engine Works', *Searcher*, 9(5), http://www.infotoday.com/searcher/may01/liddy.htm, accessed 20/10/2006.

LookSmart Vertical Search, http:looksmart.com, accessed 27/02/2007.

Lycos, http://members.lycos.nl/marc2001, accessed 12/03/2001.

Mailing List Gurus Page, http://lists.gurus.com, accessed 02/02/2007.

McGuire, M., Stilborne, L., McAdams, M. and Hyatt, L. (2000), *The Internet Handbook for Writers, Researchers and Journalists* (New York: Guilford Press.

Political Studies Association (UK), http://www.psa.ac.uk, accessed 12/12/2006.

Refdesk.com: Ask the Experts, http://www.refdesk.com/expert.html, accessed 27/02/2007.

Richard Kimber's Political Science Resources, http://www.psr.keele.ac.uk, accessed 27/02/2007.

Search Engine Showdown, http://www.searchengineshowdown.com, accessed 27/02/2007.

Search Engine Watch, http://www.searchenginewatch.com, accessed 27/02/2007.

Topica, http://www.topica.com, accessed 27/02/2007.

Topica Lists, http://lists.topica.com/dir/?cid=0, accessed 27/02/2007.

University of British Columbia, http://www.library.ubc.ca/poli, accessed 02/05/2005.

University of Texas at Austin (Web US Higher Education Institutions), http://www.utexas.edu/world/univ, accessed 20/01/2007.

WWW.InvisibleWeb, http://www.invisible-Web.net, accessed 01/10/2006.

Worldpages, http://www.worldpages.com/global, accessed 05/05/2005, renamed Yellow Book, http://www.yellowbook.com, accessed 27/02/2007.

WorldEmail, http://worldE-mail.com, accessed 26/02/2007.

5 Research Ethics

Any researcher working today has to be aware of the ethical questions that may arise in the context of what he or she is doing. What this means is that, for the contemporary researcher, it is not enough to embark on the pursuit of knowledge. There also needs to be careful consideration of any ethical or moral questions it may raise: in terms of how the research is conducted, what it seeks to discover, and what the impact of the findings may be. Most universities now require a statement on ethics from individual researchers in particular fields – medicine, the sciences and social sciences – before work can be funded or commenced.

● Core Considerations

Ethical considerations are important to researchers at all levels, and there is always potential for a research project to throw up ethical problems. One ethical issue that arises in almost all situations is plagiarism. As an ethical issue, plagiarism is also the most clear cut: you must not do it. However, there are other kinds of considerations which may bear upon your research and which require a little more thought and judgement in deciding what is ethical and what is not. Whilst the ethical framework governing humanities and social sciences is not as detailed or formalised as that of, say, medical research, there are nevertheless some ethical principles that are quite widely recognised. A glance at the Website of professional associations such as the Political Studies Association, the British Psychological Society or the British Association for Applied Linguistics will reveal discipline-specific ethical statements, to which the association believes the profession should adhere.

Whether and to what extent ethical concerns arise in your research depends very much on the nature of the particular project, but it is as well to be aware of the potential issues from the outset, as they may have some bearing on how you frame your topic. Equally, the kinds of ethical problems traditionally associated with academic research can sometimes be deepened or modified by the use of computer and internet technology. In this chapter, we will look at some of the key ethical issues that research has long been known to create and at how they arise, particularly in the context of the internet. We will also look at some ways in which these problems can be ameliorated.

In broad terms, the ethical considerations that bear upon a research project fall into two categories: on the one hand, there are issues to do with how you use and present your research findings, and, on the other, issues to do with how those findings were acquired. We will examine in turn some of the main considerations in each of these areas.

Copyright

We have noted before that any research project will require you to familiarise yourself with work done on the topic that you are addressing. There is likely to be a good deal of this material and, in the context of the internet, it is often quite easily and quickly retrieved. However, there are some issues to do with the use that you make of this material in your project. One important consideration here concerns laws of copyright. These are internationally recognised laws that protect authors of any published piece of work against the unauthorised copying of their work for purposes of publication or sale. Items protected under these laws include not only textual works, such as books or articles, but also things like images and sound. Any individual (or organisation) copying works of this sort without permission and then publishing them or attempting to sell them is in breach of the law. It is also worth adding here that when it comes to copyright issues, ignorance of the law is not considered an adequate defence against legal action.

Most people are aware, at least at a general level, of copyright. Many are less aware, however, of the fact that these laws apply just as much to the internet as they do to material produced in more traditional form (Mawhood and Tysver, 2000, p. 98). The internet often seems to be so much of a free-for-all that there is a tendency to think that no rules apply. This is not the case. As with traditional books or articles, the law allows what is called 'fair use'; in other words, it is permissible to reproduce a small part of a work, such as a short quotation or a table of information, where it is pertinent to the work being undertaken. Beyond this, however, copyright restrictions apply on the internet.

Of course, with most university projects the resulting work is not going to be published or sold and so it is unlikely to stray into copyright territory, although it is worth noting that if the work were subsequently used in a published piece, the situation would change. It is also worth remembering that if, for example, you were particularly pleased with your project and decided to put it up onto a Webpage, then you would be in breach of the copyright laws were you to have used extensive material originally produced by someone else.

Confidentiality

One further area to do with the presentation of your research findings where ethical issues may arise concerns the requirements of confidentiality. In contrast to the use of published sources, where, as we have seen, revealing the identity of the author may be an ethical requirement, in other contexts, the reverse might apply. This is particularly the case where you are engaged in work that involves interviews, focus groups or other forms of interactive research. Again, this is an area where research opportunities have been much augmented by the availability of internet-based communication (see Chapter 4). It is also, however, an area where some care needs to be taken on ethical grounds.

In these kinds of research contexts, preserving confidentiality can be very important. Publishing the names of participants can open them up to unwanted correspondence or intrusion. Further, where the subject matter of the research touches upon areas considered particularly private or sensitive, confidentiality can help avoid embarrassment or harm to personal or professional relationships. It is generally regarded as an important element in privacy rights that people have the opportunity to determine what information about them is disclosed. In addition to these ethical considerations, it is also worth noting, in a more pragmatic vein, that participants are more likely to be honest and complete in their responses if they are assured that the results will be presented in a manner that preserves confidentiality. As a rule, therefore, you should always guarantee to participants that anonymity will be preserved, or, where the nature of the research project makes this difficult, ensure that they are aware of this and are happy to proceed on that basis. In most cases, anonymity can quite easily be ensured by presenting the responses that you get in an aggregated, statistical form. Where the project requires attributing responses to individuals, the use of pseudonyms is advisable.

> **Glossary**
> **Confidentiality**: The principle that information is only accessible to authorised individuals.

Of course, confidentiality is a concern with research undertaken in any context where interviews, discussion forums and so forth are used, but research of this kind undertaken on the internet can create additional challenges. The maintenance of privacy is the principal concern that people generally have with the internet (Tavani, 2000, p. 70). This is understandable since internet technology makes the tracing of information about individuals much easier. In order to minimise the vulnerability of participants in your research to undue intrusion, you should ensure not only that names are concealed but also that e-mail addresses, URLs and other information that might give clues to identities, are withheld.

Finally, it is worth noting that internet communications cannot be guaranteed to be secure. It is possible for people to hack into e-mail archives and documents or to intercept messages. One way of minimising risk here is to use encryption software to ensure that information cannot be read by a third party, although software of this kind can be expensive. Alternatively, you might design the research so as to minimise the information potentially disclosed to intruders: for example, you might design an e-mail questionnaire in such a way that respondents return only answers and not the questions to which they are replying (Nosek et al., 2002, p. 165). In general, you need to be aware of problems of disclosure and find ways of reducing the risk of people's details leaking out: this is a basic part of the 'duty of care' that researchers have with respect to their participants.

This last issue takes us on to ethical questions concerning the way in which you acquire information for your project when it involves interaction with participants. We will now go on to consider some further issues that arise in this respect.

Informed consent

The principle of informed consent is generally held to be a basic ethical requirement in interactive forms of research. Three elements go to make up this principle: that participants are made fully aware that they *are* participants; that they are properly informed as to the nature and purpose of the research; and that they are given the opportunity to refuse to participate or to withdraw from the project. We will consider each of these in turn.

There has been quite a history of academics conducting research in a covert manner and the internet has made this approach all the easier. One no longer has to go to the lengths that two sociologists in the 1930s went to when they concealed themselves under beds in student dormitories in order to record the residents' conversations (Homan, 1991, p. 46). In an online setting, it is now possible to 'lurk' in internet chat rooms or discussion forums without ever revealing your presence, or to operate with a fake identity.

In general, however, this kind of covert research is not regarded as ethical. The methods of the sociologists mentioned above were criticised; even though they had no intention of revealing personal details of the students on whom they eavesdropped (their interest was in particular conversational forms), they were nevertheless thought to be guilty of unwarranted intrusion. Of course, there are no problems in making use of material that people have clearly intentionally published online but it is worth noting that judgements about what falls into this category can sometimes be difficult, particularly in the context of the internet. As Waskul and Douglass (1996: 131) point out, the internet tends to blur the distinction between public and private, making it difficult sometimes to determine what information should be regarded as 'fair game' for the researcher and what should not. People posting messages in chat rooms or on discussion lists are not necessarily expecting that the material will be used or reproduced outside that particular context.

In view of this, you should think hard about the information you find online and limit yourself to using only that material you are confident has been deliberately posted into the public realm. Otherwise, it is much better to seek information from participants who have been clearly informed that you are conducting research. Generally, this will not be difficult to do. If your research is based on e-mail contact or through a dedicated Website, it is easy to alert the people you contact that you are conducting research either through an introductory e-mail or though a notice posted on the site. If you are hoping to conduct research through a pre-existing forum where you cannot necessarily contact individual contributors directly, you should contact the owner or moderator of the site to explore ways in which people can be informed about your research.

However, there are some cases where things are a little trickier. For example, if your research involved children, it would be less easy to be certain that they understood what they were being told. In such cases, it is best to gain consent from appropriate 'gatekeepers' such as parents or guardians as well as from the children themselves (Homan, 1991, p. 83)

If the consent obtained from participants is to be considered genuinely 'informed', it is also necessary to explain fully the nature and purpose of the research project. Participants will need to know exactly what information you are looking for, how you intend to analyse it and what the finished project will be likely to contain before they can make a proper decision as to whether they want to take part. People may be happy to participate in research, say, about attitudes to multiculturalism but may be less inclined to do so if it is made clear to them that the researcher's real aim is to look at the prevalence of implicit racism in various social groups. Again, informing people fully about the nature of the research is important but not always a completely straightforward matter. If your research is particularly complex or technical in nature, it may prove difficult to explain it fully to participants who are not specialists in the field. In such circumstances, the researcher simply has to be as clear as possible and ensure that participants have the opportunity to ask questions about the project at the outset and as the research progresses. In these cases, as with any circumstance in which the informed consent principle is unavoidably limited in its application, the researcher must remain aware that they have an additional duty of care toward participants to ensure that they are in no way misinformed, harmed or rendered vulnerable as a result of their participation (Darlington and Scott, 2002, p. 26).

One other obstacle to fully informing participants as to the nature of the project can arise where the disclosure of such information might compromise the research itself by prompting participants to modify their responses in view of the aims of the researcher. For example, if your research involved asking participants for information on childcare or domestic activities in the home, disclosing the fact that your aim is to assess the extent to which men under-perform in this area as compared with women might have the effect of leading some of the participants to modify their responses, whether consciously or otherwise, in order to avoid providing evidence for what they may regard as an unpalatable conclusion or for fear of being thought neglectful. In cases where you might have good reasons for not disclosing fully your intentions with respect to the research, it is important that you compensate for this by providing participants with a 'debrief' once the research is complete, informing them fully as to the aims of the research and providing them with the opportunity to withdraw at that point should they wish to do so.

If your research is being conducted through a Website, this can present some problems because online communities frequently have a 'fluid' character as people come and go and there is no guarantee that all those who have participated in the research will necessarily return to the site to receive a debrief. There are, however, ways around this. You can either design the process such that you obtain an e-mail address from all participants upfront so that you can send them more details of the project later on, or, alternatively, you can arrange for a debrief page to appear automatically when a participant leaves the site (Nosek et al., 2002, p. 162).

The final requirement laid down by the principle of informed consent is that participants should be given full opportunity to withdraw from the research at any time. At the outset it is advisable to provide a consent form that participants can complete and which makes clear that they can withdraw at any point should they so wish. In online contexts, this can be attached to an initial e-mail or posted as a Webpage which they must complete before entering the main part of the site. You should then ensure that participants do have a practical and easy way of signalling their withdrawal during the course of the research. This can be done either by providing them with an e-mail contact address so that they can inform you directly or, if you are using a dedicated Website, by posting a 'withdraw' button, prominently displayed, on the site. Finally, you need to ensure that you have some appropriate way of cataloguing the responses you receive from your participants so that, should any of them withdraw, you can easily identify any information you might already have obtained from them and remove it.

Online etiquette (netiquette)

While there is no definitive statement on how to interact online, the most widely accepted rules informing 'netiquette' are discussed below and listed in Table 5.1. With this in mind, in any research of an interactive sort you should always seek to maintain appropriate standards of politeness and consideration when dealing with participants. You may also need to assume some responsibility for ensuring, equally, that participants behave appropriately towards one another if the project requires them to interact. Again, in online environments, there are specific issues to bear in mind. Communication via the internet has its own particular character which requires specific care to be taken, something that is reflected in the

Always be courteous when engaged in online communication.
Always use a clear subject heading to indicate what information you are requesting.
Never send inflammatory material when using online resources.
Always identify yourself, include information on who you are, what your interest is, how you think your recipient can help, and how to contact you.
AVOID USING ALL CAPITAL LETTERS.
Include a precise description of what information you are looking for from your participant/contact.
Be careful with humour and sarcasm!
Never use information provided by others without explicit permission or in unethical ways (e.g., to misrepresent their views).
Never forward information provided by your participant without their specific and expressed permission!

Table 5.1   Rules informing online etiquette (netiquette)

growing literature on 'netiquette'. Online communication in the form, most obviously, of e-mail has a novel character, standing, as it seems to, halfway between the formality of a written letter and the informality or immediacy of conversation (and, of course, without the body language). As a result, it is a medium in which it is easy to communicate in ways that are hasty, ill-considered or careless, and, as with a letter, once sent the communication cannot be retrieved or modified. You need to be attentive, therefore, to how you communicate online and bear in mind some basic requirements.

It is important to show respect for the people with whom you are interacting. An important element in this is ensuring that you take care in your communications. Ensure, for example, that you address people properly, as you would in a letter, avoiding overfamiliarity. You should also, as a matter of respect, avoid excessive informality in expression – the use of slang, abbreviations and so forth – as well as taking care over spelling, punctuation and grammar. And you should also be aware of tone; it is easy, when dashing off a quick e-mail, to express yourself in a way that may be ambiguous or unintentionally abrupt. It is always a good idea, once you have written an e-mail, to re-read it carefully to ensure that it meets the appropriate standards. As well as being a matter of courtesy, you are much more likely to receive co-operative responses if your communications meet appropriate standards. As well as e-mail, you should take similar care with any messages or other information that you post up on Websites.

A further principle to observe, which we have touched upon already, is respect for privacy. We noted earlier that this lays down requirements for confidentiality in terms of what you reveal about people but it also applies to the way in which you, as the researcher, interact with them. You should avoid being overly inquisitorial with participants and certainly avoid attempting to cajole them into revealing more about themselves than they are comfortable with. Again, care in communication can prevent putting people in a situation where they feel harassed or defensive. It is also as well to be clear in your communications with participants that levels of disclosure are entirely in their hands.

Treating people with due respect also means being sensitive to questions of time. Whilst your research project might be one of the main things preoccupying you, this is not so for others, who will have priorities of their own and be likely to have only limited time in which to deal with your questions or requests. In view of this, you should avoid overburdening people with excessive amounts of information or unduly long communications and try to keep the material that you send out concise and to the point. You should also be patient and learn not to expect immediate responses from people. This issue is something you should also think about when designing the research, so that you facilitate the process as far as possible by making the tasks you require of participants as quick and easy as possible. It is also best to ensure that any instructions that you provide are clear and accessible.

> **Glossary**
> **Netiquette**: Conventions that govern online communications, designed to ensure polite interactions between individuals and groups communicating with others online.

A related consideration here concerns an awareness of the technical limitations of participants. There is no guarantee that those with whom you are working will have the same level of competence with computers as you do. It is therefore important that your research design seeks to maximise ease of use and does not make too many technical demands upon participants. You should also, by the same token, be forgiving of others' mistakes and seek to respond to them politely and helpfully. Again, this is likely to make the research experience a more pleasant one for all concerned.

Another area where netiquette should be observed is where your research requires you to visit discussion sites. Aside from the requirements of honesty and openness discussed earlier on in this chapter, you also need to be aware that such sites have their own rules and you should ensure that you understand and abide by them. It is easy to upset people or undermine the discussion by inappropriate interventions. It is always a good idea to follow a discussion for a while before getting involved so that you gain a better sense of its conventions and its limits. It will also make it less likely that you irritate people by, for example, asking irrelevant questions or raising issues that the group has already dealt with.

Of course, your research may also involve you managing a discussion site or list of your own and this involves certain extra obligations. As the owner of the site, you acquire an obligation to ensure that discussion is conducted in an appropriate manner and that mutual respect is shown. To aid in this, it is a good idea to display prominently on the site a clear set of guidelines regarding appropriate modes of communication as well as the nature of, and limits to, the subjects under discussion so that all visitors to the site have a firm idea of what is expected. You will also need to ensure that you monitor the site regularly to check that those guidelines are being observed. There may be occasions, too, where you will need to intervene to remove inappropriate postings or even to ask someone to cease using the site if they are not willing to abide by the rules. Of course you will want to encourage participation on your site but in doing so you need to accept some responsibility to ensure that when people do participate they are treated properly and are not abused or offended.

A consideration of the ethics of your work requires you to step back from it a little and think about your research as more than a means to an end. Any research project that involves dealing with people on any level will inevitably throw up some ethical issues, perhaps around the acquisition and presentation of information and findings, perhaps around the difficulty of establishing an appropriate or professional relationship. In this chapter, we have tried to provide you with a general introduction to the major ethical issues you may encounter when conducting online research, as well as a guide to how they might properly be addressed. None of these basic principles of online etiquette is particularly difficult to observe and, taken together, they form a code of practice that will not only ensure that your interactions online are appropriate but will also make you a more effective internet researcher.

Exercise 1: Ethical project?

Students rarely consider the ethics of their research project as it relates either to their own work or to others, but they should! Therefore, take 10 minutes to examine your project on a step-by-step basis in terms of how and what information you are seeking. Once you have completed this, sit down and list 5–10 ethical implications that are inherent in your project. Link these directly to the use of the Net in your research.

Exercise 2: Reflection

Consider how you might address each of the points you have noted, making sure to incorporate any required changes in procedure or planning into your overall research plan. Are there any knock-on implications here? For instance, will the project take longer than you initially thought? Are you going to be able to provide full information and acquire informed consent over the internet? If you cannot acquire informed consent, is it still appropriate to proceed with your project or will you need to consider new ways to gather your data?

Exercise 3: Practice makes perfect

Write a draft e-mail to someone you will have to contact in the course of your research project, either as a potential participant, or as someone who may be able to provide you with specialist advice. In the e-mail, outline the intent and remit of your project, say how you would like them to help you, and provide any other information that might be important in order for them to make an informed decision about whether or not to participate. Read through the e-mail when you have finished, and consider what your own response to such an e-mail would be, were you to receive it. Is it appropriately addressed and signed? Is full information provided and in such a way that the person reading it will not be confused or likely to misinterpret your intentions? Is there anything you have not mentioned? Is it polite? Is it truthful? If not, how might you rewrite it in such a way as to be able to send it to someone without fear of causing offence or crossing ethical boundaries?

References and Resources

Darlington, Y. and Scott, D. (2002), *Qualitative Research in Practice: Stories from the Field* (Buckingham: Open University Press). In this text the authors have 'shared with us their stories about the qualitative research process while linking their experiences to theory and practice in human services. The difficulties, successes and new pathways created by their research findings shed new light on the complex journey qualitative researchers embark on with every new research project' – G. Edgecombe, cited at http://www.amazon.co.uk/Qualitative-Research-Practice-Stories-Field/dp/033521147X/ref=sr_1_1/026-6579488-6739635?ie=UTF8&s=books&qid=11 85202280&sr=8-1, accessed 12/07/2007.

Ebiefung, A. (2002), *Responsible Use of the Internet in Education* (Chattanooga, Tennessee: Penman Publishing). This text critically examines the key issues that are emerging with the increased use of the internet in the educational process, including the uses and abuses of the Net in academic learning and research.

Homan, R. (1991), *The Ethics of Social Research* (London: Longman). This is a basic introduction to the issues of ethics in the social research process, which effectively employs case studies to illustrate the issues as they relate to a range of different research traditions.

Israel, M. and Hay, I. (2006), *Research Ethics for Social Scientists* (London: Sage). This took offers an accessible text on ethics for social science students. It provides practical guidance on how ethics influences the research practice and is illustrated with real-life examples.

Langford, D. (2000), *Internet Ethics* (Basingstoke: Palgrave Macmillan). This text is one of the few that has been specifically designed to help students work their way through the key issues they are likely to encounter during their online research projects, including issues of data protection.

Mawhood, J. and Tysver, D. (2000), 'Law and the Internet' in D. Langford (ed.), *Internet Ethics* (New York: St Martin's Press), pp. 96–126.

Nosek, B. et al. (2002) 'Ethical Research: Ethics, Design and Control in Psychological Research on the Internet', *Journal of Social Issues*, 1: 161–76.

Oliver, P. (2007), *The Student's Guide to Research Ethics* (Buckingham: Open University Press). This text identifies and works through a range of ethical issues that students are likely to encounter when engaged in the research process. The issues covered include ethical issues involved with consent, confidentiality and dissemination, and discusses how some of the problems associated with these can be resolved.

Tavani, H. (2000), 'Privacy and Security', in D. Langford (ed.), *Internet Ethics* (New York: St Martin's Press), pp. 65–89.

Walther, J. (2002), 'Research Ethics in Internet-enabled Research: Human Subjects Issues and Methodological Myopia', *Ethics and Information Technology*, 4: 205–16.

Waskul, D. and Douglass, M. (1996), 'Considering the Electronic Participant: Some Polemical Observations on the Ethics of Online Research', *The Information Society*, 12: 129-39.

6 Key Sources of Online Information

● What are Sources?

Finding the most useful and appropriate source materials will often be the principal challenge you face when conducting your research using the internet, and is essential to the success of your project. Regardless of what you want to research, you are going to have to collect a considerable amount of information in order to answer your question. As you have already learned from producing your research strategy and plan, this information comes in a range of forms, sizes and fits. When undertaking academic research, you are going to come across three kinds of sources: primary, secondary and tertiary. Although the definition of these terms varies depending on the context of the research and the academic discipline involved, in general we can describe them in the following way:

- **Primary sources** are the fundamental, authoritative stuff of research, including the data you collect using online tools such as e-mail or your own or someone else's observations of Usenet interactions; statistics; archive material, including letters, diaries, newspaper articles etc.; works of literature or philosophy; questionnaire or survey results.
- **Secondary sources** are works about people, phenomena, works of art or literature that other individuals or organisations have complied and analysed.
- **Tertiary sources** consist of materials in which the information from secondary sources has been selected, condensed and reproduced in a convenient, easy-to-read form. For example, newspaper editors frequently report on the findings of a study based on what someone else has said or written, rather than providing information or opinion derived from having read the study themselves.

Primary sources

A primary source is an original work of some kind. It represents original thinking, observations, interviews, activities, accomplishments; reports on discoveries or events; or shares new information. Primary sources are indispensable, and should be the chief inspiration for what you write. They should, whenever possible, be consulted first hand. There is no substitute for examining a source yourself and determining what it means, rather than relying on what someone else tells you it means. This is where the internet becomes invaluable as a research tool itself. Not only has the advent of the internet, and particularly of Web-based databases, exponentially increased the availability of and access to a range of primary sources, but, with the increasing sophistication of internet software programs, your ability to generate your own primary data is rapidly becoming a possibility in many forms of academic research.

In the area of the arts and humanities, a primary source is often seen as being the original text, record (audio or visual), or document. It can be a literary or philosophical work, an information source that provides direct knowledge of an event, idea or experience, an everyday object produced by humans, an oral account or a work of art, a representation of any kind. Wherever possible, primary sources should be consulted in the language in which they were produced. When this is not possible, authoritative translations should be used (though, strictly speaking, these do not constitute true primary sources, as they are someone's interpretation of what was said).

> **Hint:** Online primary resources come in many different forms and are contained on a range of directories, databases and catalogues. As such, you should never rule out a possible source – you may already have the data you need!

In the social sciences, primary sources usually represent the first formal appearance of original research. Primary sources are original data, such as statistical information; surveys; interviews; contemporaneous news accounts; government documents; original documents, such as birth and death certificates, trial transcripts etc.; technical reports or reports of original research; patents; articles in journals publishing the data of primary research, and the main medium for the dissemination of new knowledge. Table 6.1 lists examples of primary data sources.

Literary texts: poems, novels, autobiographies, plays and their performance, etc.	Published materials: pamphlets, governmental and non-governmental documents
Diaries, letters, memoirs	Legal documents and records
Works of art and photographs; exhibition catalogues	Oral histories and interviews
Sets of data or demographic information	Questionnaire or survey data

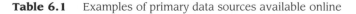

Table 6.1 Examples of primary data sources available online

Secondary sources

Most studies cannot be undertaken without secondary sources. Secondary sources consist of an analysis, interpretation or a restatement of primary sources. In other words, they reinterpret or discuss the meaning and context of primary sources (see Table 6.2). They do this in order to add to our understanding of a particular topic (often in order to update the analysis for a contemporary academic audience), using discipline-specific tools of interpretation. Any piece of research you do will, and should, incorporate or be based on secondary sources. Generally speaking, no piece of research will really be considered legitimate or thorough if the author cannot demonstrate knowledge of – or if she does not engage with – the existing scholarship: in other words with secondary sources.

With a few exceptions, the internet is an excellent source of readily-available secondary material. The beauty of this for your research is that by

Monographs and edited collections, reports, blogs (which report on what the blogger has read or seen)	Academic journal articles, magazine articles (these might even be tertiary in nature), and newspaper articles that report on findings or activities that the reporter has not directly observed or participated in
Summaries of events and shows that the reviewer attended or observed	Sources which report on or analyse objects, events, interviews or even questionnaire data that the reviewer has read directly

Table 6.2 Examples of secondary data sources available online

using the Net to engage with the secondary data and literature you will be able to begin demonstrating that you have gained a working knowledge of the extant scholarship. This will help provide a rationale for the research you are engaged in, and will also help you establish the context for your discussion and conclusions. In the humanities, the tools of interpretation used in producing secondary sources include theory, close reading, and reference to and engagement with other scholarship on the topic. In the social sciences, they include theory, qualitative and quantitative techniques of analysis, and engagement with relevant scholarship on the topic.

> **Note**: While appropriate primary data is key to the quality of your study, it is equally as important to remember that insufficient attention to secondary sources is likely to result in research lacking in depth, missing important detail, and the possible overgeneralisation of your findings.

Tertiary sources

Because tertiary sources are based on the writer's interpretation of secondary sources, they tend to contain little or no original work. It is not always easy to recognise Net sites that are using tertiary data or sources; however, one hint to keep in mind is that tertiary sources often have titles that contain phrases such as 'Concise' or 'for Dummies'. Because of their interpretation or summary nature (or the purpose they are being used for), tertiary sources are likely to be fairly useless at the latter stages of your research. Despite this, do not simply discount a site that uses them, as they can be useful when you first embark on your research project. This is because the better tertiary sources provide concise summaries of what research has been done in a field or how others have approached your subject, and thus can suggest how you might go about approaching your research.

> **Note**: Be wary when using the open Net as an information source. Many Websites are composites of a range of tertiary sources, contain little reliable or verifiable information and are generally poorly documented, if at all.

If you are very careful, some tertiary sources can be useful in the early stages of your research. For example, online bibliographies and survey articles can provide useful collations of primary and secondary sources, and may help you develop a reading list for your literature review, a fundamental step in the research process. Similarly, it is likely that you will find a range of useful starting points in online encyclopaedias and dictionaries, or sites that

	Primary source	Secondary source	Tertiary source
History	Letters from serving soldiers	Book on the US Civil War	*Concise History of 19th-Century America*
Literature	*The Untouchable*	Article on Banville's work	*Companion to Irish Literature*
Politics	The Constitution of the United States or the Declaration of Independence	Book about the role of the Supreme Court in protecting civil rights	Almanac of American Politics
Psychology	'On Female Sexuality'	Biography of Lacan	*Cosmopolitan* article
Sociology	Census data on birthrates by region	Essay on healthcare for women	*Introduction to Modern Social Theory*

Table 6.3   Examples of primary, secondary and tertiary sources in different academic disciplines

act as portals to a range of different tertiary sources. For example, when first starting out on the research trail you might be interested in going to the Internet Public Library (http://www.ipl.org) or the Resource pages of the Librarians' Internet Index (http://search.lii.org/index.jsp?more= SubTopic10). Any of these types of sites can help you start your research by pointing you to reliable tertiary resources and information.

To summarise, Table 6.3 offers examples of the different types of sources in different academic disciplines.

Online Sources: A Question of Access

Despite the technological innovation represented by the development of the internet, the requirements of research have remained unchanged. Good research is original, rigorous, contributes to scholarship and may have practical applications or effects. It relies on identifying and using appropriate sources. An appropriate source is a source that has demonstrable authority and bearing on the subject of research, and can be said to have **academic legitimacy**.

> **Glossary**
> **Academic legitimacy** means that the techniques you use to underpin your research and the sources you use provide information or data that conforms to the recognised standard of reliability and validity governing your academic discipline.

Because primary and secondary sources are increasingly available online through databases, archives and research gateways, knowledge and proficiency in the range of resources that are available for accessing different types and sources of information online is increasingly becoming an integral skill for contemporary researchers. As will be discussed in Chapter 7, the internet is increasingly becoming a viable tool for the generation of your own primary data through the use of online questionnaires, interviews and observations. However, when looking for other primary, secondary and even tertiary data, the internet has two main uses:

- establishing whether a given source of information is available;
- providing access to this source.

Strategy

The first use of the internet noted above is an essential – though often overlooked – step in the research process. The second is a bonus. The internet often allows easy, speedy access to material that might otherwise take time and effort to locate and gain access to. As discussed in Chapter 4, before you go online you need to develop a systematic and disciplined approach to compiling and accessing the scholarly resources available to you when using online technology. As part of this, you must first decide what kind of material will be most useful to you when undertaking your research. To do this we would suggest you consider the following questions:

- Which specific areas of scholarship have you identified as important to your research?
- Based on this, are there any immediately recognisable search terms or phrases you might use?
- Do you require primary material or evidence, or will secondary or tertiary material be adequate for your research needs (this should be considered in light of your stage of academic progression and the stage in your research process you are using the internet for)? For example, in the first year of your degree your research may require little more than a review of secondary and tertiary sources. However, by the time you are preparing to graduate you are likely to

have to demonstrate an understanding of and ability to generate a range of primary information, including finding and generating primary data online.

- Depending on the type of data you need, what kind of online sources will provide this? For instance, it might be possible that the data you require will be available in a particular text, which you can then search for online to see if it is available as electronic copy, or try and establish whether it is part of the catalogue holdings of your home or any nearby library. However, it may be that only access to a particular interview script will provide the data you need. It might even be that you require a range of statistical data. Establishing the existence, whereabouts and gaining access to each of these requires different types of online resources and search skills.

- Assuming that the material does exist online and is available, will you have access to the information? In other words, will the information be freely available or will there be some type of restriction placed on it? If restricted, do you have the resources or information necessary to lift the restriction?

- Finally, if you do not believe that the information exists online, or in a form that is available to you, does the internet provide you with an adequate platform for generating it?

Do not be surprised if the answers to these questions shift in the course of your reading and research: they should! However, this does not change the fact that no matter where you are in your research process, you should have a clear idea of your needs before you begin searching, otherwise you will get stuck in a cycle of surfing the Web instead of conducting directed research. To help you direct your online time, make a list of the kinds of sources you need, the topics you need to cover and any relevant search terms. If you do not do this, it is likely that your initial searches will be unfocused, and you will waste valuable time and energy on irrelevancies. At best, you will have to begin the search again; at worst, you will produce an ill-conceived and poorly executed piece of research, without academic merit.

Online Sources: Where to Start

For students and other researchers, one of the most useful places to begin searching for information on sources is the catalogue of any major research institution's main university library. Your library's homepage will probably be amongst the most useful and informative sources you will have available.

This is because most libraries have compiled and categorised the major online resources available to you through their site and listed them in easily readable and identifiable categories on their homepages. In other words, in academic research it is generally better not to succumb to the temptation to begin a search on the open Web, or worse still, by Googling. The beauty of the library is not that it is an easy shortcut to the primary and secondary resources available thorough your university but that these sources will have been previously vetted for their scholarly content and use, therefore making them sources you can consider accurate and reliable for your research.

> **Hint:** One way to remember the importance of the library to your research is to set your browser's start page to your library's homepage, at least for the duration of your research project.

Once you become familiar with the resources available at and through your library, you should begin your search proper with a thorough search of the library's main catalogue. Remember, too, that special collections are often an important source of primary material that may require you to enter a dedicated database at your library. Because of their usefulness, particularly in the Arts and Humanities, it is worth checking to see whether your library has any special collections and, if so, how you can best search and access the collection.

> **Hint:** It is useful at this stage to begin saving your searches. To do this you can either save them in your favourites/bookmarks (which you can subsequently export to a data stick or disk, so that you can access them no matter what computer you are working on) or you can open a Word document into which you can save your searches as you go along. The advantage of this is that you can anno-tate the entry, making it easy to recall what it was that attracted you to the site and how it fits into your research.

Electronic resources

In most libraries, searching the catalogue will only provide you with listings of the books, dissertations and journals held by the library, and possibly the major items in any special collections. It will not, as a general rule, be

Figure 6.1   University of Liverpool's database homepage

capable of returning an electronic version of a book; they will not return books that are not part of the library collection; and very few library search engines have been equipped to return individual chapters in books (even though they form part of the library's holdings). In order to begin producing a more comprehensive list of secondary sources that can be accessed though your library, you should move from your library's main catalogue to its selection of electronic databases and resources. For example, Figure 6.1 shows you the first few lines of the University of Liverpool's library's list of available databases (http://www.liv.ac.uk/library/electron/erdatabase.html).

Unfortunately, individuals accessing most university library electronic databases, who do not have access to the terminals in the library, and are not members of the university, are unlikely to be able to take advantage of these resources. This is because most of the major resources that a university library subscribes to are password protected – or are 'access controlled', so that only registered students and staff are able to use the resource – and thus form part of the hidden Web that is inaccessible to non-university members. However, for those of you who are allowed access, these databases and resources will form an invaluable link to valid and reliable primary and secondary resources.

Information gateways

Once you have mined the resources of your home library, it is time to move onto the open Web. In doing so you will find a range of engines and directories available to you, depending on where you are in your academic career, the research process, and the types of information you need. The key to using the different tools available to you is to remember that, while each of them can provide a window to an endless amount of primary, secondary and

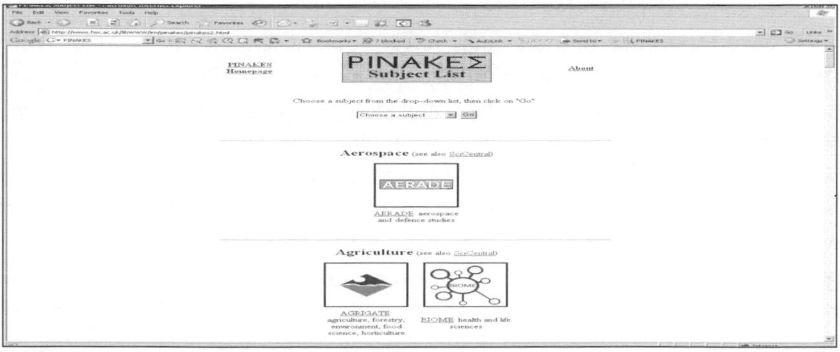

Figure 6.2 PINAKEΣ

tertiary sources in your selected subject area, the information provided will be more or less appropriate depending on your topic, the kind of information stored in individual databases or other databases linked into that network. Because of this, just as the library is often more useful for finding sources of academic quality, we would also suggest that before resorting to general search engines or directories (such as Google and Yahoo), you consider using an **information gateway**, or site designed to link you to subject-specific resources and networks.

Information gateways are useful not only because they can provide you with access to a wide range of information available on the open Web, but also because the information that these gateways link to tends to be useful for research purposes. In effect, gateways have been specifically designed to return information provided by academic institutions, libraries and research institutes. Because of this, gateways can be an effective tool in helping you locate primary sources, though they may be slightly less useful in providing access to secondary sources.

As Figure 6.2, the PINAKEΣ information gateway (http://www.hw.ac.uk/libWWW/irn/pinakes/pinakes.html) illustrates, most gateways provide two access routes to your specific area of interest. First, there will be a series of illustrated hypertext link boxes that you can scroll through; they will take you directly to the source illustrated in the box. Second, in addition to the hypertext boxes, most gateways will also offer a drop-down list, which will take you directly to the gateway of your choice.

Web rings

We often consider the Web in a linear fashion, as if it were arranged in lines going out from one page to another in an infinite line. Sometimes, however, the best way to conduct online research is to go around in circles or rings. This is because thousands of individuals have grouped together to develop **Web rings**. Web rings consist of a set of sites that have been linked together in such a way as to allow you to follow the embedded links in one page, onto the next site until you eventually arrive back at the first site. The advantages of these rings are, first, that all links take you to related information. Second, rings have been established specifically to focus on a particular topic. Third, rings have been designed by 'experts', or others, who are specifically interested in the given topic. Therefore, instead of randomly surfing the Web for information, rings allow you to collect a range of relevant information without having to utilise individual searches each time, or worry about the quality of the information you are accessing. To find a Web ring you might want to try going to: Ringsurf (http://www.ringsurf.com), RingWorld (http://www.webring.com), The Linux Webring (http://www.linuxweb ring.org), The World of Webrings (http://webringworld.org); or simply type the name of your topic followed by the phrase 'webring' into a standard search engine.

Databases

While gateways and rings do not store the information on their own sites, there are an almost limitless number of databases that do exist online. Rather than providing a set of links, databases collect and organise a range of resources, information and records related to a single subject area, in such a way as to allow the information to be easily searched and accessed. In short, a database 'is collection of information stored in a computer in a systematic way, such that a computer program can consult it to answer questions' (http://www.google.com/search?hl=en&rlz=1T4SUNA_en___GB215&defl=en&q=define:database&sa=X&oi=glossary_definition&ct=title). Because the best databases are compiled by subject specialists, they offer an excellent way to ensure you are accessing a range of quality primary and secondary sources in your area of interest. A sample of some of the better academic databases you might want to consider using (particularly in the early stages of your research) is provided in Table 6.4.

Indexes

An index is a type of database that organises its information into list form, allowing you to quickly determine if the data contained in its database is appropriate for your research needs. For example, as noted in Table 6.4, the MLA International Bibliography (http://collections.chadwyck.co.uk/home/home_mla.jsp) is an index which offers a searchable list of material published on language and literature, including articles, reviews, dissertations, monographs and edited collections. What you might find even more

Humanities abstracts	Citations of articles in all areas of the humanities
Historical abstracts	Abstracts of articles in scholarly history journals
JSTOR	Full-text database of scholarly articles
MLA	Citations to articles in language and literary studies
WorldCat	Books available in libraries worldwide. (Once you locate a book you can request it through Inter-Library Loan)
Digital dissertations	Full-text versions of PhD and Masters dissertations
ASSIA	Applied Social Sciences Index and Abstracts
Econlit	Index to books, journals and dissertations in economic theory and application
Lexis-Nexis	Legal information and full-text newspaper database
Web of Knowledge	Citation index for Science, Social Science, and Arts and Humanities
Worldwide political science abstracts	Abstracts of politics, international relations, government and public policy
Economic and Social	National Data Service providing access and support
Data Service	for key economic and social datasets
BOPCRIS	British Official Publications, 1688–1995
IESBS	Reference work for Social and Behavioral Sciences

Table 6.4   Major types of academic related databases

useful as you start your research process is that the MLA lists individual chapters in edited collections, which will often not be returned in a search of a library catalogue or, say, a more general online database such as Worldcat (http://www.worldcat.org).

Full-text catalogues

Another type of database you will find useful is the full-text catalogue. These are like online libraries, providing restricted access to 'bundles' of full-text journal and magazine articles. Because each catalogue bundles together its own unique range of journals (often based on those offered by a particular publisher, such as the Blackwell Synergy catalogue, or by subject discipline, such as JSTOR), it will be necessary for you to explore a range of these to determine which is most suited to your research needs. Keep in mind that some catalogues have been designed to thoroughly cover a very specific subject, while others have been designed to cover a range of journals representative of a broader discipline, while still others attempt to bundle together journals that represent a range of disciplines. The best way to know what is covered by a specific catalogue is to find its homepage; this will generally contain a list of the journals included in this particular bundle.

The virtue of these catalogues is that if you (or your home library) have access rights, the full-text version of your desired article can be either read directly online, saved on disk or data stick, or printed directly from the site for further (future) reference. One of the most easily used and widely available full-text catalogues for students studying at almost any major university is JSTOR (www.JSTOR.org). The goal of JSTOR and other similar full-text catalogues is to build an archive of 'scholarly materials' and to provide access to the full text of these materials. As you would expect from a full-text catalogue covering a range of disciplines, JSTOR draws its materials from a range of journals specialising in a broad range of humanities and social science subject areas. A particular strength of JSTOR is that it allows you not only to search by disciplinary area, but also to nominate more than one disciplinary area, or to select a search from a specific journal or number of journals contained in JSTOR's database. For example, a researcher working on Benjamin Franklin may find more relevant material by searching all History, Literary and Political journals carried by JSTOR, than by restricting themselves to a single disciplinary rubric or going to the open Net, where they will receive thousands of useless returns.

What we are saying is that when engaged in research, you should also be familiar with a range of specialised subject-specific databases that exist online because they have been developed to help you conduct specialised searches in a given topic area. If used wisely, subject-specific databases, such as Literature Online (LION – http://lion.chadwyck.co.uk), can be an important guide to your research and reading, especially in the initial stages of research or when you are attempting to complete a literature review.

Weblogs (blogs)

One of the most exciting aspects of the internet is that it constantly changes. This is true not only in terms of its content but also in terms of the technologies and protocols available online. One of the most recent developments you may wish to consider using in your research are **Weblogs** (blogs). A blog is little more than an online diary that you can create or access via the Web. The journal can consist of a mere text-based diary of an individual's personal thoughts, or can be as complex as a designed graphic display that facilitates discussions relating to the latest scientific discoveries. As such, blogs can be considered a small (or not so small) personal database.

What makes blogs interesting from a research perspective is not only that you can develop and post your own blog in order to create your own little 'soapbox', but that you can also use a blog to encourage the collection of information, or even try to mobilise a group of people. Blogs can also be the subject of your research, because at their base they form 'a collection of digital content that, when examined over a period of time' can help you understand and 'expose the intellectual soul of its author or authors' (Stone, 2004, p. 35). While this online diary will be of use to anyone interested in conducting ethnographic studies, there are also blogs dedicated to almost every subject under the sun. In fact, some of the more influential blogs, such as the *Daily Kos* (http://www.dailykos.com), have not only helped candidates for election raise money but have been able to put issues onto the political agenda.

What allowed the development of blogging was the advance in software capable of embedding HTML codes without the individual having to know the tags or the conventions governing their use. Thus, blogging came about because of the ease with which Web pages can be made. In fact, not only can stand-alone programs such as Dreamweaver help almost anyone develop their own Website, but a range of online sites have recently emerged that are designed to instruct the prospective blogger. Individuals with little or no technical knowledge, knowledge of HTML, or even an understanding of the software program being used, can learn how to develop their online journal, including how to embed interactive zones where readers can make their own comments.

> **Hint:** Technorati (http://www.technorati.com) and Google Blogs (http:// www.google.co.uk/blogsearch?hl=en) are two tools capable of finding blogs.

Chat and instant messaging

A final resource you might consider using are programs that have been designed to allow you to use the Net to conduct real-time communications. Two of the most useful of these are the range of Chat programs that are available on the Web and any of the growing number of Instant Messaging (IM) programs. Both of these technologies allow you to communicate, rendezvous, connect or collaborate with others by doing little more than typing (or video-linking) in real time. As such, the flow of the conversation appears more natural than in most e-mail communications or when operating via the listserv network.

> **Glossary**
> **Instant Messaging (IM)**: A software program that allows for real-time typed communication between two or more people operating on their computers at the same time – the most common program being Microsoft's Instant Messenger.

Initially, most instantaneous discussions took place in spaces that required you to log in to the discussion in order to participate. However, as a researcher, it is likely that you will want to avoid having to constantly log in to a dedicated chat room. It is also likely that you will find that many of the topics being discussed (and how they are being addressed) in these rooms to be quite frivolous. This is where other forms of real-time communications come into play. For instance, by using instant messaging technology you can actively engage in substantive real-time conversations. The key to any of these services, whether it be in the form of a chat room, instant messaging, or video technologies such as Skype, is that they allow you to contact anyone currently logged in to your service and have a typed real-time conversation with them.

Online broadcasts (podcasts)

Anyone who has an iPod® (or similar device) will be aware of online broadcasting, or 'podcasting'. This is simply another way to refer to the publishing of files on the internet. The difference is that instead of having to continually monitor the file for changes, you can subscribe to it and receive new files every time they are posted (much like a RSS feed).

While most of you have probably use online broadcast technology to receive, download and subsequently store music files, online broadcasting is quickly becoming a valuable source of information for anyone interested in conducting online research. Not only are a great many arts, cultural and political programs available as podcasted auditory files (readily available for free through places such as the iTunes music store), but there are also a growing range of visual broadcasts available to help in your research endeavours. Beyond the widely entertaining and occasionally informative YouTube (http://www.YouTube.com), there are any number of broadcasts dedicated to arts and cultural issues (such as the feed available though Cool Hunting http://www.coolhunting.com/video), news feeds (such as Reuters hourly updates http://www.reuters.co.uk), and thousands of other topics.

Finding Primary Sources and Archive Material Online

Although your literature review should include primary sources, it will, as we noted in Chapter 5, primarily involve discussion of secondary sources and material. However, if you have gone about your literature review properly, you should be sitting on a large list of citations, footnotes and bibliographies, which indicate relevant primary sources and where they are or might be located.

When looking for primary source material that has already been collected, catalogued and placed online – as opposed to the primary data you will generate though the use of interviews, questionnaires and observations – the best place to begin is with the specialised databases discussed above and in Chapter 4. In addition, however, we also suggest that you become familiar with a set of tools that have been developed and placed online specifically to help you locate the primary data sites hidden in the Invisible Web. Terry Abraham (Figure 6.3) has compiled one of the best. The Repositories of Primary Sources reports to have catalogued over 5000 primary sources databases, from across the full spectrum of academic disciplines, covering 'manuscripts, archives, rare books, historical photographs, and other primary sources for the research scholar' and for which 'All links have been tested for correctness and appropriateness' (http://www.uidaho.edu/special-collections/Other.Repositories.html). As you might imagine, having such

Figure 6.3   Terry Abraham's Repositories of Primary Sources

resources available at your fingertips makes the research process one that academics in years gone by could only have dreamed of.

> **Hint:** When looking for primary source data it is worth beginning your search by thoroughly exploring the databases and gateways provided by your library, as these will have been vetted for their academic merit, currency and accuracy.

Primary source portals are useful because they can often provide you with the information you need without you having to dedicate the time and resources necessary to collect your own primary data. They are a particularly important resource for anyone wishing to study national or regional data that has already been compiled in major national or international surveys.

When considering where you may find primary source data it also pays to be creative. For example, many primary source databases are embedded into sites sponsored or operated by international organisations and other university libraries. By way of illustration, let us examine three different sites dedicated to cataloguing and providing links to online primary source documentation. First, many of the agencies and institutions sponsored by, or affiliated to, the United Nations produce primary source material. Much of this material can be accessed for free online, or purchased at a reasonable price directly through the UN. What is good about the UN archives portal (Figure 6.4), is that it links you directly to its sub-agencies and affiliated organisations. This subsequently allows you to gain access to the sub-portals of these agencies and organisations, providing you with a whole range of other primary source documentation.

Second, as discussed, most university libraries provide online access to a range of primary source Websites. As illustrated in Figure 6.5, the University of Michigan has developed one of the most comprehensive portals to primary data available on the Web. Its Documents Center (http://www.lib.umich.edu/govdocs/index.html#doccen) provides you with links to thousands of primary source Websites containing high-quality qualitative and quantitative data from across the globe.

Third, a very under-utilised online documentary resource are churches. Many churches maintain primary source materials that are available online (though often for a small fee). For example, the Church of Jesus Christ of Latter-day Saints (the Mormon Church) maintains one of the largest genealogical libraries in the world (http://www.familysearch.org). Anyone

Figure 6.4 UNESCO archives portal

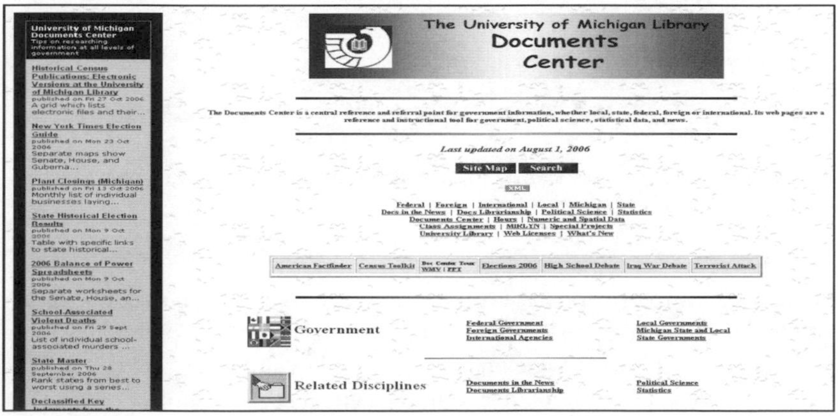

Figure 6.5 University of Michigan's Documents Center

looking for documentation on a particular individual or family might want to consider the resources held by religious as well as civil organisations.

What we are trying to stress is not that any individual site will provide you with all the primary data you will need (nor even the majority of it) to answer your question, as many projects will require you to conduct your own surveys or observations in order to collect the data you need. Rather, we are suggesting that when looking for primary and secondary sources, the internet provides a range of resources that are limited only by your ability to

Type of organisation	Example of the data that can be accessed
Governments	Census returns and other statistics; material relating to writers and artists; politicians and other individuals or organisations of note
Public libraries	Local government documentation, court records, records of births and deaths, personal papers and other materials related to local history.
Non-governmental organisations	Archives and libraries pertaining to the organization's goals and activities.
Business and non-profit organisations	A range of publicly available records.
University libraries, research institutes, museums, societies	Significant archive holdings.
Individuals	Many collect records and personal papers, which they archive and place online as private collections.

Table 6.5   Types of sites likely to provide links to primary data

figure out how to use and access them and that, as a general rule, the larger, better-funded, and/or more public-minded the individual or organisation, the more likely it is to provide online access to its catalogues and collections. For those of you who are interested in pursuing these ideas further, Table 6.5 provides some of the more useful types of agencies and organisations that collect and catalogue primary source material.

When the primary data you can access is not adequate to your needs, and you do not have the means to generate the data yourself, it may be necessary to arrange an archive visit. Before making a visit to an archive, however, you should use the library or archive Website to research the costs involved and what will be required in order to gain access to the documents you are interested in. For those of you who cannot find an appropriate Website for the archive you are interested in consulting, it is worth consulting Archives Made Easy (http://www.archivesmadeeasy.org) before embarking on your archive trip. As illustrated in Figure 6.6, this Website is hosted by the London School of Economics and Political Science (http://www.lse.ac.uk) and aims to

Figure 6.6   Archives Made Easy

maximise the usefulness of archive research trips by providing details of the costs and processes involved in an archive visit.

Evaluating Websites as Sources of Data or Information

Because of the importance of primary and secondary sources to your research project, it is vital that you learn how to evaluate the quality of information provided on the sites you visit. While we will return to this in a later chapter, we want to conclude here with a brief discussion of some of the initial steps in determining if the information, particularly the primary source material you access online, is appropriate to your study. This is particularly important because, unlike library-based resources which have been selected, catalogued and shelved based on specific criteria to ensure their academic quality and merit, you must be able to determine whether you can use a Website and its information as either a primary or a secondary source for your project. The first question you should ask yourself is whether the Website is actually relevant to your research topic. If it is relevant you should be able to state exactly how it is relevant and how you wish to use it. In deciding answers to these two core questions you should be guided by a series of sub-questions. Does the site:

- reproduce hardcopy documents, such as private correspondence, manuscripts, books, or other documentation, which you would otherwise have to access through archive research, interlibrary loan or other means?

- provide access to official documentation, statistics or the public record?
- provide access to research or information gathered by reputable individuals or organisations working in the same or related fields?
- provide audio or visual files featuring individuals, works or discussions that you could legitimately cite in support of your argument?
- form part of a body of evidence you are accumulating as part of your research, which you will subsequently be able to analyse, and which may inform your conclusions?

If you cannot answer 'yes' to at least one of these questions, then the Website you are considering probably does not contain any useful primary source material. Therefore, you will next have to consider if the site contains any useful secondary or tertiary information. One final test you might use is to ask yourself is whether you can legitimately cite this Website as evidence of a social, material or representative reality, and be taken seriously? If you conclude that this is not possible, it is probably best to dump the Website into the dustbin of research history.

If you determine that a Website contains useful material, your next task is to evaluate the content. This part of the process is the same for virtual sources as for other forms of primary source material. However, because much of the information placed on the Web does not undergo the same screening process as the information contained in scholarly books and journals, the need for evaluation is even more important.

First, you need to determine the usefulness of the site to your research. Any gaps in the information provided, any shortcomings in the methodology used in its production, any assumptions underpinning it that may have skewed the results or may no longer hold, should all call into question its use as a source of research data. In addition, you should also consider whether the information on the site supports or contradicts what you have already collected, and how this affects its relative importance to your project. Overall, we believe a useful way to begin assessing this is to use the types of questions raised in Table 6.6.

Once you have considered the Website and the information contained within it under these headings, it is then necessary to consider the information in relation to the other online (and offline) sources you are using. For instance, does the information:

- provide an exception to the other sources you are using?
- provide exemplification, to be added to your other sources of evidence?
- illustrate a rule or norm you are trying to establish?

The context	Who produced the site?
	When was the site produced, and last updated?
	What is the purpose of the site?
	What audience does the site target?
	Who has access to the site?
	How do I know?
Checking the source	Is the information provided on the site correct?
	Can it be verified?
	Is relevant information missing or excluded from the site?
	If it is missing, for what reason or to what purpose has it been excluded?
	How do I know?
Analysing the source	Who or what is represented on the site (people, organisations, actions, events, or personal viewpoints)?
	How are they represented (e.g., visual images, oral files)?
	What kind of vocabulary is used, and to what effect?
	Is the tone polemical, informative, satirical etc.?
	Is a political, cultural, theoretical or other position stated or possible to infer?
	What effect does this have on the representation and interpretation of material on the site?
	What bearing, given the answers to the questions above, does it have on the research being conducted?

Table 6.6   Evaluative questions

These questions form part of the process of Website evaluation, and can be useful for a range of researchers, from those seeking relatively straightforward information from newspapers or government statistics, to those studying online communities or e-activism. In all cases, it pays to maintain as much critical distance as possible from the sources you are using.

Exercise 1: Podcasts for academic research

Find and work your way through three different podcasts that are directly related to your research topic. Discuss what you found, how you found it and how useful it was to your research. If you cannot find three sites, say what you did to try to find them and why you think they are not available.

Exercise 2: Website evaluation

Go to five of the Websites you have visited (or intend to use in your research), and evaluate each site, according to the evaluative techniques discussed in this chapter. Based on these evaluations, discuss what you discovered about each site and decide whether you would (or will) use it. If you intend to continue using the site, discuss why the evaluation suggests that the site was usable in the research process.

Exercise 3: Maximising your time

Make a list of the relevant information you have found through your online searches. How much of this will you be able to access online? Is there any essential material you will not be able to access online? If so, make a plan detailing how you intend to gain access to this material, including details of how long this might take and what you will need to do beforehand. Lastly, consider if there is any way this material could be substituted or augmented by material you can generate or access online.

● References and Resources

ArchiveGrid, http://archivegrid.org/Web/jsp/index.jsp provides links to historical documents, personal papers and family histories held in archives around the world.

Archives Made Easy, http://www.archivesmadeeasy.org is dedicated to providing access to and information on physical archives around the globe.

Archives for Research on Women and Gender, http://www.lib.utsa.edu/Archives/WomenGender/links.html.

Biblioteca Virtual Miguel de Cervantes, http://www.cervantesvirtual.com is a jump site to thousands of classical texts from Spain and Latin America in digital format. Links to publishers, libraries, archives, and other resources.

British Library, http://www.bl.uk is the homepage of the British Library.

Documenting the American South, http://docsouth.unc.edu. These are archives created by the library of University of North Carolina and include texts, images and audio files relating to Southern history, literature, and culture from the Colonial period through the first decades of the twentieth century.

Euro Doc, http://eudocs.lib.byu.edu/index.php/Main_Page

Family Search, http://www.familysearch.org, accessed 28/02/2007.

History.Com, http://www.history.com offers both audio and video files of historic events listed in a video gallery (which contains audio speeches) you can search using a keyword engine.

History World, http://www.historyworld.net is a collection of histories divided into three primary sections: World History, Timelines and Specialist Articles.

INFLANET's National Libraries of the World Address List: http://www.ifla. org/VI/2/p2/national-libraries.htm

Internet History Source Book Project, http://www.fordham.edu/halsall. This is a collection that provides links to historical texts for Ancient History, Medieval Studies and Modern History. There are also some thematically based subsets that include African History, East Asian History, Indian History, Jewish History and History of Science.

Latin America Network Information Center, http://info.lanic.utexas.edu/

Library of Congress, http://www.loc.gov/index.html, accessed 28/02/2007. This is the homepage of the Library of Congress. Not only does it provide access to one of the most complete collections of texts but it also provides extensive links to a range of national and international resources.

Library of Congress: The American Memory Collection, http://memory. loc.gov/ammem/index.html, accessed 28/02/2007. This is a resource provided by the Library of Congress and is an excellent resource for anyone interested in the study of America and American history.

Literature Online, http://lion.chadwyck.co.uk/, accessed 28/02/2007.

London School of Economics, http://www.lse.ac.uk, accessed 28/02/2007.

MLA International Bibliography, http://collections.chadwyck.co.uk/home/ home_mla.jsp, accessed 28/02/2007.

National Archives United Kingdom, http://www.nationalarchives.gov.uk/ default.htm

National Archives United States, http://www.archives.gov/index.html

Perseus Digital Library, http://www.perseus.tufts.edu

PINAKEΣ, http://www.hw.ac.uk/libWWW/irn/pinakes/pinakes.html, accessed 28/02/2007.

Portugal's Memória – Biblioteca Nacional Digital, http://purl.pt/401/1, accessed 10/06/2007. This is a full-text data archive related to art, science, law, education, history, language, literature, music, and other areas.

Repositories of Primary Sources, http://www.uidaho.edu/special-collections/Other.Repositories.html, accessed 28/02/2007

School of Oriental and African Studies (SOAS) *African Archives and Manuscripts* http://www.soas.ac.uk/library/index.cfm?navid=1423. This archive provides one of the UK's most complete collections of manuscripts and other primary data sources available to researchers of African history and culture.

UNESCO Archives Portal, http://www.unesco.org/cgi-bin/Webworld/portal_archives/cgi/page.cgi?d=1, accessed 10/07/2007. A sub-unit of the UN. This portal provides access to the documents and resources produced and commissioned by UNESCO.

United Nations, Document Centre, http://documents.un.org/welcome.asp?language=E, accessed 07/07/2007. This site provides either direct access or linked access to a range of documents that have been produced or commissioned by the United Nations and its associated agencies.

University of Liverpool Library, *Electronic Resources Portal,* http://www.liv.ac.uk/library/electron/erdatabase.html, accessed 27/02/2007.

University of Michigan, Document Center, http://www.lib.umich.edu/govdocs, accessed 28/06/2007. The Document Center is one of the largest portals on the Web. It provides links and access to an extensive range of primary source material, covering a range of qualitative and quantitative data sources and academic disciplines.

Women Working 1800–1930, http://ocp.hul.harvard.edu/ww, accessed 30/03/2007. This contains digitised resources selected from Harvard University's library and museum collections. These materials address the role of women in the US economy between 1800 and the Great Depression, and include books, pamphlets, photographs and manuscripts.

Wordcat, http://www.worldcat.org, accessed 28/02/2007. This site claims to provide its users 'access to over 1 billion items in more than 10,000 libraries around the world'. This includes access to music, videos and articles, in addition to articles and journals.

7 Using the Internet to Generate Individualised Datasets

With the ever-increasing supply of online resources, the Net makes the development of your initial question, and the collection of secondary data, considerably easier than it was in the past; possibly too easy for those inclined to take shortcuts. As mentioned before, the resources available through your home library are going to prove invaluable to all of you who learn to mine them efficiently. However, as good as your home library is or as proficient as you become at finding data, you may need to move beyond the confines of what others have said and written about your topic when answering your research question. To do this you are either going to have to collect your own primary data or find and interpret existing primary source material differently.

As discussed in Chapter 6, you can find a range of primary data sources online. For instance, the University of Essex houses one of the largest quantitative data archives in Britain (JISC/ESRC Data Archive, http://www.data-archive.ac.uk). Similarly, many governments issue primary data, such as the US Census Bureau (http://www.census.gov) and the UK Office of National Statistics (http://www.statistics.gov.uk). Although a range of statistical databases is available to you, do not overlook the possibility of using the Net as a means of collecting primary qualitative data. For instance, the University of Michigan's Library offers a range of links to qualitative data sites though its Document Center http://www.lib.umich. edu/govdocs. Dedicated databases and archives of personal journals, diaries and letters have also been placed online by a number of individuals and institutions. As part of this, it is worth remembering that a range of image and audio files have also been archived and placed online. These can be used for the purpose of primary analysis. For instance, someone interested in studying the images or personal papers emerging out of the Great Depression could turn to the New Deal Network (http://newdeal.feri.org/ index.htm), which offers a range of audio, visual and written databases. Similarly, anyone interested in media studies should consider using the image data (both moving and still) available at the Media Resource Center (http://www.lib.berkeley.edu/MRC/primarysources.html).

While the types of primary data available online are almost limitless, and can prove invaluable to students interested in analysing primary research, many projects are going to involve research questions that are not amenable to previously collected data, or the data that has been made available online. In these instances you are going to have to find ways to use the existing online resources at your disposal in order to generate, collect, and subsequently analyse your own primary data. It is the purpose of this chapter, therefore, to introduce you to some of the key ways you can use the Net to generate your own primary data.

To give you a taste of what is to come, let us provide you with a few examples of how you might consider using the Net to generate your own primary data. Have you ever considered using a relevant chat room to conduct an online observational study? Similarly, have you ever considered using a chat room or listserv to find participants to take part in a study, either in one-on-one interviews or in a focus group format (Bradley, 1999; Bradley, 2000; Write et al., 2000)? To collect survey data, you can use any range of online software, including instant messaging, e-mail communication technologies, and online phone technologies (Couper, 2000; Dommeryer and Moriarty, 1999; Schonlau et al., 2001). Virtual spaces can themselves constitute and provide primary source material. For instance, bulletin boards and Usenet groups provide an opportunity to engage in virtual fieldwork, whether that occurs though simple observations of group interactions, participant observation of online interactions, or even using group interactions to conduct an analysis of the group's dialogue/discourse (Coombes, 2001).

It is clear that the Net is altering the way students are interacting with each other and their professors (for information on how you can interact appropriately online, see the discussion of netiquette in Chapter 5). It is also true that the Net is changing how students are conducting their research (though not always for the better if the desired outcome is an improved understanding of the topic under question). Equally, the most important aspect of this is the growing potential of the Net to help the typical student generate and collect primary data.

Part of the reason for this has little to do with the technology itself but rather the potential the Net has for reducing the costs traditionally associated with the administration and analysis of research observations, interviews and questionnaires. The financial and time costs typically involved in these activities used to prevent the typical student (and some academics) from being able to collect primary data for their research projects, particularly when these projects only lasted a few weeks, or at most a couple of months.

Another aspect of the Net's increased popularity in the generation and collection of primary data relates to its ability to increase the ease of data collection. When compared with the efforts that used to go into the development, dissemination and collection of postal questionnaires, or the time and organisation involved in conducting random sample telephone interviews, the internet can be (provided you have the necessary technological capabilities) positively cheap and simple. All told, with a little technical know-how and some effort on your part, the Net provides you with a powerful tool for generating and collecting your own primary source material. The ability to design the instruments for the collection and then collecting your own primary data is one of the primary advantages the internet provides students interested in advancing their own research skills. It is also helping to bring students into the realm of research that was not that long ago reserved for the academic researcher working in a think-tank or major research university. Clearly, then, this has the potential to help democratise the overall learning and researching process.

Questions for Consideration

Before you even turn on your computer, open a Web browser, search a Website, sign up to a mailing list, interact with a newsgroup, or attempt to make observations of an online interaction for the purpose of generating and/or collecting your own primary data, we believe that you should consider six core questions:

1 What do you want to learn (why are you interested in generating your own primary data)?
2 What are the most appropriate tools for gathering this information (questionnaires, interviews, observations, or some other technique)?
3 How should the instrument be developed (should you use open- or closed-ended questions; should you have structured or unstructured designs)?
4 Is the technique amenable to online implementation (what are the differences between the online and offline community; how will these differences influence your findings; if going online who should participate and how can you draw the sample)?
5 What are the most appropriate and productive ways of making contact with potential participants (e-mail, newsgroups, mailing lists, online advertisements)?
6 What would be the best way to implement the study (Web-based techniques, e-mail techniques, Skype, instant messaging)?

Regardless of your answers to these questions, you should use them to help you to focus on the most appropriate online techniques for gathering or generating your primary data. The importance of these questions comes to light as soon as you begin to realise that, although we live in the 'information age', there is still a relatively small online population composed of a fairly narrow range of individuals (see: Internet Usage World Statistics, http://www.internetworldstats.com; US Census Bureau 1995, 2002, 2006 and 2007). Not only is the online population not a mirror image of the offline population, but computer-mediated-communication (CMC) can also result in substantially different interactions from face-to-face (FTF) communication. Not only are the visual and cultural cues that exist in FTF communications missing in CMC, but even the use of volume and speed of presentation is missing. All of these factors make your answers to these six questions all the more necessary (see: Herring, 1996; *Journal of Computer Mediated Communication*, http://jcmc.indiana.edu; Thurlow et al., 2004).

What Do You Want to Learn?

Before jumping online you need to ask yourself what it is that you actually want to learn and whether going online will help you. The answer to these questions will help you decide whether the internet is an appropriate medium for the collection of your primary data, whether the population you need to interact with is available online, and how you might be able to contact your online sample or make the necessary observations. Understanding what you want to learn will also help direct you to the most appropriate tool for the compilation of your primary data. For instance, what you want to learn can dictate whether your data needs are best met by conducting an online survey using an attached questionnaire, or whether you could better become involved in the observations of online interactions occurring in a chat room or bulletin board. While we discussed some of the ethical issues involved in conducting online research in Chapter 5, we want to be clear right now that your data needs can dictate the types of techniques you implement and these will themselves involve you in ethical considerations. For example, it is

TIP Use this question to determine whether the information you generate needs to be qualitative or quantitative. This will help you determine the most appropriate instrument for your research and how to administer it. For example, your data needs should help you decide whether an in-depth interview is appropriate or whether a closed-ended questionnaire would provide more appropriate data.

possible that your research question might require you to conduct observations without the prior knowledge of those being observed or even get you involved in conducting surveys without informing your subjects of the true reason for conducting the research or revealing the conclusions you are trying to discover.

Similarly, if you are interested in learning about 18–24-year-olds' perspective on the differences between the British Labour and Conservative Parties in relation to their views on immigration, it is probably going to be more appropriate to conduct an online focus group than to conduct an analysis of party documents. However, if your question involves analysis of how an individual in charge of a government department or program understood their role in relation to the implementation of a given policy, it is probably going to be more appropriate for you to conduct an online interview with the individual in question than administer a questionnaire to a random sampling of civil servants.

In coming to terms with your information needs, you will need to determine the tools most likely to provide you with the appropriate data. At a general level, these will consist of **online interviews**, the distribution of **questionnaires**, or some form of **online observation**.

Online Interviews and Questionnaires

Although they may require some practice and a lot of skill, online interviews consist of little more than a directed discussion involving two or more individuals, mediated though online technology. The primary purpose of conducting an online interview is to collect information that only the individual or group being interviewed can provide. Like interviews, questionnaires are also used to collect information from an individual or group, but not though discussions. Instead, online questionnaires require participants to independently answer and return a questionnaire, consisting of a series of questions you have designed to elicit the data you need. Regardless of whether you use interviews or questionnaires, you will have to decide not only who should be targeted as a participant, but also how best to deliver the interview or questionnaire to your participants. In relation to the conduct of your interview, there are three general techniques available to you:

1 Utilise your e-mail program to conduct either synchronous or asynchronous question-and-answer sessions.
2 Use one of the many instant messaging packages to conduct real-time question-and-answer sessions.

3   Use one of the online video conferencing/telephone software packages to conduct real-time, synchronous question-and-answer sessions.

In relation to the delivery of your questionnaire, three general techniques are available:

1   Embed your questions in an e-mail sent directly to an intended participant.
2   Attach a file to an e-mail you send directly to your intended participant.
3   Develop a dedicated Website and then direct participants to the site, where they can fill in the questionnaire and submit it.

As a general rule, interviews are conducted in an interactive fashion, in which the interviewer and the interviewee can, and often do, interact. Questionnaires, on the other hand, are self-administered and returned to the researcher.

Finally, when carrying out online interviews and questionnaires, a range of different survey designs can be adopted. Of these the three most popular are the **structured**, **semi-structured** and the **unstructured survey**. Each design simply refers to the degree to which you provide a structure to the interview or questionnaire.

In completely **structured** designs, questions will be set in advance, arranged so that one question leads to the next, and will always be presented in this order regardless of the answers provided or individual involved in taking the survey or answering the interview questions. In completely structured survey designs most of the questions will themselves be closed-ended. Figure 7.1 provides an example of a closed-ended questionnaire. Notice that the questions are closed, follow a basic logic structure, and only allow for one answer.

In contrast to the structured design illustrated in Figure 7.1 (which was developed with a simple word-processing program obtained online), it is

---

Do you believe that the most important aspect of the immigration debate is:

• How the media portrays immigrants ☐

• How politicians discuss immigrants ☐

• How your friends view immigrants ☐

Figure 7.1   Online structured questionnaire using closed-ended questions

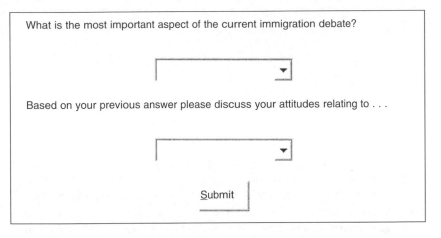

Figure 7.2   Online semi-structured survey using open-ended questions

often preferable to use an unstructured design. In these instances the researcher enters the interview with a general set of issues or categories they want to explore but, instead of having a set of specifically worded (or even ordered questions), the researcher uses fairly open-ended questions, in an attempt to explore with the participant their understanding of the issue under consideration. The idea is to use the answers received to one question to develop a new question or an entirely new line of questioning, so that an in-depth understanding of the situation can be gained. For example, instead of providing a predefined set of responses, as in Figure 7.1, the survey illustrated in Figure 7.2 has been constructed to allow the participant to express, in their own words, what they see as important. This allows participants to let you know what issues should be covered in more depth.

Given these parameters, you should understand that closed-ended research structures tend to be used to collect data that can be quantified and/or easily compared across participants. As such, closed-ended survey designs tend to be used to gather data through structured questionnaires. On the other hand, unstructured designs tend to be used to collect qualitative data that is difficult or impossible to quantify and compare statistically. As a result, unstructured designs tend to be more appropriate for interview settings as they allow you to diverge from the interview schedule and develop follow-up questions when necessary.

Falling between structured and unstructured survey designs are the semi-structured. Semi-structured interviews and questionnaires fall along a continuum ranging from those that are almost completely structured, using

---

Note: The number of response categories you provide and where you position a response can influence the responses you receive. For example, if you provide an odd number of response categories you allow participants to sit on the fence by selecting the middle response category each time. Therefore, if you want to force a participant to take a position on an issue you should provide an even number of response categories.

---

formalised structures and mostly closed-ended questions, to almost completely unstructured designs using primarily open-ended questions and/or 'other' fields. For example, you might want to start your interviews or questionnaires with a series of closed-ended questions in order to gather demographic data and establish the parameters of your study but then integrate more open-ended questions in order to collect in-depth information on particular topics. Similarly, by mixing open- and closed-ended questions into a single interview you can provide the interviewee with structure while giving yourself the freedom to add supplementary questions in order to 'probe' for more information when an answer appears to contain more information than the initial response revealed. In sum, the primary purpose for using the semi-structured design is that it allows you to provide structure and track issues that are of interest to you, while allowing you to seek further clarification and elaboration when necessary.

A final type of interview made possible by recent technology that you might consider using, if appropriate in your research, is the focus group. An online focus group involves the interviewing of a group of individuals drawn together using real-time software (such as instant messaging, bulletin boards and dedicated conference suites). The purpose of conducting online focus groups is to facilitate interactions between participants. This is done in order to discover how consensus positions can be built amongst participants, to probe opinions and attitudes though discussions, or to explore issues involving agreements and disagreements. When considering the use of focus groups it is worth keeping in mind that the primary research advantage to using real-time software is that it allows participants to respond immediately to what is sent, allowing for 'live interactions'. This immediacy, however, can present a problem in that it can be difficult to moderate and organise, and its success will often depend on the typing and reading skills of those involved. On the other hand, although asynchronous interactions are easier to organise and moderate, and allow individuals to come in and out of a discussion to suit their timing needs, they tend to lack the spontaneity that is required of true focus group research.

● Question Structure: Open-ended and Closed-ended

In addition to considering how they fit into your overall research design, when constructing your surveys you are going to have to consider how to compose specific questions. While there are no hard rules governing how you design individual questions, at a general level it can be argued that the more structured you want the results to be, the more likely it is you are going to have to rely on closed-ended questions. This is because closed-ended questions make it easier to compare answers across participants and to quantify answers for statistical analysis. The reason closed-ended questions allow you to make these easy comparisons and subsequently quantify the answers is that they limit the range of responses available to a participant to a small number of predefined categories. The most closed-ended questions will limit responses to a single 'yes' or 'no' response. Table 7.1 presents the basic types of survey questions that might be used.

For student research, the **multiple-choice** design is often the most fruitful. The multiple-choice design allows you to develop a range of response categories (or possible response options), and then instruct your participants to select the best answer from amongst these options. For example, if you are interested in why students avoid eating at the student union you could develop a very simple tick-box form that you attach to an e-mail asking for

Type of question	Best used when . . .
Open-ended	respondents' own words are important.
Closed-ended	you need to rank ordered data; desired response choices are 'known'; you need to quantify results for statistical analysis.
Multiple-choice	there are multiple, but finite, number of options.
Ordinal	answers can be ranked in relation to each other.
Categorical	answers are categories and each response falls into one category.
Numerical	numbers are the best possible response categories.

Source: Adapted from: http://coe.sdsu.edu/eet/Articles/surveyquest/index.htm

Table 7.1 Basic types of survey questions

Why don't you eat at the University Pizzeria?	(Please tick one box)
Food is too expensive	☐
Its location is inconvenient	☐
The quality of the food is poor	☐
Not enough choices	☐

Figure 7.3   Standard closed-ended question tick-box form

an e-mailed response, or that you embed into the actual message of one of the newer HTML-enabled e-mail programs. The advantage of using multiple choice questionnaire design is not just that it can be easily attached or embedded into an e-mail but that it is easy to develop and will provide you with data that is easily analysed since you pre-developed the response categories, and are collecting closed-ended data (see Figure 7.3 for an example).

Multiple choice questions are fairly easy to design; however, when your question requires you to be able to rank order your responses, you will have to use **ordinal** designs. For example, if you are interested in ranking the reasons students do not eat at the Union you might present your questions as shown in Figure 7.4.

Often in answering your question you might need to use a range of categorical questions in order to force respondents to place themselves into a

Please write a number between 1 and 4 next to each item: 1 should indicate the item that is most important to you, and 4 the least important. Use each number only once.	
Why don't you eat at the University Pizzeria?	
Food is too expensive	—
Its location is inconvenient	—
The quality of the food is poor	—
Not enough choices	—

Figure 7.4   Closed-ended questions used for ranking purposes

single category. This might occur in instances when you need to know the gender balance of your participants, in which case you would ask them to respond whether they are a female or a male. In a similar vein, you might find that you need to collect data in the form of real numbers. For example, it might be important to know the age range of your participants. In this instance you could include a question that asks your participants to state their age to the nearest year.

Closed-ended questions tend to be easier to respond to and analyse than open-ended questions, particularly for students just learning how to use the Net to administer interviews and questionnaires. However, if your research question is amenble to the use of unstructured questions, it is worth considering if the inclusion of open-ended questions would add to the quality of your research. Unlike closed-ended questions, which force respondents to select from a predetermined range of responses, open-ended questions allow the participant to respond in their own words, and as they deem most appropriate, therefore allowing you to collect unique, in-depth, qualitative data.

The hard part of using open-ended questions is designing them. Students often design questions in such a way as to encourage yes/no answers. The real trick to using open-ended questions is to spend time considering what you want to learn and then converting this into questions that encourage participants to provide extensive responses. You also need to do this in such a way as to avoid causing the respondent to inflect their responses in a particular way. The wonderful thing about computer-administered surveys is that they can help reduce participant bias, as you will not have to worry about what you are conveying through your body language or gender bias, or any other visual signifier a respondent may pick up on (unless of course you choose to utilise an online video conferencing or phone package).

However, computer-mediated communication (CMC) will require you to consider not only how you phrase your questions but also how your audience may receive and interpret them. Often what one group of online users expects and understands from a question, another group will not. Because CMC loses the cues that help participants interpret open-ended questions in face-to-face communications, if you suspect when using CMC that participants are answering questions in such a way as to provide you with what they think you want, or that generates a response that they think is acceptable rather than telling you what they actually believe, you will need to develop a new set of questions (or engage in a round of follow-up questioning capable of teasing out their actual opinions and understandings).

While in-depth, context-rich data may be important to your study, it is worth remembering that the use of open-ended questions (and unstructured

> **Glossary**
> **Generalisability** refers to the extent to which you can use your data to make claims going beyond your immediate study. **Reliability** involves the ability of someone else to conduct your study (in the same way) and come to the same conclusions. As a general rule, generalisability and reliability tend to be more associated with quantitative studies – though both are important in qualitative studies.

designs), as a general rule, reduces your ability to generalise your findings. This is more problematic for the novice researcher than for the more experienced. Because open-ended answers are harder to analyse, there is a distinct possibly that the reliability of your conclusions may be called into question by a more seasoned researcher.

Online Observations

Unlike online surveys, where you are using the personal knowledge and opinions of your participants as the basis of your data, observations are carried out in order to record events, interactions, activities, etc., without the researcher directly questioning the individuals or groups involved in the activity or event being observed. The goal is to collect data that is not dependent on the knowledge or opinions of those being observed. Online observations do not require you to observe only individuals or groups. It is just as possible to observe a Website, a collection or presentation of documents (see how different archives are displayed or collated, etc.), or even photos or videos, as it is to observe the actions of an online group or community.

There are two general ways to collect data though the observation of online events: participant observation and non-participant observation. In the latter you make observations (with or without the knowledge of the observed), while trying to be 'invisible' to the observed, while in the former, you become actively involved in the activity or event you are observing.

> **Glossary**
> **Lurking** is the process of following discussions occurring on message boards, in newsgroups and chat rooms, or any other interactive system, without actively contributing to or participating in the discussion itself.

When engaged in online observations, particularly participant observation, and observations in which the object of the observation knows it is being observed, it is very important to do everything you can to avoid introducing personal, cultural or political preconceptions, prejudice or partiality into your observations. 'Bias' is often used as shorthand for the way in which observations or other techniques of data collection or analysis may be inflected by hidden or subjective factors. While bias can be introduced in any number of ways (not least in the sample you select for your study), the reason it is important to do as much as you can to minimise it, is that it can, unknowingly or knowingly, influence your study. This is particularly true if:

- you allow your own beliefs and actions to shape how you interpret what you observe;
- your conduct and behaviour in an online event alters the actions of those being observed;
- your observations are known to the participants of an online event and they subsequently alter their behaviour in response to the process of being observed.

Because of the problems associated with objectivity and bias, students often find it easier to remain objective when engaged in non-participant observations, whether conducted 'covertly' or with the knowledge of those being observed. This is because you are not trying to become involved in the observed phenomena and, therefore, you are able to sit back and watch what is going on instead of trying to participate, observe and understand all at the same time. For instance, if your question is intended to discover how individuals behave when interacting online, one possible starting point is to examine the actions of a newsgroup rather than trying to become actively involved. Another possibility is to observe whether individuals behave online in the ways they self-report within a self-administered questionnaire. Finally, you might be interested in observing whether a group behaves online differently than they do offline. To do this you might observe the behaviours of your classmates in a classroom situation and then compare this to their behaviour when engaged in one-to-one e-mail exchanges or online group discussions.

While observations often sound as if they will be easy to do, it is important to consider what you want to observe, how you can best go about this, and what will be the best sites for making these observations before actually jumping in. For instance, one possibility would be to post an item to a newsgroup and observe how members (or the member in question) react. Similarly, rather than making a posting, you could simply lurk online, observing how the group (or person in question) interacts, without calling the group's attention to your presence. You might even want to become actively involved with the group to observe who responds to different stimuli, and how they respond.

> **Glossary**
> **Message board** is a site that uses online software technology in order to facilitate asynchronous discussions. A **chat room**, on the other hand, is a type of online forum that has been developed to facilitate synchronous conferencing,

Another possibility for an observational study emerges out of questions interested in discourse and dialectal analysis. For example, if you are interested in the difference between online verbal interactions and offline line interactions, you might set up a discussion group and then observe how participants' online interactions vary in comparison to their in-class interactions or even out-of-class interactions. Similarly, if your research question is concerned with how language affects understanding, you might be interested in observing how people respond to different Web pages based on the language structures used on two comparison Web pages (or set of Web pages).

The collection of primary data is one of the key ways you are increasingly going to be able to distinguish your research from that of your fellow students. In this process the Net provides a range of new opportunities. These are embedded in the technologies and techniques associated with the adaptation of the traditional survey and observational tools that have underpinned the research process for generations. In this chapter, we have outlined some of the more important tools for generating primary research data online. As important, however, are the skills of knowing how to use these tools, and to determine if and when they are appropriate. It is to these issues that we now turn.

Exercise 1: Finding people

Go online and find three different types of people finding tools. Use these to demonstrate that you are able to find and make contact with:

- three academics working in your area of research who are not associated with your university or organisation;
- three online groups interested in and currently discussing issues associated with your area of research. One of these should be a mailing list;
- then, without actually making contact, discuss how you would go about making contact with them either though online contacts or through more traditional means, depending on which you decided was more appropriate (and why).

Exercise 2: Making an online observation

Sign up to the mailing list you have identified in part 2 of Exercise 1 above. Lurk for a while, saving each mailing as you receive it. Now consider the information you have gathered in the following way:

1. What kinds of subjects are typically dealt with in the correspondence? Can you determine from this what kind of material or topic it would be appropriate to introduce, and what kind would be inappropriate? Why?
2. How would you describe the online community? Academic; student; professional; general public; political; special interest? Is it possible to know or infer things like sex or nationality?
3. How would you describe the interactions: formal, informal, discursive, conflictive, supportive?
4. Do you consider the amount of material you have gathered sufficient evidence of your conclusions to justify them?

Exercise 3: Try interacting

Once you have completed Exercise 2, try to engage in online interactions with the group you have signed up to. In these follow the rules of Netiquette. Discuss what types of responses you received, if any. If no one responded discuss why and what you could do to increase the likelihood of your messages stimulating a conversation.

● References and Resources

Bradley, H. (2000), 'Getting the Information You Want: How to Find and Sign Up for Mailing Lists and Electronic Newsletters', *Smart Computing Learning Series*, 6: 58–62.

Bradley, N. (1999), 'Sampling for Internet Surveys', *Journal of the Market Research Society*, 41: 387–95.

Coombes, H. (2001), *Research Using IT* (Basingstoke: Palgrave Macmillan).

Couper, M. (2000), 'Web Surveys: a Review of Issues and Approaches', *Public Opinion Quarterly*, 64: 14–23.

Dommeyer, C. and Moriarty, E. (1999), 'Comparing Two Forms of E-mail Survey: Embedded vs. Attached', *Journal of the Market Research Society*, 42: 39–50.

Herring, S. (ed.) (1996), *Computer-Mediated Communication: Linguistic, Social and Cross-Cultural Perspectives* (New York: John Benjamins).

Internet Usage World Statistics, http://www.internetworldstats.com, accessed 09/05/2007

JISC/ESRC Data Archive, http://www.data-archive.ac.uk.

Journal of Computer Mediated Communication, http://jcmc.indiana.edu, accessed 07/07/2007.

Media Resource Center, http://www.lib.berkeley.edu/MRC/primarysources. html, accessed 15/07/2007.

Michigan, *Document Center*, http://www.lib.umich.edu/govdocs, accessed 05/04/2007.

New Deal Network, http://newdeal.feri.org/index.htm, accessed 12/07/2007.

Schonlau, M., Fricker, R. and Elliott, M. (2002), *Conducting Research Surveys via Email and the Web* (MR-1480 (California: Rand).

Thurlow, C., Lengel, L. and Tomic, A. (2004), *Computer Mediated Communication* (London: Sage). This text has been designed to introduce students to CMC by having them perform a range of tasks. The core intention of this text is to help students get used to the nature and impact of the internet within the communication process.

UK Data Archive (formerly the ESRC or the Essex Data Archive), http://www.data-archive.ac.uk, accessed 02/02/2007.

UK *Office of National Statistics*, http://www.statistics.gov.uk, accessed 01/10/2006.

US Census Bureau (1995), Survey of Internet Usage, www.census.gov/mso/www/npr/Inet95fullreport.pdf, accessed 09/07/2007.

US Census Bureau (2002), Computer and Internet Usage by Age and Disability Status, www.census.gov/hhes/www/disability/sipp/disab02/ds02f6.pdf, accessed 09/07/2006.

US Census Bureau (2006), Social Abstract of the United States 2006, www.census.gov/prod/2005pubs/06statab/infocomm.pdf, accessed 05/06/2007.

US Census Bureau (2007), Social Abstract of the United States 2007, www.census.gov/prod/2006pubs/07statab/infocomm.pdf, accessed 07/07/2007.

Waddington, H. (2004) 'Types of Survey Questions', *Encyclopaedia of Educational Technology*, http://coe.sdsu.edu/eet/Articles/surveyquest/index.htm, accessed 28/02/2007.

Write, J., Amorosao, L. and Howard, P. (2000), 'Research Methodology – Methodology and Representation in Internet-based Survey Tools', *Social Science Computer Review*, 18: 179–95.

8 Is Your Study Amenable to Online Implementation?

Once you have established what your primary data needs are and the most appropriate methods for collecting that data, you will need to decide whether or not the Net is an appropriate tool for compiling your data. While it may be easy to conduct observations, interviews and questionnaires online, it will not always be appropriate. Rather, you are going to have to decide whether or not the internet population offers an appropriate conduit for drawing your sample. This may not pose a problem if your study involves interviewing specific known individuals or making observations of online events. It may be more difficult to determine if your question requires you to survey a range of unknown actors or make observations of items or events that occur both online and offline. In these instances, as discussed in the previous chapter, you will have to decide: (1) if the types of individuals you are interested in contacting operate online, and (2) if they are online, what the best technique for drawing a sample of this population from the internet will be.

Answering these questions will involve considering what is available online and who operates online. Once you have decided that what you need is available online, you are going to have to decide whether the online community will provide an appropriate sample for collecting your primary data. To answer this you need to consider whether the individuals, groups and organisations operating online, or the situations and information that can be observed, could distort your data, and thus introduce **bias** into your results, making any conclusion you arrive at unreliable, misleading, or even prejudicial (see Chapter 7). One of the key ways bias can be introduced into your results (depending on what you are trying to discover) is through failing to consider the difference between the same or similar events occurring both online and offline. Often, events occurring in these different arenas do so for different reasons or unfold in different ways. Similarly, the results of online data and the conclusions generated can be unreliable because 'a large fraction of the general population does not have access to a personal computer or is otherwise unable to participate in an Internet-based survey' (Schonlau et al., 2002, p. 14). Therefore, if your research requires you to generalise beyond your particular study, or to comment on the population as a whole, you must understand whether and how different representations and under-representation can be adjusted for (or corrected) within your study or its findings.

> **Glossary**
> **Representativeness** is an indication of how accurately the individuals or observations used in your study speak for all the people or observations you could have used or made.

These issues are compounded by others involving the **representativeness** of those individuals or phenomena you are able to access, interact with or observe online. To pick up on a point made in Chapter 7, when you are considering the appropriateness of the internet as a means of compiling primary data you should always bear in mind the demographic composition of the individuals operating online: most are English speaking, come from Western industrialised nations and higher-income households. Within this sub-group there is a gender and racial imbalance, with white men under 35 years of age, with higher educational levels, over-represented online. Further compounding issues of who is operating online are questions of the computer 'literacy' of those who are actively involved in online activities. For, while it might be possible to draw an 'unbiased' sample from the total population of internet users engaged in the activity or event you are interested in investigating, it might not be possible to use online technologies uniformly with this group, due to differences in, say, the adequacy or proficiency of individuals' computer and typing skills (Graham and Marvin, 1996; Mann and Stewart, 2000).

Because of these mitigating issues, and unless you have been assigned a sample or participant list, with prior knowledge of its research advantages and disadvantages, you are going to have to consider how to draw your sample. In this, it will be important to ensure that your sample is capable of providing the data you need to answer your research question, and in such a way as to minimise any unintended bias. To do this you are going to have to carefully determine how best the online population can be sampled. The **sample** is itself composed of nothing more than the individuals, groups, organisations, sites or events that you use in the generation of your data. This is drawn from the total possible **population** of individuals, groups, organisations, sites or events that you could use. When selecting your research sample you can use either random or non-random sampling techniques.

Random sampling tends to be used when you are interested in conducting a statistical analysis capable of being generalised to the entire population. This is because random sampling helps to minimise the bias that could

> **Glossary**
> A **sample** is a sub-group of the entire population you are interested in study-ing. The **population** consists of the total number of cases that could be subject to your study.

be introduced into your study by who you survey, what sites you include, or which events you choose to observe. To generate a random sample you will need to use sampling techniques designed to ensure that anyone (or anything) from the overall population that could be examined is just as likely to be selected for inclusion in your study as the next individual or event. Using proper random sampling techniques will allow you to have a high degree of confidence in your ability to generalise beyond the confines of your individual dataset.

If you are less interested in being able to generalise your findings, you will probably want to, or at least be able to, draw a **non-random sample**. In these studies you actually want to select your sample based on particular criteria, such as whether you are confident you can gain access to the sample, or based on prior experience of using a given technology to contact people.

> **Note**: It is important that you are conversant with the way data has been gath-ered when using information in existing databases. Otherwise, you may use it inappropriately or draw inappropriate conclusions. Worse, you might unknow-ingly use information that is inappropriate to your data needs.

While the individuals and situations selected for non-random sampling can provide a great deal of detailed data on that particular group, bear in mind that because the information is drawn from a non-random sample, it should not be considered valid for generalisations. Neither is it suitable for use in quantitative studies, particularly those interested in testing a hypothe-sis. Without going into a detailed description of every possible technique we point you towards, Table 8.1, which highlights some of the key techniques available. For more information on sampling and the internet see: Best and Krueger (2004); Mason (2002); McQueen and Knussen (2002); Salkind (2004); Schonlau et al. (2002); Wood (2003).

Once you have determined the best sampling technique for your project, you will need to consider the size of the sample required. As a general rule, the more confident you want to be in your findings the larger your sample should be. The primary exception to this is when your research involves

Random sampling techniques	Non-random sampling techniques
Simple: Involves ensuring that each element of a population has an equal chance of being selected.	**Accidental**: Involves drawing a sample from the available population.
Stratified: Involves drawing equally sized simple random samples from every stratum available in a given population.	**Quota**: Involves sampling individuals and groups from different sections of a population to find a good balance.
Proportional stratified: Sampling that attempts to represent a characteristic in the sample in the same proportions as it exists in the population.	**Theoretical**: Involves drawing a sample from the group you think knows the most about the subject under investigation.

Table 8.1   Key types of sampling techniques

non-probabilistic samples. This is because studies using **non-probabilistic** sampling do not attempt to generalise. Rather, they are designed to select participants based on availability, willingness to participate, knowledge of how they can be contacted, etc. Thus, while who you select, or what you observe, will influence your results, the actual size of the sample does not.

Because the larger your sample, the more confidence you will have in your results when engaged in **probabilistic** sampling, the internet (despite its limitations) becomes a viable tool. This is because: 'Regardless of the research design . . . There are tens of millions of prospective participants online . . . [and] the marginal cost of contacting an additional individual is extremely low' (Best and Krueger, 2004, p. 21). So, as long as you are confident in your sampling decisions, the internet is likely to prove a valuable tool for generating the primary data you need. This is particularly true if you are interested in researching groups that would traditionally be hard to reach or find but are available online. For example, several studies have been conducted into the activities and behaviours of drug users that would not have been possible without the internet. Similarly, a range of studies have been conducted with women and minority groups who have traditionally been excluded from more traditional offline studies (see McCoyd and Kerson, 2006; O'Connor and Madge, 2001; Sills and Song, 2002).

Making Contact with Participants

Once you have determined the type of data you need, the most appropriate method for collecting this data and the most appropriate sample, you will need to recruit your participants. One of the first tools you should consider using is your institution's e-mail. Most universities, public institutions and professional organisations have e-mail databases. The data they contain can be accessed by almost anyone within the organisation, and, in the case of universities, by almost anyone with access to the internet. Therefore, once you have established that your study is amenable to the use of individuals working or studying at a given institution, you should be able to use an existing institutional e-mail list.

> **Glossary**
> **Portal** is a Website that acts as a gateway to a range of different online services and tools on a single page.

While some studies can use pre-existing e-mail databases, others will need to rely on more general sources. In these instances, a range of Web-based e-mail databases and directories are available. When working through these a good starting place is often your home portal. This is because many browsers have homepages that integrate e-mail- and other address-finding tools. Alternatively, if you do not use a portal with an e-mail-finding tool when you enter the internet, there are a range of dedicated e-mail-finding sites. So, you might consider sampling the abilities of sites such as Langenberg (http://person.langenberg.com), World E-Mail Directory (http://worldE-mail.com), or Ultimate E-Mail Directory (http://www.theultimates.com/E-mail).

Finally, if you have a research budget (and can stretch it), you might consider whether it is worth avoiding the aggravation and time involved in compiling your own list and simply purchase a list from a commercial e-mail service. For instance, one of the larger providers is Americaint (http://www.americaint.com/custom_extractions.htm). The advantage of Americaint is that it sells different types of lists across a range of categories

> **Hint:** Web-based e-mail databases are only as good as the compiler. They are often outdated because people tend to change providers on a regular basis, and many only include the addresses of those who have voluntarily added their information.

and prices. Getresponse (http://www.getresponse.com/leads_offer.html has a range of lists priced by their sizes and intended audience.

At times, none of the above resources will prove adequate for your study. In these instances you will have to find alternative ways of contacting individuals. In this, mailing lists and newsgroups not only allow you to keep up to date with emerging debates and look into past debates, but they also provide you with an alternative way of locating and recruiting potential participants. When using these forums, it is important to remember that the quality of participants (and thus your potential recruits) ranges from the good, to the bad, to the downright ugly. Because of this, it is often good to study the archives of the group, to 'lurk before you leap'. Similarly, remember that different forums can be used in different ways. For instance, when looking at mailing lists, you are going to encounter moderated and unmoderated lists. Moderated lists depend on a moderator to determine the acceptability of a message before it is forwarded to the list, ensuring that the information and discussions reflect a level of quality that is seldom reached in unmoderated lists. While moderated lists are clearly better than unmoderated lists, it is often difficult to use moderated lists for recruitment purposes. This is because most moderators are cautious about using their lists for this purpose, or are forbidden to do so. The best strategy is to approach the moderator and try to demonstrate how your research and use of the list relates directly to the group and its interests. At a minimum, though you will have to consider the ethical issues involved, you can always develop a list of e-mail contacts that you can subsequently use by taking note of those individuals who are actively involved in discussions or in making postings to the list. Figure 8.1 demonstrates how you might make an approach.

While not all mailing lists allow you to forward requests for help, newsgroups offer an open conduit for contacting individuals. Not only can you participate without having to join, but you can also post a request for participants to take part in a study or arrange for participants to take part in a discussion once you have gained their agreement. In addition, with a little tact, almost any forum can be used to draw the attention of potential participants to a Website you have dedicated to your study. In these instances you are doing little more than posting linking information, with a request for interested individuals to visit the site. These 'advertisements' need not be confined to newsgroups, but can be placed on any range of Websites, including as a paid advertisement on sites you expect your target population to visit.

A final method you might consider for the recruitment of participants involves designing and placing an advertisement directly onto the Web, then waiting for participants to respond. Placing advertisements on the Web has

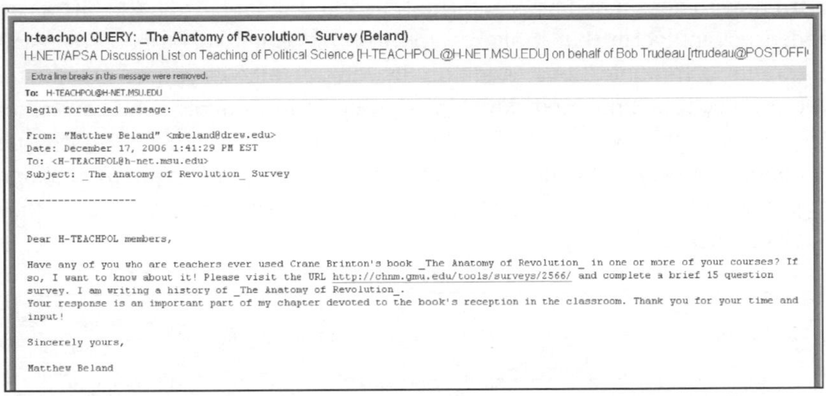

h-teachpol QUERY: _The Anatomy of Revolution_ Survey (Beland)
H-NET/APSA Discussion List on Teaching of Political Science [H-TEACHPOL@H-NET.MSU.EDU] on behalf of Bob Trudeau [rtrudeau@POSTOFFI

Extra line breaks in this message were removed.

To: H-TEACHPOL@H-NET.MSU.EDU

Begin forwarded message:

From: "Matthew Beland" <mbeland@drew.edu>
Date: December 17, 2006 1:41:29 PM EST
To: <H-TEACHPOL@h-net.msu.edu>
Subject: _The Anatomy of Revolution_ Survey

Dear H-TEACHPOL members,

Have any of you who are teachers ever used Crane Brinton's book _The Anatomy of Revolution_ in one or more of your courses? If so, I want to know about it! Please visit the URL http://chnm.gmu.edu/tools/surveys/2566/ and complete a brief 15 question survey. I am writing a history of _The Anatomy of Revolution_.
Your response is an important part of my chapter devoted to the book's reception in the classroom. Thank you for your time and input!

Sincerely yours,

Matthew Beland

Figure 8.1 Illustration of the use of a mailing list to recruit study participants.

advantages in terms of time, money and ethics, but it introduces a number of other issues. For instance, in relation to sampling, you will have to consider who it is that is visiting the Website, who it is of those visiting the site that decide to participate, and even who is linking to your site, and what this may suggest to potential participants about the study or their role in it.

Online Implementation Techniques

A final set of issues you will need to consider when using the internet to generate and collect primary data involves selecting the most appropriate resource for administering the observation, interview or questionnaire. While any of the forums discussed thus far can be used to collect primary data, to administer a survey you are, as a general rule, going to be reliant on a form of e-mail or e-mail-related technology, such as instant messaging and discussion forums, or you are going to have to administer your research using a dedicated Website.

E-mail and e-mail-based technologies

When conducting an online survey, e-mail or some form of e-mail-based technology is, generally speaking, an easier mode of administration than using a dedicated Website, which you will have to develop and publicise specifically for this purpose. E-mail is also easier to use in that most people operating online use e-mail and therefore you will not need to teach your participants how to use it; just as importantly, you are not going to have to learn how to design and place information onto the Web itself. E-mail has an added advantage in that it allows you to engage in synchronous or asynchronous communications. Additionally, e-mail allows you to administer your survey to a single individual or a group of individuals, who can either respond straight away, or at their leisure. Similarly, unlike face-to-face and telephone survey techniques, e-mail allows your participant to respond regardless of where they are physically located (providing, of course, they have online access).

> **Note**: Spam filters are now a necessary element of any e-mail system. Because of this, you are going to have to consider how you address an invitation to participate in your study, and which site you send your e-mail from. Many filters have been set up to eliminate bulk communications regardless of their purpose. Therefore, you are more likely to be successful in your recruitment efforts if you utilise your university account to initiate and carry out your e-mail interactions.

Just as e-mail and e-mail-related technologies allow you to engage in synchronous or asynchronous communications with an individual or group, most e-mail programs also offer a range of options for administering your surveys. Included here are:

- individual contacts between yourself and your participants;
- collective communications between yourself and your participants;
- collective communications between your participants (e.g., focus group);
- the ability to write a questionnaire directly into a message that is subsequently sent to your participants (who answer the questions in a return e-mail);
- the ability to develop a survey with an outside software program (such as Microsoft Word or Excel), and then attach it to an e-mail you send to your participants.

While e-mail may be easy to use, is widely available, and offers multiple ways of administering your survey, each technique associated with e-mail administration has its disadvantages. For example, one of the most problematic aspects of using a standard e-mail program to conduct synchronous interviews is that you are dependent on the typing and screen-reading abilities of your participants. The worse these are, the more onerous they are going to find the medium to use in an active way, and the less likely they are to want to participate. Regardless of his/her computer skills, a participant can choose not to respond to a given question when asked online. Similarly, there is no guarantee a participant will be willing or able to remain online long enough for you to complete the collection of your data. If you have written a questionnaire into an e-mail there is nothing you can do to compel a participant to complete the questionnaire or to complete it as you instruct, particularly if operating in an asynchronous fashion. You are therefore almost completely dependent on the goodwill of your participants.

Glossary
Spam is an unsolicited bulk message sent generally to your e-mail (though it is increasingly appearing on blogs and in wiki's). **Spamming** is the process of producing and indiscriminately sending these bulk messages.

Additionally, even when an individual has the skills necessary to participate in your online survey, there still remains the possibility that if you attach a survey or document to an e-mail, your participant will not have the necessary software needed to open the attachment. Sometimes, when participants are able to open an attached survey they will find that their edition of a program does not open the attachment correctly. When this happens, the formatting you have used to write your survey or embed objects is lost, often making it virtually impossible to interpret what was written.

Finally, when administering your survey through an e-mail program, you will find that many of the tested techniques associated with face-to-face communication for providing incentives to participate to complete the survey, for determining truthfulness, for assessing how at ease a participant is – or even who the participant is – disappear. Because of these limitations, it is advisable that you consider how to adjust your interview style, or the length, appearance and presentation of your questionnaires to maximise your participants' willingness and ability to fully participate in your survey.

Hint: Even if you are not able to use e-mail to administer a survey, it is worth considering whether e-mail can be used as a cost-effective way to check a fact, make contact with an individual who might otherwise be difficult to reach, or as a way to make a first contact with potential participants who subsequently participate in more traditional face-to-face or pencil-and-paper processes.

While these issues may seem to call into question the use of e-mail technologies in the administration of online surveys, many of the emerging video and audio conferencing technologies are starting to help address these issues. For example, Skype offers one-on-one video calling that can be used to conduct interviews (which might help eliminate the need to embed a survey and have the participant return it), and there are also programs that allow you to broadcast images to a limitless number of users (some of which do not even require you to be housing the images or software on your computer – such as Linksys http:///www.linksys.com), which offers a dependable way to conduct group interviews or focus group interactions. The primary advantage offered by these technologies is that they can help bring some of the visual and auditory cues back into the online interaction that are lost in the e-mail environment – particularly the survey environment. They can also help you overcome some of the issues associated with the self-administration of questionnaires, as you can now contact participants and conduct the survey much as if you were using a standard telephone technique.

Web-based administration

While it is not the intention of this text to teach you how to write your own Web pages, it is important to realise that e-mail and e-mail-related technologies offer only one route for the administration of a survey or observation. It is just as possible to develop a dedicated Website. The nice thing about this is that you no longer have to be a programmer or even know HTML tags to develop a Web-based questionnaire, forum or observational platform. Rather, a range of software programs exist that insert the HTML tags needed for your Web browser to know how and where to display a particular piece of information within the browser window. In fact, programs such as Dreamweaver allow you to develop Web pages based on word-processing-type interfaces, in that what you see (on the screen) is what you get (**WYSIWYG**). Even more friendly are the growing number of Websites that offer predesigned Web forms (Wufoo, http://www.wufoo.com –minimum charge attached; The Form Assembly, http://www.formassembly.com; JotForm, http://www.jotform.com – both free but not as flexible as Wufoo). These sites not only have predefined forms but offer a range of options you can use to 'personalise' the form in order to make it more appropriate for your purposes.

While some of the issues relating to the use of e-mail administration hold true for Web-based surveys, such as the need to rely on the goodwill of the participant to complete any given element of the Web document or to interact honestly, three additional issues emerge when using the Web:

1   How will participants be directed to the Website?
2   Will access to the Website (or any of its components) need to be controlled, and, if so, how?
3   What will be the best design for the Website and its interactive areas?

Issues of representativeness and sampling will be important for the gener-alisability of a Web survey (particularly if you do not control access to the site), but directing potential participants to your Website is fairly easy. For instance, one of the easiest ways to direct people to a Website is through a direct e-mail invitation. This invitation can contain directions or site infor-mation in the main text message, or it can provide a link that takes your participants automatically to your Website. For those sites that have been designed to control access through the use of a password, your initial or follow-up e-mail messages can also contain this information (or direct your participant to where they can obtain access information or create their own password). Don't forget that e-mail invitations can be supplemented or augmented by an online advertisement placed directly on the Web or on appropriate Websites. You might even consider issuing invitations to mailing-list and newsgroup participants.

Regardless of how individuals come to your site, you need to decide what areas and activities different participants will be allowed to access once they are there. This is not as complicated as it may sound because most of the programs that allow you to convert (or write) your documents into HTML also provide a step-by-step process for establishing a password protection system. For example, in Microsoft Word all you have to do is access the toolbar 'Web Tools' and find the password button. By pressing this button you will be able to insert (and format) a password directly into the Web page. The key will be to ensure your participants have access to the password, or the ability to access the initial page and then create their own.

> **Note**: Not all e-mail programs are able to make automatic connections to embedded Web addresses. Because of this, it is always worth using the actual address as the link. This will allow any individual who is interested in your study to 'cut and paste' or type the address directly it into their Web browser's address bar.

As part of your decisions concerning access and question control, you will also have to decide whether your survey will allow participants to answer questions out of order, or leave blank entries, or whether it will force each answer to be completed before participants are allowed to move forward.

The more complete the survey the more usable the data. This, however, must be weighed against the fact that if you force participants to complete answers they do not want to, or that they cannot, you risk losing their participation all together. From your point of view, it will be even more important to consider what to do with your results if you force participants to answer each question (or set of questions) before they can advance through the survey, because if you force them to answer every question there is a reasonable chance that they will not be answering the 'undesirable' questions truthfully. It could also be that, despite your best efforts, some of your questions are inadequately or inappropriately formulated. If so, and you insist participants answer them anyway, your results may be seriously flawed. Equally, if you decide to let participants skip questions you will have to consider the impact this may have on your ability to interpret your findings.

> **Hint:** On average it has been estimated that people read a computer screen at a rate 25 per cent below the rate at which they read a written text. Because of this, we strongly advise you to minimise the amount of text you require your participants to read – at least 50 per cent less text than you would if you were writing the same document offline.

Finally, unlike e-mail, which exists as an independent program you can use to administer your survey research, if you want to take advantage of the Web, you are going to have to develop a Website. The first issue you are going to have to consider is the Website's visual layout. This involves not only the font and font size, but also the colours you are going to use and the spacing you use between lines of text and the formatting of the page itself. Secondly, you need to consider whether to include images, and, if so, how best they can be used. For instance, you might want to attract people to your project with a dramatic homepage image, which leads them to a detailed description of the project. Similarly, you might want to embed tables, images, or even audio and video clips directly into a questionnaire or interactive zones. The key to this process will be using the appropriate images and data, and considering where these images should be placed on the page, how large they should be in comparison to other Web elements, and what other types of players (e.g., Real Audio), programs (e.g., Java), plug-ins (e.g., google image viewer) or viewers (e.g., Chinese text viewers or symbol viewers) will be required for your participant to access these additional elements.

Before developing your Website it is worth consulting other sites to see what they have done and how they have gone about developing their interactive components. For those of you who have not developed a Website before, it is possible to access a range of 'style sheets' or Web page templates that will take you through the process of developing your site. However, when using a Web page template, it is worth remembering that while it will greatly reduce the problems associated with Website design and construction, it is possible that your participants will be using a browser that does not support the template, especially if they are using an older browser. The problem is not that nothing will come through but that what is designed may not be displayed as you designed it, potentially eliminating your participant's ability to access or view the information needed successfully to participate. While there are no hard and fast rules governing how you design your Website, some basic conventions that may prove useful include:

- keep your sentences, paragraphs and questions short;
- use special font characteristics more often than you normally would (e.g, use bold-face type to highlight key words and phrases) in order to catch the attention of your participant;
- never use more than 100 words per page;
- try to use sections to break up your text and tasks;
- use as many headings as you believe appropriate – remember, a heading will simply scroll off the screen so it is hard to have too many.

Overall, the idea is to ensure you have variation in any lengthy segments of text, and that you call attention to important words and phrases. You want your readers to read what you have written before they respond or move on (i.e., click to another page or scroll down the screen), and you want to design your site to facilitate the ability of your participants to navigate through its various sections and processes.

We hope we have demonstrated in this chapter the strategic ways in which you can adapt the internet as a tool to help you generate primary data through the use of established methods. Like more traditional methods of conducting interviews and questionnaires, you need to consider important issues around size, sampling, representativeness, ease of administration, and so on, when using the internet in this way. The internet also generates its own set of considerations, which you need to deal with as part of your research design as well as when you begin to consider the nature and meaning of your findings. If you are at the stage at which you can begin to reflect on what these might be and how you might address them, you are well on the way to developing a professional relationship with the internet as one of your core research tools.

Exercise 1: Who to contact?

Every project is different and, as such, will require you to contact a unique range of participants or observational sites. In light of your research project, discuss what group of online users or sites would best help you gather the data you need to complete your project. Based on this, discuss how best you can make contact with these groups or find the sites you need for your observations.

Exercise 2: What to ask?

With your research question and a target group in mind, devise a set of closed-ended questions to elicit some of the information you will need in order to be able to answer your question. Now reflect on the questions you have asked and the options for answering you have provided. Are there any problems of bias you can foresee arising here? Answer specifically with regard to the fact that you will be using the internet to administer this.

Exercise 3: Administration?

How might you best administer this questionnaire, and why? What could you do to augment your results using internet technology?

References and Resources

Americaint: Buy E-mail Lists, http://www.americaint.com/custom_extractions.htm, accessed 28/02/2007.

Best, S. and Krueger, B. (2004), *Internet Data Collection* (London: Sage). This text describes how to go about using the internet to collect data for a range of different projects. Importantly, it discusses the problems of online data collection and suggests ways to work your way around them.

Coombes, H. (2001), *Research Using IT* (Basingstoke: Palgrave Macmillan). This text examines how you can combine computer technology and academic research in order to enhance the usefulness of both.

The Form Assembly http://www.formassembly.com, accessed 06/07/2007.

Get Response, *E-mail Marketing*, http://www.getresponse.com/leads_offer. html, accessed 28/02/2007.

Graham, S. and Marvin, S. (1996), *Telecommunications and the City: Electronic Spaces, Urban Places* (London: Routledge).

JotForm http://www.jotform.com, accessed 01/06/2007.

Langenberg.com: Find a Person & E-mail Search, http://person.langenberg. com, accessed 28/02/2007

Mann, C. and Stewart, F. (2000), *Internet Communications and Qualitative Research* (London: Sage).

Mason, J. (2002), *Qualitative Researching* (London: Sage).

McCoyd, J. and Kerson, T. (2006), 'Conducting Intensive Interviews Using E-mail', *Qualitative Social Work*, 5(3): 389–406.

McQueen, R. and Kunssen, C. (2002), *Research Methods for Social Science* (New York: Prentice-Hall).

Nielsen, J., 'Be Succinct!' http://www.useit.com/altertbox/9703.html, accessed 15/02/2001.

O'Connor, H. and Madge, C. (2001), 'Cyber-Mothers', *Sociological Research Online*, 5: 4 (http://www.socresonline.org.uk/5/4/o'connor.html).

Pedley, P. (2001), *The Invisible Web* (London: Aslib-IMI). This text examines the Invisible Web using examples to address issues involved in using and finding the material contained in the sites that are hidden from most conventional search tools.

Salkind, N. (2004), *Statistics for People Who (Think They) Hate Statistics* (London; Sage).

Schonlau, M., Fricker, R. and Elliott, M. (2002), *Conducting Research Surveys Via E-mail and the Web* (MR-1480) (California: Rand). This is an excellent text examining the pros and cons of conducting surveys online. It does this through a review of the literature associated with online surveys, using this as a basis for a discussion of the differences between online and offline application processes and results.

Sherman, C. and Price, G. (2005), *The Invisible Web* (Medford, NJ: Cyber Age Books). This text addresses the issue of the materials that exist online but are hidden from most standard search tools. Not only does it discuss the types of materials contained in the Invisible Web but also how students can go about finding and accessing this material.

Sills, S. and Song, C. (2002), 'Innovations in Survey Research', *Social Science Computer Review*, 20(1): 22–30.

The Ultimate E-mail Directory, http://www.theultimates.com/E-mail, accessed 28/02/2007.

US Census Bureau, http://www.census.gov, accessed 28/02/2007.

Walliman, N. (2005), *Your Research Project*, 2nd edn (London: Sage).

Wood, M. (2003), *Making Sense of Statistics* (Basingstoke: Palgrave Macmillan).

Worldmail, http://wordE-mail.com, accessed 28/02/2007.

Wufoo http://www.wufoo.com, accessed 1/05/2007.

9 Data Analysis

In the social sciences, the online research process, like more traditional methods of generating primary material, allows you to collect raw data. That data, however, is part of the process of conducting research and not the end point, or output. To give your research project meaning, you will have to identify actual findings: the underlying trends, patterns and relationships within the data, a reading of which will be presented as part of your research conclusions. It is only through analysis of your data that you will be able to answer your research question or hypothesis.

This chapter provides you with a brief examination of some of the generic processes involved in the analysis of your raw data. The purpose is not to teach you all you will need to know about data analysis. Instead, we would like to introduce you to the mechanics of organising your data in preparation for analysis, whether by hand or with the assistance of a software package such as NUD*IST (suitable for qualitative studies) or SPSS (suitable for quantitative studies).

● Data Analysis: A Brief Overview

At the generic project level, the first step is to reduce the amount of raw data you have collected. Your aim is to work with a manageable amount of the data most relevant to your research question. Once you have established a working dataset, you will need to convert, or code, your remaining data into a usable format. How you do this will depend on how you collected your data and how you intend to analyse it. This is because the nature of qualitative data and quantitative data are very different, and therefore require different types of analysis, which are discussed later.

As a result of the differences between qualitative and quantitative data, you will need to rely on a range of different techniques of analysis tailored to fit your research project. Before turning to these techniques, however, we issue a warning: in order for your findings to be considered reliable and valid, and whichever technique(s) you choose, you must demonstrate a combination of unbiased, balanced and well-judged analysis, for it will be this analysis that will inform your findings and overall write-up.

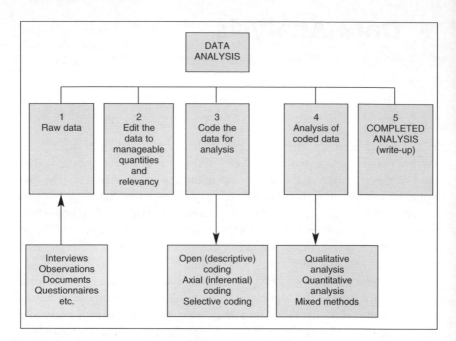

Figure 9.1 General steps in data analysis

Figure 9.1 is a representation of the general process you will have to complete in order to be in a position to analyse your data, regardless of how you went about gathering it or the particular analytic technique you intend to use. As we note above, before you begin your analysis, the first thing you must do is reduce the amount of information you have collected to manageable levels. As a general rule, you should retain only the data most relevant to your study – in other words, the data you require in order to be able to answer your research question.

As Figure 9.1 indicates, once you have reduced the amount of data you are dealing with to manageable proportions, the next step in the analytical process consists of using a more or less standard set of procedures to convert your raw data into its analytical format. This is the process of coding your data. The coding of data can involve turning the information you have into numbers for statistical (quantitative) analysis, or developing specific categories from the written data or observations in preparation for a qualitative analysis.

First, however, you need to consider how your data helps you answer your research question. When coding your data, you will need to be as honest or 'true to the data' as possible. Remember, it will be your codes and coding procedures that ultimately determine the underlying reliability of your analysis. Because of the importance of your coding procedures to your analysis, it is essential that you view your data in a balanced way, and apply as clear and objective a judgement as possible as to how you apply your codes. Ultimately, the data you choose to use in your analysis and the values you attribute to it will determine what claims you can make.

Unfortunately, the internet does not provide a quick and easy way to help you code your data. Coding will require you to use your best judgement based on what you learned in the process of reading for your literature review. This should have introduced you to the kinds of codes typically used in the kind of study you are undertaking, including their uses and shortcomings. Coding can be complex, with certain datasets overlapping, and, depending on the nature of the research project, with a large number of categories and subsets. To help you keep track of your codes or qualitative categories, you might want to consider using a database – Excel, for example – to record events, quotes, occurrences, etc. This will make tracking your data much easier and help clarify the connections that may be critical in the final analysis.

Once you have your basic codes and categories established, you are ready to begin the analysis of your data. Whether you intend to undertake qualitative or quantitative analysis, whether with the aid of a software package or by hand, your aim is to analyse your data in such a way as to ensure you present as true and objective a picture of it as possible. This is true whether your final analysis supports your initial beliefs or not.

● General Differences between Qualitative and Quantitative Data Analysis

As we discussed earlier, qualitative and quantitative research are very different in their data collection techniques and their ontological emphasis. Basically:

> Quantitative research is . . . concerned with the collection and analysis of data in numeric form. [Because of this] [i]t tends to emphasise relatively large-scale and representative sets of data . . . Qualitative research . . . [on the other hand] is concerned with collecting and analysing information in as many . . . non-numeric [forms] as possible. It tends to focus on exploring, in as much detail as possible, smaller numbers of instances or examples which are seen as being interesting or illuminating, and aims to achieve 'depth' rather than 'breath'.   (Blaxter et al., 1996, p. 60)

As a result of these differences, and despite the common necessity of balance, judgement and objectivity in the analysis of either qualitative or quantitative data, there are differences in the techniques associated with each. The first, and most obvious, difference is that quantitative analysis involves the numeric representation of data, while qualitative analysis generally involves the analysis and presentation of non-numeric data.

Second, because quantitative data is numeric, it tends to be manipulated statistically in order to describe and explain underlying patterns and relationships, including variation, magnitude and correlations. On the other hand, rather than relying on statistical manipulation, qualitative analysis involves the grouping of data into categories in order to discover underlying meanings and relationships (though statistics can also be useful components of an overall qualitative analysis).

Third, as a general rule, researchers undertaking quantitative analysis have to design studies so as to 'impose order' on the data before it is collected. This allows the researcher to quickly and efficiently code the data while it is being collected. This in turn facilitates a relatively fast analysis, because datasets can be fed directly into an ever-increasing range of statistical software packages. While order is imposed before data is collected in quantitative studies, qualitative analysis tends to allow, or even require, the researcher to look for order in the data after it has been collected. This is because, according to qualitative researchers, the important aspects of an event tend to emerge while it is under way. Thus, while it is possible to develop 'general categories' in qualitative studies, it is not (always) possible to predetermine what you are looking for. These differences often lead to qualitative analysis being seen as a means of gaining an 'insider's perspective' on the data. The researcher is actively looking for deep understanding. On the other hand, quantitative analysis, which has order imposed on it by the researcher, involves the use of an 'outsider's perspective' to more objectively understand and analyse a given situation.

Qualitative data analysis

Research in the arts and social sciences involves the study of social and cultural life, and lends itself to qualitative approaches. If you are conducting a qualitative research project – in other words, collecting data generated from an 'insider's' perspective' – one of the questions you will subsequently face concerns the type of analytical technique that will be most suited to answering your research question through examination of the data you have collected. This question arises because of the variety of qualitative data that can be collected and categorised using interviews, observations, documentary, linguistic, and other types of studies. This variety has led to the development of a number of related analytical techniques, including documentary and textual analysis, grounded theory analysis, narrative and conversation analysis, discourse analysis and semiotics, to name but a few.

While allowing for a rich tradition of investigation, this methodological diversity has eliminated the possibility of a universal analytic technique emerging. Because of this, it is particularly important to be clear on what the purpose of your study is from the outset. This will enable you to determine whether the analytic techniques you select are appropriate for finding answers to your research questions. Remember, you need to select techniques that are: appropriate for the honest representation of the data, transparent in design, explicit in their application, and applied systematically across all of your data.

Because of the methodological diversity of qualitative analysis (for a good brief review see: Ratcliff, http://don.ratcliffs.net/qual/15methods.pdf), we have provided some basic information below on how to approach the analysis of your data (for more information on how to undertake qualitative data analysis see: Kent, 2001; Miles and Huberman, 1994; *Qualitative Data Analysis Links* http://www.unige.ch/ses/sococ/qual/qual.html; Silverman, 2001; Wetherell et al., 2001; Wolcott, 2001). Despite the range of techniques that exist for the analysis of qualitative data there are some common steps that most academics accept as core practices.

The first of these steps appears straightforward. As discussed, you should go through the data you have collected and eliminate as much of it as possible. This can be quite difficult, however, because you are not trying to reduce the data in order to present a selective reading, or to eliminate data that does not support a predetermined outcome. You cannot reduce the data in such a way that it will cause you to arrive at or present a partial or skewed reading of a given situation, through deductions arrived at through insufficient data or the lack of contradictory or counterfactual evidence.

Your goal in reducing the mountain of data you have collected is to 'find the "slice of cake" that fits your own enquires so you can report on this usefully' (McKenzie et al., 2001, p. 245). In other words, when you sit down in front of your interview transcripts, field notes, videos, documents, etc., you will need to go through the data methodically in order to find logical and useful paths. These should be the paths that encompass the main themes emerging in the data: observations that seem to be recurring, or the range of ideas that come to light as you sort through your primary material. The selection of your final sample will require you to use your knowledge of the subject (gained during your literature review and data collection processes) to find patterns, relationships and regularities. In other words: 'From the whole range of your data you need to draw some relative generalisations' (ibid., p. 247). These generalisations will also eventually form the basis of the categories and concepts that you will use to analyse the data. Remember, however, that at this point you are not attempting to reach conclusions but to establish a base on which to construct your analysis.

> **Glossary**
> **Coding:** The process of labelling (or tagging) your data is known as coding. The labels you use to separate pieces of data are known as the individual **codes** (or tags). Codes can be anything from a single word to a complex idea incorporating a range of related concepts.

Once you have condensed your data to a manageable quantity, started to establish the main themes, found recurring responses, and considered any of the main counter-themes that might be hidden in the data, you will be ready to begin developing the concepts and categories that will inform your analysis. This is known as the **coding** process. The codes or tags that you develop at this stage will form the base of the categories you will subsequently use to organise and analyse your data. Use your initial labels – the paths, themes or patterns you have identified at the selection stage – to develop a more advanced system of categorisation, which can be used to help you summarise your data. The codes you decide upon should do this by pulling 'together themes, and by identifying patterns' in such a way that 'early labels become an essential part of subsequent analysis' (Punch, 2005, p. 199). For example, if you have engaged in observing the activities of an online chat site, you might develop a set of initial tags for:

- the types of messages left by men who visited the site;
- the types of messages left by women who visited the site;
- the type of individuals who left messages on the site in a 24-hour period.

As you go through the data based on these initial descriptive codes you might begin to notice a pattern to the times of day men were more likely to visit the site, or that the topics men discussed were different from those that interested women. From these observations of the data you will begin to develop a set of inferential codes that you can use to help you distinguish patterns in the data. From these overall patterns, you will be able to develop a final set of codes dedicated to setting out what exactly you have discovered.

In qualitative analysis, coding is a process of breaking apart your data into smaller categories and then recombining it into a new meta-code that can explain what it is you have found. Because of this, when engaged in

> **Hint:** Because most word-processing and database software allows you to change the colour of your text or background highlighting, when coding your data you might try using different colours to indicate different codes or categories. For example, if you are coding for how men interacted on a chat site you might try using pink, while using yellow to indicate how women interacted.

coding it is likely not only that individual items or words act as codes, but that as you advance through the coding procedure you will be using phrases and ideas to classify the information you include in any given section.

When developing codes, different types of analytical techniques will require you to develop different kinds – and combinations – of codes. For instance, some researchers (particularly those relying on quantitative analysis) will enter the research situation or look at their data with a set of pre-developed codes. Others (particularly those relying on qualitative techniques) may go into a research situation or enter their data with a only a very general coding framework, and allow this framework to develop and become more complex as they explore the data. Still other studies will enter the research situation or examine the data with no predefined codes, allowing the codes to emerge from the data.

As illustrated above, when engaged in coding you will have to look through the data more than once so that you can build up a pattern of codes that will guide you to the most appropriate answer to your research question. The first level of coding (or first sweep though your data) will primarily be dedicated to developing codes capable of helping to describe and summarise different segments of the data. Using these descriptive and summative codes, you can subsequently go through your data and begin to develop a range of higher-level (order) codes. This will require you to move away from description and summation and towards the initial interpretation – to escape the confines of the basic data and attempt to 'discover what it is saying'. Therefore part of the process involved in developing higher-level codes is an initial analysis of the data. In other words, 'second-level coding tends to focus on pattern codes established during the first sweep. A pattern code is inferential, a sort of "meta-code," which pull[s] together material into smaller and more meaningful units' (Punch, 2005, p. 200). Finally, using the patterns or meta-code that emerge from the data, you should be in a position to develop a 'core' concept capable of pulling 'together your developing analysis' (ibid., p. 211).

> **Hint:**   Codes, regardless of whether they are quantitative (and thus established prior to data collection) or qualitative (established in the process of analysing the data), must be applied consistently across all of your data.

In summary, the analysis of qualitative data requires you to read through your collected data carefully, looking for themes that you can subsequently categorise and code. Bear in mind when doing so the reason why you made a particular observation or asked a particular question. This should help you maintain the perspective and focus you will need to read through and appropriately code your data. Once you have your codes you will be ready to conduct the final analysis by using your codes to discover the meaning that your responses and observations offer. To do this you will need to find ways to cluster your data so that they present a truthful and coherent story which feeds back into your general 'theory' as to what occurred. It is worth keeping in mind that no analysis is going to be worth its effort unless you can 'convince your audience(s) that the procedures you used did ensure that your methods were reliable and that your conclusions were valid' (Silverman, 2001, p. 254).

Quantitative analysis

Qualitative analysis requires you to undertake an in-depth examination of the written, symbolic, spoken or visual world, using words and images as your primary data and the principal way of discussing your findings. Quantitative analysis, on the other hand, relies on the researcher converting oral, written or visual data into numbers, which are subsequently analysed using statistics, and then used to help the researcher describe what occurred (or is occurring). As such, unlike qualitative analysis, in which almost any online material can be converted into data, quantitative analysis requires the data you collect to conform to specific rules associated with statistical analysis. In other words, your data must adhere 'to the requirements of each operational step of the research process', so as to ensure that it can be converted into valid and reliable statistical information (Kumar, 1996, p. 223).

> **Note**: Because of the growing quantity and functionality of statistical software, the universe of quantitative analysis is available to anyone, regardless of their mathematical abilities. The key is not mathematical proficiency, but rather knowledge of when different types of statistical measurements are more or less appropriate.

Quantitative and qualitative studies require you to sort through your data once it has been amassed. Use careful judgement to guide you through the selection process and remember that even if your data is valid, if you do not retain an appropriate or representative sample of what you collected in the first place, your results are unlikely to be reliable or valid even if your statistical techniques are flawless. Regardless of the quality of your statistics, if the underlying data is questionable, your whole analysis is questionable.

Once you have sorted through your data, what you are left with will need to be coded (or placed in its appropriate numeric form and category). It will be this quantified data that you analyse. If your dataset is small enough, or your analysis involves the use of fairly simple statistics, it will often be possible to calculate your measurements by hand. However, if you have a large dataset and your data is amenable to more advanced statistical analysis, you may need to enter your raw numbers into a statistical software package capable of computing the statistics you can subsequently use to understand the underlyng trends in your data (for a good starting text see: Miller et al., 2002; Wood, 2003).

One of the easiest places to begin using statistical analysis is through the integration of basic **descriptive statistics** into a more general qualitative analysis. This is because descriptive statistics are fairly easy to construct, yet they allow you to quickly describe and display basic relationships between variables. By this means you can use statistics yet avoid having to engage in some of the more advanced analytical techniques associated with **inferential statistics**.

Take one example. Your research question may be concerned with investigating whether 'there is a relationship between the time of day you observe a chat room and the number of men using it?' or whether 'there is a relationship between educational level and chatroom use'. Rather than describing your findings in a lengthy paragraph (or more), descriptive statistics allow you to indicate that between 10:15 and 1:30 in the morning, men are 25 per cent more likely to be involved in chat room activity than women. Similarly, rather than detailing every instance of correlation in relation to educational level and chat room use, you could summarise your findings to indicate that college-educated men are 70 per cent less likely to be actively involved in chat room discussion than those with only an A-level (high school) education.

While quantitative analysis depends on use of the correct collection and coding procedures, it is just as important to understand and then determine which statistics are appropriate for your study. This can only be decided in the context of the type of data you collected, how you collected it, and what you want to say with reference to that data. As illustrated in Table 9.1, on a

Categorical			Continuous
Constant	**Dichotomous**	**Polytomous**	
Book	Yes/No	Age	Income (in £)
Human	Good/Bad	old	Weight (in kg)
	Rich/Poor	young	Height (in cm)

Table 9.1   Types of data

general level, data can be divided between categorical and continuous. **Categorical data** (data that can be separated into specific, mutually exclusive categories based upon some common characteristic), is most commonly associated with qualitative analysis. However, it can also form the basis of descriptive statistics when it is appropriate to count the occurrence of a particular category, and subsequently calculate measurements such as the mean or standard deviation. While categorical data is most often associated with qualitative analysis, **continuous data** (data that can take on an almost limitless number of values and can be meaningfully subdivided into increasingly smaller increments) is tied directly into quantitative analysis because it can be analysed for statistical inferences.

> **Note**: There are three basic types of variable categories: **constant**: each variable can take on only one value or category; **dichotomous**: each variable can have one of two values or categories; **polytomous**: where a variable can be divided into a number of different categories.

It may be useful at this point to illustrate how statistics can be used in the analytical process. Let us start with the presumption that most undergraduate studies in the UK use more descriptive statistics in the process of data analysis than they do more advanced statistical procedures, which often require the use of computer software packages such as Minitab or SPSS. We will also assume that, of the range of descriptive statistics that are available to students, most will be concerned with integrating measurements of central tendency, or the typical value of the variables they are investigating, rather than more advanced forms of descriptive statistics. Based on these assumptions, let us take you though a basic example of how you might use statistical (rather than linguistic) analysis of observations of chat room interactions.

Glossary

Mean is calculated by adding up the sum of the variables and then dividing the number by the number of observations.

$$\frac{3+5+5+7+5}{5} = 5.$$

Median is calculated by lining up the observations in numerical order and then finding the exact middle (exactly half the observations are above the number and half below).

3, 5, 5, 5, 7 = 5.

Mode is calculated by finding the most common value. In the previous example this would be 5.

Briefly, using data drawn from the observation of a chat room, it should be possible to design a study around a count of the number of men using the chat room. For instance, you could use this count and compare it to the number of women using the same service (dichotomous categorical data analysis). Using your findings, you might want to further analyse the information to discover the average number of men engaged in a discussion at any given time. To do this you will not only have to count the number of men engaged in discussing an issue over the course of a given period, but you will also have to decide whether the **mean** (arithmetic average), **median** (middle value) or **mode** (most common value) best describes the 'typical value' of their participation. You might want to expand the analysis of your observations to include some form of statistic relating to the spread or distribution of the number of men actively participating in a chat room over a given period. You could then compare this to the same spread for women, which will help provide you with information as to whether or not there are times that are more representative of male chat room participation, and times more representative of female.

To use any form of statistics you need to know more than simply when, and possibly how, to calculate them. You also need to understand what the statistics are telling you. For instance, a **spread** (the distance between the highest and lowest observed value in your dataset) that consists of two or more **modes** tells you something very different from a set of values which includes only a single mode, particularly if they have the same **mean** value. Similarly, you will need to consider what it means if you have two datasets with the same mean but very different **standard deviations**. Even more important information might be conveyed if you discover that your distribution exhibits an unusual skew (the degree to which the distribution varies from perfect symmetry around the middle value) or kurtosis (how peaked your distribution is).

Selecting the appropriate statistics for use in your data analysis will require you to have a thorough understanding of the type of data you have collected, the kind of data analytical techniques it is amenable to, and what it is you are trying to discover in the course of your research. For example, while it might be appropriate to use a measurement of spread in relation to interval data, it makes little sense to discuss spread in relation to categorical data. In fact, when using categorical data it is not appropriate to discuss any form of central tendency beyond the simple mode. This is because categorical data is collected in such a manner as to provide no arithmetical relationship between one category and another. It therefore makes little sense in such cases to discuss anything more than the number of observations that were in each category and what the most common observation consisted of.

If we move beyond descriptive statistics, we find a range of more advanced inferential statistics. These have developed in line with advanced mathematics and can be used to help you begin to understand and predict how variables interact and have an impact upon each other. The more sophisticated you want your inferences to be, the more advanced your statistical analysis will have to be. The key here too, however, is that different types of statistical techniques are useful for finding out different types of information. Therefore, different inferential statistics are going to be more or less appropriate for an analysis intended to determine what the data you have collected is telling you.

The type of investigation you can engage in using complex statistical analysis ranges from looking for relationships between variables using cross-tabulation, or groups of variables using one-way and two-way ANOVA analysis, to techniques that have been designed to help you examine relationships between variables, such as correlation analysis and regression analysis, all the way to the use of stepwise regression to examine how the loss of a single variable affects the variance of the total analysis. The key to successfully using these techniques is not that you can use them to draw inferences from your data. Rather, it is to remember that your ability to draw inferences will depend on the nature of the data you have collected, how you have gone about quantifying this data, and whether you have used the appropriate statistical measurement for your data and analytical purposes. The quality and reliability of your inferences will therefore rest on your ability to demonstrate that what you calculate did not simply come about by chance but was a real consequence of what you were observing. In other words, you must always remember that statistical analysis does not prove 'facts'. Statistics allow you to demonstrate the probability that what you conclude is in fact more than a construct or outcome of your measurement or observational techniques.

This chapter has provided a brief introduction to the kinds of data analysis techniques you may find helpful when you come to consider the data you have collected. While we have concentrated on statistical analysis here, it is useful to remember that, although useful in both quantitative and qualitative studies, statistical analysis is just one way of examining information or producing useful categories from which you can derive particular conclusions or support contentions or hypotheses. It may not be the only or most useful approach to your data, particularly if you are engaging in qualitative study. We do hope, however, that even basic consideration of the data you collect through the lens of statistical analysis will help you to view the data and its meaning with more clarity, and perhaps facilitate further, qualitative techniques of analysis.

Exercise 1: Your ontology – how does it influence your views of data gathering?

No matter what your project, sit down and discuss five general pros and five general cons of utilising qualitative data gathering techniques. Then do the same for quantitative techniques. Based on your discussion, consider which technique more completely fits your ontological predispositions.

Exercise 2: Coding

Make a list of the data you intend to or have already gathered in the course of your research project. Would you describe this as qualitative or quantitative data? How much of it do you really require? What kind of coding will you need to use to start breaking it down? Would databases be useful in this process? Be specific as to how/why/why not.

Exercise 3: Statistics

Regardless of whether you have collected quantitative or qualitative data, consider if and how converting some of the data you have to statistical format might assist in its eventual analysis. If you believe it will help, state why; if you believe it will not, then explain why not.

Will you be able to do this by hand, or will you require specialised software? Be specific in your answer.

References and Resources

Blaxter, L., Hughes, C., and Tight, M. (1996), *How to Research* (Buckingham: Open University Press). This text provides a practical guide to conducting research in the social sciences. It offers a range of tips and exercises and is an excellent text for testing your understanding of different research techniques.

JISC: Plagiarism Advisory Service, http://www.jiscpas.ac.uk/turnitinsignup. php, accessed 28/02/2007.

Kent, R. (2001), *Data Construction and Data Analysis for Survey Research* (Basingstoke: Palgrave Macmillan). This text offers an easy-to-follow guide to survey data analysis for students in the social sciences (particularly marketing).

Kumar, R. (1996), *Research Methodology* (London: Sage).

Mason, J. (2002), *Qualitative Research*, 2nd edn (London: Sage).

McKenzie, G., Usher, R. and Powell, J. (2001), *Understanding Social Research* (London: Falmer).

Miles, M. and Huberman, M. (1994), *Qualitative Research,* 2nd edn (London: Sage).

Miller, R., Acton, C., Fullerton, D. and Maltby, J. (2002), *SPSS for Social Scientists* (Basingstoke: Palgrave Macmillan). This text provides students with a basic but thorough guide to the use of SPSS using cases drawn from the British Social Attitudes Survey. This text offers an extremely practical guide to the use of SPSS for the undergraduate and graduate student just starting out on the road to statistical analysis.

Phillips, L. and Jorgensen, M. (2004), *Discourse Analysis as Theory and Method* (London: Sage). This text offers a comprehensive overview of three different discourse traditions and their uses within the research process.

Punch, K. (2005), *Introduction to Social Research: Qualitative and Quantitative Approaches*, 2nd edn (London: Sage). This text is a very good introduction to academic research, taking students through the issues and techniques associated with the qualitative and quantitative research traditions.

Qualitative Data Analysis Links, http://www.unige.ch/ses/sococ/qual/ qual.html, accessed 12/07/2007.

Ratcliff, D., *15 Methods of Data Analysis in Qualitative Research*, http://don.ratcliffs.net/qual/15methods.pdf, accessed 16/07/2007.

Silverman, D. (2001), *Interpreting Qualitative Data: Methods for Analyzing Talk, Text and Interaction* (London: Sage). This text has been designed to introduce students to the fundamental concepts associated with qualitative research, including the key methods available for analysing qualitative data.

Strauss, A. and Corbin, J. (1998), *Basics of Qualitative Research: Techniques and Procedures for Developing Grounded Theory*, 2nd edn (London: Sage). This text offers a practical guide to the process of developing grounded theory using a range of illustrative examples to clarify the core methodology involved in the process.

Wetherell, M., Taylor, S. and Yates, S. (2001), *Discourse as Data: A Guide to Analysis* (London: Sage). This text offers a clear, step-by-step guide to the processes involved in different types of discourse analysis.

Wolcott, H. (2001), *Writing Up Qualitative Research*, 2nd edn (London: Sage). This text provides practical advice on how to go through data and find the best bits to use in an analysis and write-up. Importantly for new researchers, it offers a concise discussion of some of the key considerations and methods for integrating underlying theory and methods into a project write-up.

Wood, M. (2003), *Making Sense of Statistics* (Basingstoke: Palgrave Macmillan). This text provides an accessible introduction to statistics, explaining what different statistical results mean and why different methods work, rather than trying to take you through the minutiae of the underlying mathematical processes. The text also offers basic guidance in how to design, structure and analyse your results.

10 Writing-up Your Research Paper or Dissertation

Many students find the writing-up stage to be the most daunting step of any research project. Regardless of how well-developed and coherent your research plan was, or how well you carried it through, if you do not write up your methodology and results in a coherent, systematic way, emphasising your conclusions and the reasons you have arrived at them, the project as a whole will inevitably suffer. Additionally, although you will have reflected on your work throughout the research process, often the writing process is one of continued discovery that helps crystallise the meaning of the research in your own mind. Remember, you are not unusual if you find that you are not really sure of what you think until you have written it down: few people are.

Although not technically a component of the online research process, this chapter focuses on the ways and means of writing-up your research project, suggesting ways in which you can ease the pain, while maximising the quality of what you produce. Where appropriate, this chapter also discusses how you might use some of the newer online resources to help you with the writing process (for more information see Appendix D).

The academic writing process involves more than coming to terms with your own beliefs and thoughts; it is about organising large amounts of information, primary and secondary material, and a range of ideas and conclusions. It is also about presenting a coherent, tenable and well-structured argument. The way you organise your writing will ultimately form the framework underpinning your essay or dissertation.

Because organisation is so important to the development of a coherent argument, we suggest that you consider staging this final part of the research process in order to:

- minimise the minor difficulties of writing-up;
- formulate a coherent argument;
- avoid errors of fact;
- avoid incomplete information; and
- most importantly, avoid inadvertent plagiarism.

The Stages of Writing-up

The revision stage

Before you begin to write-up your results, sit down once again with your proposal. Revisit the original question and the theoretical framework you began with. Ask yourself how it guided your research, and why. Note the elements of your theoretical reading that shed light on the overall project, or on specific elements of that project. Decide whether your project has been about testing a theory, or whether it has involved the use of theory as a tool of interpretation.

At this stage, you may want to consider developing a database to help you systematically organise and display your thoughts. There is a wide range of software tools, from databases to simple word-processing programs, that can be used for this purpose. For instance, you might consider using a word-processing program to develop a simple table in which rows represent concepts and corresponding column cells are filled in with the information you have relating to the concept. Another strategy might be to use each sheet in a database program to cover a single concept, and use each cell to fill in the evidentiary bases supporting that concept. No matter what technique you use to organise your basic database, once you have developed it you should be in a position to begin to condense these initial thoughts about authors, works, theoretical position or even simple ideas into more concrete categories.

> **TIP** When condensing the information in your database it is always a good idea to have a cell indicating the part of the project the information is relevant to, and why.

Continue filling in and condensing your cells in this fashion so that your database gets more and more detailed. The key is to make sure that the details you include help you understand how each individual piece fits into your overall research project. This will require you to include cells dealing with all the issues that you faced when developing and carrying out your project: Was it possible to carry out the research using the methods you described initially? What methods did you actually use? Were they successful? If relevant, what data did you gather? Was it qualitative or quantitative? If you are working in the arts or humanities, note the primary sources you have settled on or discovered, and describe their interest or relevance to the overall paper.

Next, consider your other reading. Over the course of the research project you will have developed a bibliography composed of all the primary and secondary sources you have consulted. You will also, in all probability, have made copious notes. Revisit these, sorting thematically. Decide which are the most relevant and why. Which will you refer to or quote from? Which provide useful general or background information, but will probably not need to be referenced directly in the final write-up? Make editorial notes of this kind on your bibliography, using the knowledge you have gained in the course of the research process to decide on the relative importance of individual works, data or other material. If you have taken notes on your original reading and stored them in a database already, so much the better.

TIP For those of you who are unable to carry a computer with you everywhere you go, you might try using one of the growing number of Web-based word-processing programs. The advantage of using one of these is that no matter what computer you are using, as long as it has internet access you will be able to work on your database, particularly if you store the information in one of the online storage sites. While it is unlikely that online word-processing packages will replace your desktop version, they can help the 'mobility' of the writing process, and are handy ways to write collaboratively without having to be in the same room, or even country, as your colleagues (for online word processing see Zoho Writer, http://www.zohowriter.com or Writely, http://www.writely.com, and for online storage facilities see I(2)Drive, http://www.i2drive.com).

If not, then you might want to consider transferring some of the main points into your database, including bibliographical details and their whereabouts so that you can locate them if needed during the write-up process. This will greatly increase the ease of reference when it comes to searching out a quote or elaborating an idea when you are actually writing-up. You should now be in a position to begin ordering your database material so that each section begins to reflect its overall relevance to the project, and you can therefore move on to the planning stage.

The planning stage

Having revisited the research you have done and clarified the process in your mind, you can move on to planning your research paper. It is here that you will begin to decide the form your research paper or dissertation will take. In other words, you will need to begin to consider the actual layout that you will use. Thus, you should spend time considering details such as:

- Should you use individually developed chapters?
- Would it help to divide the project or chapter up using subject headings?
- Should your material be presented as an undivided narrative?
- Will you need to include tables of data and, if so, what form should they take?
- Does your project need to include research-relevant appendices, illustrations, or copies of primary material?

While considering these issues do not forget that all of your decisions should be taken in light of the work you have undertaken and the specific argument (or arguments) you want to make. How you plan your argument and layout must also be compatible with the kinds of data or other information you have collected, and how you went about collecting it.

TIP When you arrive at the planning stage your database should be complete (or only missing very minor aspects). If you are not sure, you might insert a checklist of what you have done and what remains to do into your database. This will help you decide whether or not you are in a position to make a viable writing plan.

We advise you to take these early steps because without a coherent layout and structure, the most inspired argument will be difficult to express and may confuse readers. Equally, without a well-focused, critically informed and intelligently argued line of reasoning, even a perfectly laid out research paper will lack academic merit or interest. Thus, while often skipped or skimped upon, planning is actually one of the most important aspects of the writing process.

> **Note**: Different people and different research topics involve slightly different approaches. If you are interested in learning more about this, we suggest you read Chapter 6 in Crème and Lea (1997), Greetham (2001) and Peck and Covle (2005). Each of these texts contains useful discussions on how different writers and disciplines approach the writing process.

Decide what your main argument is

Once you have established your database, reviewed it, and made a preliminary plan, you will finally be in a position to begin formulating your main argument. This is equivalent to producing a thesis statement – in effect, the line of reasoning you are using and the conclusion to which this inevitably leads. At this point you should write your main argument at the top of your database (or each of the individual sheets contained within it). This will help you to develop that argument, and stick to the point when you are actually writing-up. It is important that you know in your own mind what your opinions are, but what you write about your argument at this stage need not be comprehensive. It should take the form of a statement or a number of statements relating to the research question.

It is also useful to double-check at this stage whether the argument you wish to make is relevant. Think about whether the material you have collected in the course of your research is sufficient to make a strong and legitimate case. Place your statements of argument alongside your initial question and decide whether they match up. If they do not complement each other, you may need to revise one or the other, in order to ensure the coherence of the final write-up.

Again, we are not trying to tell you that the argument you are making at this stage will never change; it may change in the course of making it. However, keeping your thesis statement and question in mind throughout the process of writing up does help to keep you on track and prevent irrelevancies from creeping into your work.

> **TIP** Try to 'nutshell' your argument by writing down three or four sentences which explain exactly what the research paper is about. For help on how to do this, you can go online and examine the abstracts in a database associated with your academic discipline (e.g. *ABC-CLIO Historical Abstracts and America: History and Life* or the *Applied Social Science Index and Abstracts*).

Assemble your evidence

Having drafted a basic thesis statement, you need to test its merit. The first step is to think about whether or not you have sufficient evidence to sustain the argument you wish to make. It is often useful to brainstorm around your argument, bringing the research you have done and what you have learned in the course of that research into play. Write down the main points of your research, some of the ideas you have and themes you wish to pursue. Do these support the argument you wish to make or not? Overall, is there enough evidence to sustain the argument over the entire paper or dissertation? Is there counterfactual evidence you will have to address? Are there gaps in the research or theory that you will need to acknowledge or fill? Think about whether the material you have collected in the course of your reading is sufficient to make a strong and legitimate case. If not, revise your opinions in line with the evidence, or do more reading.

Break it down

From the revision stage, you should already have a list of key terms that need to be addressed, points you wish to make and key works you have covered in your reading. Make a list of paragraph headings, using keywords and arrows in flowchart format. Start with the introduction and move logically through the argument you intend to make on a point-by-point basis. Limit each paragraph to one idea or argument. When you have run out of material or points to make, decide whether you have covered enough to come to a conclusion.

Next to each paragraph keyword, make a keyword list of supporting evidence, argument, and material to be cited in each paragraph. Include examples, empirical evidence, theoretical argument etc. as appropriate. It is helpful to use a spider or tree structure to link these thoughts, which are in effect branches of your argument, to the central question. You can then move on to make subsidiary trees or spiders from the nodes you have produced. These should include supporting theory, themes or argument, evidence you wish to call on, or conclusions you wish to support.

Refer to your database for this, which is where a lot of the hard work in this area will already have been done. Specifically, take the information in your database and start moving it into either a drawing program or the flow-chart (diagram) function that exists in most word-processing programs. For example, in Microsoft Word you can build fairly complex visual and textual diagrams by clicking on the Drawing icon (or by going to the Insert drop-down menu), and then clicking on the Insert Diagram option. From here you can build your own diagram by selecting the type of chart you want Microsoft Word to insert. If you would rather have more control over the representations and directions of lines and boxes, you can also develop your own flowchart by using the text boxes and line functions found in the drawing toolbar. To display this, you go to the View dropdown menu, clicking on the Toolbars item and then clicking the Drawing button (for more information see Appendix E).

> **Hint:** Not only are database and word-processing programs easily integrated into your write-up, but if you consider using a graphing program (or the charting capacities of most word processors) you will easily be able to edit your work – without having to make the cut-and-paste (or erasure) mess that is required of hand-crafted charts.

Decide on layout

By tracing the path or paths of your argument, you are establishing the logic by which the paper will proceed, and determining what it is you need to cover. Once you have your argument sketched out, you can begin to break it down into its constituent parts. These parts are the pillars of your argument, and will provide logic to what you write. For a dissertation, this will typically involve separating your work into chapters, and require you to include an introduction and a conclusion. Individual chapters should operate both as independent blocks of writing dealing with a theme or a number of related themes, and as key building blocks of the argument as a whole. A research paper, on the other hand, is typically not broken into chapters; however, it does work according to the same logic, albeit informally. Like the dissertation, it needs an introduction and a conclusion, though these are more likely to be flagged in some disciplines than others.

CHECKLIST

1. Does my plan include the opportunity to discuss relevant literature, including:

   - scholarship to date
   - relevant theory
   - secondary literature on key areas
   - primary source data
   - methodology (if relevant)
   - ethics (if relevant)?

2. Am I clear what my argument is and does it relate directly to the research question?

Political or sociological studies, for example, often use section headings to guide the reader or assist in structuring arguments relying on different kinds of evidence or covering a number of themes. Literary criticism and history, on the other hand, use such section headings less frequently, if at all. Regardless of the disciplinary norms, however, your plan should include such section headings, though these may be omitted from the final draft.

Timeframe

The next step is to consider how much time you have at your disposal to complete your write-up. It is critical that you know whether you are working to a strict deadline or whether you have a more flexible completion date. Check what that deadline is and remind yourself of how long (in terms of words or pages) the finished piece of work should be. If you are not working to a fixed deadline, it may be helpful to give yourself one. Be realistic. There is no point in setting deadlines you are unlikely to meet, and failing to meet a set deadline can begin the slippery slope to non-completion.

TIMETABLE

Date of final submission: Total time available:
Deadlines: Introduction:
            Chapter 1:
            Chapter 2:
            Chapter 3:
            Conclusion:
Date for completion of first draft:
Date for completion of second draft:
Date for completion of proofreading:

Once you have established your submission date, it is useful to break your writing time down by deciding on a number of interim deadlines. For example, as you can see from the timetable chart , you might consider developing deadlines for finishing your introduction, individual chapters or sections and, importantly, your first draft. Remember, your first draft deadline should give you enough time to make at least one major revision, as well as to proofread the text and double-check all references. When setting interim deadlines, it will be important to consider the relative importance, and the relative difficulty, of writing individual sections or chapters. We would advise you to dedicate more time to chapters or sections you believe will be more important to your overall project or that you think will be harder to draft. It is also worth noting, as you will have gathered from your own readings, that introductions and conclusions are normally the shortest chapters or sections of the final paper. What is less obvious, however, is that they often require the greatest amount of revision. For introductions in particular it is useful to allow time for at least one major rewrite before the deadline for the first draft, as introductions often need to be tackled twice: once at the beginning of writing up, and again at the end. Finally, remember that it is sometimes the technical details that slow you down. Allow plenty of time at the end for putting together and checking: bibliography, tables, diagrams, charts or other forms of data illustration. The mechanics of setting these up can often be time-consuming, and require many different configurations to get correct.

> **TIP** When compiling source material or a framework to be used in your essay or dissertation, do not cut and paste from a Website. If there is no way around this, immediately include a full citation and mark it out as 'borrowed material'. If you do not clearly indicate that the material is not your own you run a risk of plagiarism by inadvertently incorporating pieces of the text into your own work.

Your audience

Once you have your plan and the relevant notes to hand – divided up by chapter – you are ready to begin writing. Consider who you are writing for. This will be determined by the kind of readership you envisage for your work. Ask yourself if your audience will be:

- a specialised audience of academics in the same field;
- a government body involved in making or evaluating policy;
- a course tutor evaluating the quality of your independent study;
- a PhD panel or journal editor who will decide whether or not your work contributes to scholarship in the field?

Each of these audiences will use different rubrics to assess your work. In all cases, however, you will need to convince them of your competence as a researcher, the persuasiveness of your argument, and the legitimacy of the scholarship you present. Because of these multiple criteria, it is vital that you develop a good working plan before you begin to write; one that you are confident addresses all these adequately should also satisfy the criteria of your audience.

The introduction

No matter what kind of academic script you are producing, you will need some kind of introduction. Without it, your work will lack a frame, appear unanchored, and leave a gap for the reader. Inevitably, a weak introduction will undermine the academic standing of even the best-argued piece of work. The function, layout and content of introductions vary hugely across the disciplines. One of the main distinctions is between humanities-based research and social science research. The former typically requires the introduction to anchor your research and make it relevant to extant scholarship. If there is a gap in the scholarship that you are going to address, then it needs to be stated and explained here. Any sources you have consulted and intend to call upon should also be mentioned. You should also indicate your critical position, and make it clear whether your work will involve the

> **Hint:** To minimise the chance of error or lack of clarity in your writing:
>
> - Use the Spellcheck.
> - Ensure that your word-processing program is set to the standard language of your country.
> - Avoid using slang, jargon or colloquialisms.
> - Abbreviate as little as possible.
> - Use the active rather than passive voice.
> - Avoid using 'I: it overpersonalises your work and can appear to weaken your argument.
> - Remember that online grammar checks are useful but not foolproof.
> - Use a thesaurus. This will help you to develop your vocabulary, finesse your writing and avoid repetition.
> - Acknowledge all sources quoted, referred to, or drawn from and ensure they appear in your bibliography.
> - Know the citation, reference and bibliographical format used in your discipline.

reinterpretation of well-known material, or will call upon new sources, or sources not previously considered by this branch of scholarship. Avoid stating what you will do, though for longer pieces of work, such as a dissertation, you should give a brief overview of individual chapters.

While there is a general rule against using 'I' in the writing process, in some social science disciplines the researcher is often required to engage in a certain amount of self-reflection. In fact, in fields such as anthropology, sociology and social history, legitimation of the research process involves discussion of the position of the researcher, and how that may or may not have influenced the research process. For this reason, the introduction to any project in these disciplines should include an overview of the methodology and methods used. It should also indicate how these relate to the overall argument, and where in the write-up discussion and evaluation of the role of the researcher and the effectiveness of the research methods employed is to be found.

In writing your introduction or chapter, begin with your plan. What key terms, issues or questions did you decide required attention in this piece? What key works from your reading need to be included or discussed? What evidence can you marshal in support of the argument you are making, and how might you best include it?

WHAT DOES AN INTRODUCTION DO?

It:

- introduces the topic or research question;
- provides an overview of what the piece is about;
- relates the research presented to other research or scholarship in the field;
- explains the rationale behind the piece, noting, if relevant, any gaps in scholarship;
- states the argument in brief;
- gives an indication of how the argument will be made;
- introduces (if relevant) the methodology and/or methods;
- explains (if relevant) the writer/researcher's involvement in the research process and whether and how this affects the information generated or the interpretative scope;
- indicates the sources used;
- states (if relevant) the scope and limitations of the overall project.

Organise the sheets in your database or the rows in your tables so that they appear in the same order as the points you wish to make and start writing the introductory paragraph. From here you can move logically through the argument you intend to make on a point-by-point basis. Remember, good writing will limit each paragraph to one idea or argument. When you have run out of material or points to make, decide whether you have covered enough to come to a conclusion. Ask yourself if the argument is properly stated, supporting points made, and appropriate examples and analysis included. If you think you have covered all relevant ground, then write a concluding paragraph which makes it clear to the reader exactly where in the argument this chapter is placed and, if relevant, where you intend to go next.

See Appendix D for tips on beginning paragraphs and writing-up.

> **Note**: Fresh ideas or examples may occur to you in the course of writing. In these instances you might consider using an electronic Post-it note, which are electronic versions of yellow Post-its. There are two basic versions of electronic Post-it notes. One can be downloaded and run directly from your computer (see *ATnotes* http://www.atnotes.free.fr); the other are online Post-it services that store your note in an online database (see *ChimeNote* http://www.chimenote.com).

Using charts and diagrams to present data

Just as we suggested you consider developing a diagram to help you map the relationships between the different parts of your project, consider whether this might also be useful within your write-up. Remember, diagrams and charts can be useful if you want to include visual aids to help explain a conceptual relationship. You may have to include a chart in order to help your reader understand and interpret any dataset that you need to include in your write-up. For instance, many readers find written information about quantities, statistics, rates of change or trends difficult to digest. However, it is fairly easy to clarify these with the inclusion of a chart. Charts are also particularly helpful if you want to discuss the datasets you have developed in the course of a quantitative research project. Your charts and diagrams should be designed in such a way as to help your reader understand your interpretation of the data. (Appendix E offers a guide to generating diagrams and charts.)

The charts and graphs used in this text represent an attempt to present an easily comprehensible schematic for understanding a written argument. Presenting material schematically and in summary form allows it to be understood without difficulty and to be easily referred to again and again. If properly constructed, charts and graphs can provide you (the researcher), as well as your intended reader, with greater clarity about the data itself. Although there appears to be an almost limitless range of possible graphs, charts and diagrams, we recommend the following nine types as those most likely to be of use in your write-up. These are, in no particular order: Venn diagrams, cycle diagrams, radial diagrams, organisational charts, pie charts, bar charts, line graphs, area graphs, and a special subset of the line graph, the X–Y graph.

Venn diagrams are ways to illustrate visually how different ideas, datasets, concepts or items intersect and overlap. They do this by building a series of intersecting circles, where the intersection indicates the size and degree of overlap between the items in question. The diagram itself can be as simple as two slightly overlapping circles, all the way to complex multi-ringed diagrams more akin to advanced crop circles than academic diagrams.

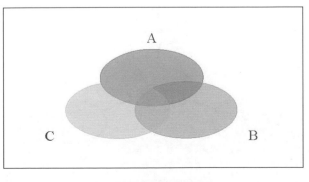

Venn diagram

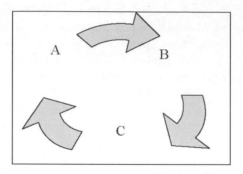

Cycle diagram

While Venn diagrams allow you to illustrate interaction and overlap, **cycle diagrams** allow you to illustrate processes that involve continuous cycles. For example, the policy-making process can be thought of as a circle, starting with the realisation of a problem, moving to the development of a policy to address the problem and its implementation, which subsequently leads to new problems that require new policies.

Radial diagrams are probably going to be most useful to you if you decide to try and illustrate your argument with examples of how different elements relate to each other while planning your write-up. This is because radial diagrams allow you to illustrate the relationships between a range of elements and a core element or concept. They are very useful for showing how component factors or conceptual outlines fit together into an overall argument or claim.

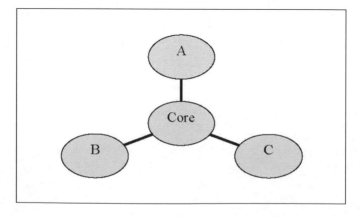

Radial diagram

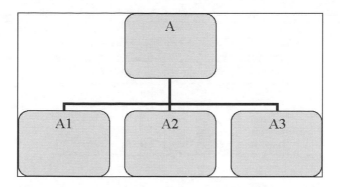

Organisational chart

An **organisational chart** is much like a radial chart. Instead of illustrating how items relate to a core element, however, these charts use boxes and links to illustrate hierarchical relationships between the elements of the diagram. For example, if you are interested in illustrating how different individuals fit into an organisation, you could start at the top and work your way down through the layers of subordinate positions. In general, these diagrams are very useful for illustrating structure.

Pie charts are circular charts, divided up into sections which indicate size or frequency. They are useful if you are discussing parts of a whole category, such as the distribution of set resources, the profile of a population etc., as they show the sizes of parts that make up the whole. While they are a useful device that you have probably come across before, remember when considering their use in your write-up that although pie charts provide clear snap-shots of particular situations, they cannot show change over time. They are therefore not useful in illustrating trends, though two or more pie charts can be used to demonstrate differences in the same or similar groups at different times.

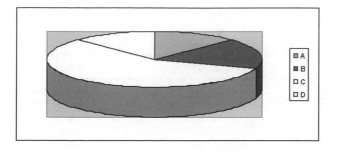

Pie chart

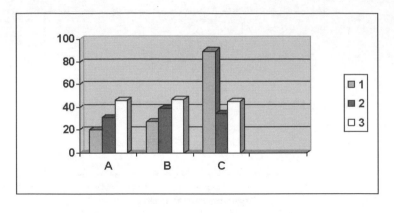

Bar graph

Probably the most widely used graphs are **bar graphs**. These graphs are a very good way of illustrating comparisons between classes or groups of data, aspects of different groups, or changes over time in a single group or a variety of groups. Bar graphs are particularly useful when observed or recorded changes are large. For smaller changes, you might consider using line graphs.

Line graphs are typically used to illustrate changes in the same group over time, or for different groups over the same period of time. Because of their design, they are often considered easier to read than bar graphs, particularly when your research involves tracking small changes or illustrating trends.

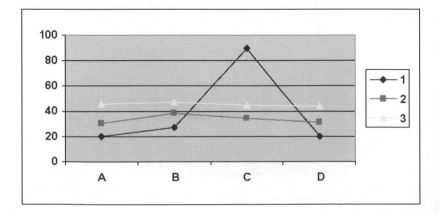

Line graph

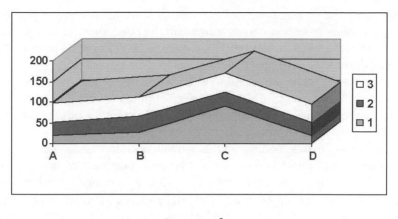

Area graphs

Area graphs tend to be used to track changes over time but are layered to help illustrate differences. This makes area graphs particularly useful in illustrating the difference between two or more groups in the same overall category over time.

A sub-group of the line-graphs are the **X–Y graphs.** As their name implies, X–Y graphs are specifically used to illustrate the relationship between two different things. In simple terms, X–Y graphs work by plotting changes in one variable along the X-axis and the other variable along the Y-axis. The resulting graph illustrates the impact a change in one variable has on the other, if any. If one variable increases in response to increases in the

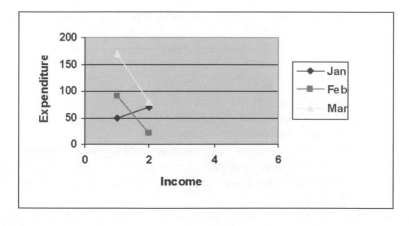

X–Y graphs

other, then the variables are said to have a positive relationship. If one variable decreases in response to an increase in the other, then the variables are said to have a negative relationship. If there is no discernable pattern, then the variables may have no direct relationship to one another.

Charts and graphs are useful tools because they help you display visual information. Because of this, they can assist you in coming to terms with your own data so as to better explain and interpret it for others. However, neither charts nor graphs can take the place of well-reasoned, well-explained arguments. Because of this you will need to ensure that any chart or graph that you use is accompanied by an explanation of its relevance, and, if necessary, a detailed analysis of what is indicated by the chart or graph in the context of the overall project. (For more information on how to generate and insert diagrams and charts into standard word-processed assignments, see Appendix E.)

Writing a conclusion

Whether you are writing a 500-word abstract or a 10,000-word dissertation, you will need to arrive at one or more conclusions. A conclusion must be more than your opinion or a simple summary of what you have already said. It requires you to draw on your data and/or your argument in order to derive reasoned and reasonable answers to your research questions, answers supported by the evidence you have encountered in the course of the research. A conclusion must always be legitimated by your data and emerge from the arguments you have mustered in answering your question. Because of these requirements, it is vital that you consider what you have in fact argued within your paper before you draft your conclusion. Make sure your conclusion:

- restates the key argument (or arguments) you develop in your paper, but in brief;
- provides a brief, but comprehensive, overview of what the piece was about;
- states your conclusions with reference to:
  - the evidence you have provided;
  - the methodology or methods used;
  - any other relevant scholarship;
  - the theoretical frameworks used to underpin your research;
  - if relevant, your individual involvement in the research process;
  - if relevant, the scope and limitations of the project and its findings;
- and, if relevant, discusses some of the possible directions that might be taken in future research.

While there is nothing wrong with referring to previous discussions, arguments or evidence, do remember that a conclusion should conclude, not summarise. In other words, having read the conclusion, your reader should be the wiser with regard to your research project and its findings than s/he would have been had s/he stopped at the final chapter.

TIP To double-check whether you have written an adequate conclusion, read through what you have written, and try to summarise it in two or three sentences. If you find yourself rehearsing your methods or referring to evidence without inferring anything new, then you will probably need to go back and clarify the conclusions you have reached.

Completing the first draft

Having worked through your plan, inserted all relevant data and charts, and drafted a conclusion, you will have completed the lion's share of the writing-up – your first draft, the basis of what you will submit. Unfortunately, you are not yet done. You must read through the paper at least one more time, paying particular attention to the introductory and concluding paragraphs.

The first part of your job is to read through your draft and check whether you need to include more material or whether there are particular parts of the argument that you consider weak or in need of rewriting. When making alterations, one of the more useful ideas is to take advantage of the Comment functions and the Track Change function found on most word-processing

---

CHECKLIST

When you have finished writing, read through your first draft, ensuring you address the following on a chapter-by-chapter basis:

- Does the chapter address the overall question and the chapter topic? Where and how?
- Is the chapter comprehensive? Does it cover/include all relevant primary and secondary material? Does it address key issues?
- Is the chapter coherent? Are your points clearly made and supported by relevant examples or evidence?
- Is all the material included in the chapter relevant? Is the argument sustained throughout?
- Does the chapter flow? Does each paragraph follow logically and in order from the previous one?
  - Is each paragraph coherent?
  - Is each sentence clear, grammatically correct and each word correctly spelt?
  - Does the chapter come to a conclusion?

programs. Using these, you will be able to insert comments without actually changing the text itself and track any changes that you do make to an earlier draft. Consider as you proceed the general integrity of the argument, the relevance of the examples you have used and the coherence of your explanations. It is also useful at this stage to focus on the clarity and conciseness of the piece. Remember, all academic writing should be clear, concise and unambiguous – you are writing for a particular audience with a particular academic objective in mind. See Appendix D for writing tips.

THINGS TO LOOK OUT FOR:
REASONS FOR LACK OF CLARITY IN WRITING

- Sentences which are too long and contain too many points
- Overuse of jargon
- Insufficient information
- Excessive or inappropriate use of the passive voice
- Inaccurate or confusing use of pronouns
- Misuse of words
- Inaccurate or insufficient punctuation
- Lack of a fully conjugated verb

Part of the discipline of academic writing is the ability to stick to a given word length. Not reaching the required word length maybe considered by your assessors as an indication that you have not conducted the research properly. Overshooting the mark, on the other hand, may raise concerns about your ability to focus on your topic or present a coherent argument. Wiring to a specific word length can be a challenge when you are dealing with a complex topic or a lot of information. However, both the clarity and concision of your work – putting things in a nutshell, using as few words as possible – depend to a large extent on developing your writing style. Being as concise as possible will help demonstrate to your

---

THINGS TO LOOK OUT FOR:
REASONS FOR LACK OF CONCISION IN WRITING

- Repetition
- Poor vocabulary
- Overuse of the passive voice
- Clumsy phrasing
- Redundancies
- Oversimplifications

reader that you are in command of your topic, and prevent irrelevancies and misunderstanding (see Appendix D for tips).

Peer review: feedback as a tool for improving your writing

Any piece of academic writing you submit for assessment, be it a one page-essay or a dissertation, will generate some kind of feedback. In the course of writing up a dissertation, for example, you will receive feedback and guidance from your supervisor which, properly used, should enable you to improve what you have written and to move forward with your research and argument. In most cases, however, feedback is received as part of the assessment process. While comments on your essay script can be useful in future pieces of writing, they usually come too late to improve the piece of work submitted.

Nevertheless, learning how to use feedback to improve your work is an important skill. Providing feedback to someone else also allows you to develop critical skills that will assist you in improving your own work and writing style. In the final stages of writing up, you may therefore wish to consider cooperating with a colleague in peer review of one another's work. Peer review allows you to read, comment upon and provide feedback to one of your class colleagues, and to have them do the same for you. Received feedback can help you to improve your writing before it is finally submitted, as it will help you to identify your strengths, provide insights into your approach and indicate potential for future improvement. Learning how to give feedback can improve your ability to evaluate your own work as well as that of others.

Note: When working with others during the write-up stage of your project, it is just as necessary to indicate where they have been involved in the writing as it is to acknowledge the works of others you use. If you use their words it is **plagiarism** not to acknowledge it, and if you work too closely with them in redrafting your project it could be considered **collusion**.

Peer review can put you in the position of both teacher and learner. When acting as a reviewer, keep at the back of your mind exactly how you would like others to approach your work. How would you like them to address you and your ideas, either through writing, in person or through a video link? It is important to be positive and encouraging. At the same time, the key objective of the peer review process is to learn how to provide and receive constructive feedback. It is nice to have someone say: 'This is really interesting; I really like it', but it isn't really any more helpful than having someone say: 'What nonsense!' As a reader, try to be generous, honest and thorough.

The process of reviewing someone else's work should help you to identify weaknesses in your own work in the future by becoming aware of what a reader looks for. As a writer, try to avoid defensiveness.

> **TIP**   Take a note of particular queries or questions you would like your reviewer to consider when looking over your paper. Give these to your reviewer along with your essay or chapter.

Constructive feedback is intended to help you: it is not personal criticism. Both providing and receiving feedback can help to place your own work in an evaluative context. It helps you to develop a critical eye for your own work in terms of its argument, structure, focus, presentation and writing style, and thereby to improve your performance in future written work.

GUIDELINES

Read the essay through in order to get a general idea of the topic and argument. Read the essay a second time:

- responding to the special requests of the author;
- marking passages that were enlightening or enjoyable to you as a reader with a tick ✔;
- marking passages that were unclear or left you wanting more information with a ?;
- indicating material you think might not belong in the essay or paragraph, because it distracts from overall coherence with a ~;
- indicating lack of logic or flow between paragraphs with a];
- circling any errors of punctuation, spelling or grammar;
- noting questions or comments that will help the author.

The Net can prove itself extremely useful in the peer review process. This is especially true for those engaged in independent study – writing a dissertation, for example – which means you are not in a class or lecture situation, with colleagues you can easily ask for comments or swap your written work with. Word documents can easily be attached to e-mails and sent to a reviewer, who may be a fellow student or an expert in the field whom you are asking to check for, say, any factual errors. You can ask your reviewer to go through your work using their own word processing Comment function to make suggestions, or they can make suggested alterations with the Track Change function switched on, allowing you to view the original and the suggested changes on the same script once it has been returned. Those more technically inclined may consider sending the assignment to the reviewer and using an online video chat service, increasingly available through university computing facilities, to discuss the project. This is particularly useful for those engaged in the presentation of visual material. Normally, after a simple registration process you can download and begin using one of these programs providing you have the relevant technology installed. If you already use a Webcam program, there is no need to register for a dedicated service. However, if you are interested in high-quality images and hassle-free interactions, you might consider signing up for a service such as SightSpeed (http://www.sightspeed.com), which offers one of the best image reproduction facilities on the Web.

TIP If you get to the end of a piece of writing to discover that you have exceeded the word length but do not wish to cut out sentences or paragraphs, edit by removing as many adjectives and adverbs as possible.

For those involved in collaborative projects, online word processors not only allow your entire team to work on the same document, but are equally useful as part of the process of peer review. For example, you can use the online program to jointly write up a draft and then allow your reviewer to access the document and make suggestions and changes. You can access and review the work of your reviewer almost instantaneously.

Equally, do not overlook the possibility of using tools such as online spreadsheets to help you write up your results and receive feedback on a draft piece of work. Spreadsheets such as Xcellery (http://www.xcellery. com) and EditGrid (http://www.editgrid.com) are available online (although Xcellery requires you to have locally installed versions of Excel before you can engage in collaborative exercises), and many allow multiple users to access them, enter data, and manipulate the data online. Not only can you use these online tools to help you develop your datasets or store ideas that you share with others before you begin writing up your final draft, you can also allow your reviewer access to your 'raw data', helping them to 'fact check' your analysis. This may be particularly useful to those involved in statistical analysis. Providing your reviewer with access to your database can help him/her understand your graphical interpretations and presentations, often more thoroughly than they will through your writing alone.

Submitting the final draft

Having revised your work, you will eventually arrive at the point at which you are ready to submit. Before you do, it is worth doing one final review to ensure that your work is coherent, complctc, properly referenced and laid out in the appropriate form. Pay particular attention to your introduction and conclusion. They should set out your argument in general terms, and clearly engage with the question asked. They should also complement one another.

Writing-up is the final stage of the research project, and produces the end product by which the quality, success or failure of your work will be judged. We hope in this chapter to have provided some guidance as to a systematic way you can approach the writing up of your research. As with everything else, writing style, coherence and the ability to construct an appropriate argument improves with practice. Any piece of work will benefit from a systematic approach, however, one in which you are rigorous in the standards you apply to yourself. As you are checking over your work for the final time, remember that everyone's writing style is individual, but make sure that your meaning is clear, that your work is properly paragraphed and can be easily read and understood. In this way, you can maximise the results of your hard work over the course of your research project. (Appendix D offers some useful writing tips.)

CHECKLIST

Citation
- Are all quotes, summaries and references (oral, written or Web) fully cited, using the appropriate stylesheet? If there are references for which you do not have full citations, you need either to find the full citation or omit the reference.
- Are all the Websites cited still available? If not, you will need to include the date on which they were last accessed by you in your citation.

Bibliography
- Do all the works cited appear in the bibliography?
- Are all the items in the bibliography cited in the text?
- Have you conformed consistently with your chosen stylesheet?

Style
- Use double or 1.5 spacing, 12 pt and a standard font unless otherwise advised.
- Do a final proofing, focusing on spelling, punctuation and grammar.

Layout
- Ensure you have inserted a title or title page.
- Ensure you have inserted page numbers and that the pagination is consecutive, particularly between chapters.
- For dissertations, ensure you have an index page, detailing the contents.
- Ensure all figures, diagrams or illustrations are numbered and indexed.
- Are you within the word limit?

Coherence
- Do the introduction and conclusion complement each other?
- Do they address the title directly?
- Is the title appropriate to the finished paper or dissertation?

Exercise 1: Understanding feedback

Take an assignment you have recently completed and review it using the feedback you received. What positive points were made about the essay? What were its shortcomings? Try and understand why you received the feedback you did, and consider how you might improve the piece by rewriting it.

Exercise 2: Peer review

Find a partner interested in peer review and exchange essays or chapters. Review the work using the notation indicated earlier. In addition, try to make constructive comments on the following: focus, structure, argument, spelling and grammar, evidence of reading, bibliography and citation. Give the essay a notional grade (2.1, 2.2), reflecting how you think an assessor would mark the piece of work as it currently stands. You should also indicate a potential grade – what you think the work could receive if appropriate substantive, structural or stylistic changes were made.

Return your essays to one another and talk your colleague through the comments you have made, addressing the questions they raised. Read your reviewer's responses, listen to what is said, perhaps taking notes or clarifying questions, before going away to sort out your essay.

Exercise 3: Final check

Before finally submitting your essay or dissertation, read through it one more time. When you have finished, read through the introduction again. Introduction and conclusion should dovetail, with your discussion coming full circle while remaining clear and coherent. If they do not, consider whether it is your introduction or your conclusion that needs a final revision before submission.

● References and Resources

Crème, P. and Lea, M.R. (1997), *Writing at University: A Guide for Students* (Buckingham: Open University Press). This is a good guide to the generic writing process with specific examples drawn from across a range of different academic disciplines and projects.

Gibaldi, J. (2003), *MLA Handbook for Writers of Research Papers* (New York: MLA). This text has been specifically designed by the Modern Languages Association to provide anyone interested in honest academic work with the guidelines necessary to write-up and properly handle other people's research. It includes information on basic writing techniques, including how to outline, spell, punctuate and document any of the sources you have used during your research.

Greetham, B. (2008), *How to Write Better Essays*, 2nd edition (Basingstoke: Palgrave Macmillan). This text has been designed to help students studying across a range of academic disciplines understand and successfully navigate the writing process.

http://nces.ed.gov/nceskids/createagraph/, accessed 1/3/2007.

http://mathforum.org/alejandre/spreadsheet.html, accessed 10/3/2007.

http://42explore.com/graphs.htm, accessed 5/3/2007.

Lipson, C. (2005), *How to Write a BA Thesis* (Chicago: University of Chicago Press). This text offers students a step-by-step guide through the process of crafting their final-year dissertation. It is aimed at students writing their dissertations in the humanities and social sciences, and incorporates illustrations of how to use all three of the main citation systems used in these disciplines: MLA, APA and Chicago.

Microsoft Office Word Help.

Peck, J. and Coyle, M. (2005), *The Students Guide to Writing*, 2nd edition (Basingstoke: Palgrave Macmillan). This is a good guide to the generic writing process, and a good starting point for students unsure of their writing abilities.

11 Plagiarism and Citation

Once you begin writing up your findings, you have to decide how and when to cite the information you find and use. When citing material you need to consider the problem of both intentional and unintentional plagiarism. Proper address to these issues lies at the heart of honest work. Despite the significant expansion in research opportunities the advent of the internet has allowed, many academics consider its use by students as marked by a decline in academic standards. There is an increasingly widely held view that the more students turn to the internet for information, the more likely they are to engage in forms of plagiarism, from cutting and pasting from Websites to purchasing academic essays online. For the academic reader, plagiarism is often remarkably easy to detect. A simple entry into Google for 'internet plagiarism' returns over one million sites discussing the issue, and offering solutions or ways to detect it within student work. Universities are also developing increasingly sophisticated methods of using technology, including the internet, to filter student work for plagiarism before it ever goes to an assessor. An entire range of software programs have been developed to help teachers and academics discover if a student has plagiarised from an online source.

Many students are not fully aware of the seriousness with which plagiarism is viewed and their own level of responsibility in ensuring they do not engage in it. Many students in whose work plagiarism is detected may not have actively decided to cheat; in fact, many apparently 'genuinely believe that it's okay to take someone else's writing, make a few changes, and then present it as their own' (Southon, 2001, http://www.freesticky.com/ stickyWeb/articles/plagiarism.asp, accessed 1/3/2007). It is not. But because of the ease with which it is possible to plagiarise from online resources, particularly with the cut-and-paste facilities offered through most word-processing programs, plagiarism is flourishing. We would like to use the remainder of this chapter to discuss what plagiarism is, how to avoid it, and how to make sure you use proper citation techniques.

Plagiarism

Plagiarism is an issue of great, and increasing, concern in higher education. This practice may be defined quite simply as passing off others' work as your own. It is, in this sense, an act of theft. It also constitutes a form of fraud in relation to the institution and potentially contributes to a devaluation of the qualifications that other students work hard to acquire. It also represents a lack of achievement for the individual who engages in it, a devaluing of knowledge, learning and academic endeavour. For an academic, plagiarism is the most shameful of accusations.

It hardly needs saying, then, that plagiarism is an unacceptable practice that is treated very seriously in all academic work at whatever level. Plagiarism has always been a potential problem in academic environments but in some ways the emergence of the internet has made the practice easier and more prevalent. With the sheer amount of material available online, and the ease with which such material can be cut and pasted into another document, the temptation to plagiarise is all the greater. There are various reasons why students are sometimes tempted to plagiarise. Often, of course, it is just a cynical attempt to get a better mark without putting in the corresponding effort. Sometimes, however, it may be due to a student's lack of confidence in their own ability; and sometimes it may be the result of simple panic as a student realises they have not left enough time to meet a deadline. Whatever the reasons behind acts of plagiarism, however, they are always regarded as unacceptable and universities have in recent years tightened up considerably their procedures for detecting and punishing plagiarism.

> **Glossary**
> **Plagiarism**: The intentional or unintentional use of someone else's work or ideas without proper permission or citation.

At its most extreme, plagiarism can take the form of appropriating entire pieces of work, or extensive passages from existing pieces, and presenting them as, or incorporating them into, a finished project. Again, with the rise of internet technology and the ease of cutting and pasting, this has become a temptingly easy way of cheating and one that is seen as carrying less of a risk than copying from a book in the library with which the lecturer may well be familiar. Universities have responded to this by the use of online technology itself as a mode of detection and deterrence. Many institutions now operate software packages (such as the JISC Turnitin software program – http://www.jiscpas.ac.uk/turnitinsignup.php) that will scan student work and search the internet for matches in order to detect instances where work has been copied. The result is generally a report that will identify any passages in the piece that match another source, will give Website addresses for the sources used and will produce an overall indication of the level of plagiarism that has taken place. Increasingly, student essays and projects are put through this sort of scanning procedure as a matter of routine before they are accepted for marking. Of course, such systems are not foolproof and do not have access to everything on the internet; but they are generally regarded as being effective enough – and sufficient of a deterrent – to be worth using. One further development that the internet has heralded is the emergence of online agencies that will sell essays to students. Generally, these will be either essays from a store of prewritten pieces covering a wide range of topics or, in some cases, essays written by anonymous authors specifically for the particular assignment. These do not come cheap and they carry no guarantee of quality.

Copying entire works or extensive parts of works produced by others is not the only form that plagiarism takes. Academic convention allows for the reproduction of short quotations or pieces of information from other works and this is generally regarded as a legitimate part of the process: most academic books or articles you care to look at will contain these imported elements. Using material in this way allows you to do a number of things. It enables you to:

- demonstrate that you have researched the field;
- provide support for an argument that you are making or illustrate a point;
- and can allow you to show how your work compares or contrasts with other work on the subject.

It is therefore a useful element in a rounded project. The important thing always, however, is to ensure that any material used in this way is fully acknowledged through appropriate citation of the work from which the material has been taken and of its author. Where no such acknowledgement is given, this again constitutes a form of plagiarism, is unacceptable and is likely to incur penalties. It is important, therefore, that whenever you quote from another source, or import information including items such as tables or graphs, you clearly indicate that you have obtained the material from elsewhere. Where you are directly quoting, you should either use the conventional quotation marks or, in the case of longer quotes, present them as an indented passage. In both cases the material should be followed by a clear citation (we will return in more detail to citation later on).

Of course, you may not always want to quote directly from a source. It may be more appropriate to put the material into your own words; and, indeed, this is often a good idea because it shows that you have grasped the point and meaning of the material that you are using. Where you are paraphrasing in this way, however, you should generally put in a citation for the source that you have employed. The only exceptions to this are occasions where you are stating things that are held to be common knowledge. For example, if you were to state in the course of an essay that *Hamlet* is one of Shakespeare's most studied plays, or that the US political system incorporates a separation of powers, these are statements that you are likely to find in numerous other works, but are held to be so widely known as to require no citation. However, beyond these elements of common knowledge, any more specific point, argument or researched information that you obtain from another source should be cited. Similarly, when using empirical data from another source, whether in the form presented in the original or as adapted for your own presentational purposes, the source should always be noted. In this way you will be able to avoid any allegation of plagiarism in your work.

A further point is worth making about avoiding plagiarism. It will help enormously if (as has been recommended in other chapters of this book) you keep full and accurate records of sources in the course of researching your project. Having proper references for notes you have made and material you have gathered will not only save you time later, it will also reduce the temptation, in a case where, for example, you have a useful quotation but no reference for it, simply to drop the quotation marks and pass it off as your own. Further, having full records of this sort will help you avoid unintentional plagiarism. It is easy, sometimes, to have an idea, an argument or a form of words in your mind that you have acquired from somewhere else but which you come to think of as your own. This is a common and to some extent unavoidable feature of academic work, particularly where the research is being conducted over a sustained period. Where you have full and accurate notes and references, it is a much easier matter to check back and see whether what you have in mind is actually original.

Glossary
Copyright: Official recognition of the ownership of a piece of work or idea.

Another area that merits consideration in this context concerns the implications of working with other people. **Collusion** between students in producing assignments is something that may also be regarded as plagiarism. Of course, there is nothing wrong with students undertaking collaborative study:

the ability to work with others may be regarded as an important transferable skill and indeed some universities include group projects amongst their assessments. However, it is important that any individual assignment that you produce is genuinely your own. Questions of collusion generally arise where students have taken it upon themselves to share out the work on an assignment and then collaborate on producing a final piece. Markers tend to look closely in cases where different students are submitting pieces that are suspiciously similar. Collusion sometimes also occurs when a student, taking pity on a friend who has perhaps not put enough work in, allows that friend access to their own assignment so that they can reword it and submit as their own. Whilst this may seem like an act of generosity, it is nevertheless participation in plagiarism. So, there is nothing wrong with collaborative study – talking things through, kicking around ideas or sharing information about sources – but when it comes to the actual production of a piece of individually assessed work, you need to ensure that it is the fruit of your own efforts.

> **Glossary**
> **Collusion:** Act of collaboration in which two or more individuals work on the same project without acknowledging their interactive efforts.

One final point is worth emphasising in relation to plagiarism. As noted earlier, whilst many acts of plagiarism are cynical attempts at cheating, this is not always the case. Sometimes it occurs when students are lacking confidence in their own ability, or are otherwise struggling with their studies, and plagiarism becomes a tempting way around the problems that they are encountering. In such circumstances, it is always better to consult with your tutor, welfare officer, or other relevant members of staff. Universities want their students to do well and staff will always be happy to offer advice where it can usefully be given. Additionally, most universities now have very well-developed advice and counselling arrangements for students with academic or personal problems, generally operated by trained professionals. There is a good deal of help available and it is always better to make the most of the help and support that is on offer than to resort out of desperation to measures that you may well later regret.

Citation

As was mentioned earlier on, clear and full citation is an essential part of any piece of academic writing. Whereas in other fields, such as those of popular non-fiction or journalism, expectations in this respect are looser, in academia full rigour is demanded. Proper citation is also more than just a way of avoiding any suspicion of plagiarism. The provision of clear and comprehensive citation shows that you have researched the field properly and that you are aware of the useful sources. It also provides the reader with the opportunity to follow up the discussion by going back to the sources that you cite, something which gives the reader the sense that you are confident about the work that you have produced, such that you are happy for the research process that you undertook to be open to scrutiny through reference to sources. Finally, proper citation is an important part of the presentation of your piece of work and gives the impression of a professional job done.

For all these reasons, then, good citation is essential and you need to be aware of the requirements. When it comes to citing traditional sources, there are a number of different citation systems – you need only browse through a few of the academic journals in your field to see how they vary. It is also likely that your own department or institution has its own published guidelines on appropriate systems of citation and you should make sure you consult these. However, probably the most prevalent system now in use, and one of the easiest to employ, is the Harvard system. In this system, citations are made in the text rather than in footnotes or endnotes and mention, in brief form, the author, year of publication and (where appropriate) a page reference. This can be employed when quoting directly or when paraphrasing or otherwise referring to a particular source. For example: 'Toleration has lately fallen on hard times; it is a virtue that has fallen from fashion because it goes against much in the spirit of the age' (Gray, 1995: 18). Or, 'It has been argued that the virtue of toleration has become less fashionable in recent times' (Gray, 1995: 18). Or even, 'Gray argues that toleration is a virtue that has fallen from fashion in the current period' (1995: 18).

In each case, these specific in-text citations will lead a reader who might want to follow them up back to the full reference for the source that will appear in the bibliography. Here they would find:

Gray, J. (1995) *Enlightenment's Wake: Politics and Culture at the Close of the Modern Age* (London: Routledge).

Thus, the reader is able to make easy reference to the full details of the source, such as author, date of publication, title, place of publication and publisher. This system can also be used for articles and chapters in edited books. So, for example, an in-text reference to: (Finlay, 2006: 390) might lead back, in the bibliography, to the following article:

Finlay, C. (2006) 'Violence and Revolutionary Subjectivity: Marx to Zizec', *European Journal of Political Theory,* 5(4), pp. 373–97.

Here the reader can find author, title, name of the journal, volume and issue number, and pages. Similarly, for a chapter in an edited collection, an in-text reference to: (Randall, 2002: 113) might lead back to the following bibliographical entry:

Randall, V. (2002) 'Feminism', in D. Marsh and G. Stoker (eds), *Theory and Methods in Political Science,* 2nd edn (Basingstoke: Palgrave Macmillan), pp. 109–30.

So here we find author, date of publication, chapter title, editor(s), book title (edition if applicable), place of publication, publisher and pages.

You may also sometimes want to cite material that an author has themselves gleaned from another source. If so, the citation should take the form: (Coole cited in Randall, 2002: 111). This would take us back to the bibliographical reference to Randall used in the previous example. Following these conventions will provide you with the means to give authoritative citations and references.

When it comes to internet sources, the rules are a little less hard and fast than they are for traditional sources, partly because online documents do not always provide quite the same publication information. It is also the case that internet documents are frequently moved, removed or modified and so it is hard to be sure that the citation information that you provide will enable the reader to recover the document, or to recover it in the form that you encountered it. For this reason, it is a good idea to save any online sources that you use so that you can produce them later should you be asked to verify the source. When it comes to citation, on the whole it is generally best to stick to the principle of keeping the in-text reference brief and providing a fuller set of publication details in the bibliography. Sometimes this is rather easier said than done if the online document does not give a lot of detail about internet sources. For the in-text reference you should provide:

- name of the author (whether an individual or an organisation)
- date the document was posted or last modified, or, if this is not available, the date you accessed it
- page number (if available).

For the full bibliography reference, you should try to provide:

- name of the author (whether an individual or an organisation)
- date the document was posted or last modified (if available)
- document title
- full URL
- date you accessed the document.

An in-text reference: (Smith, 2001: 3), would lead to the bibliographical reference:

Smith, W. (2001) 'Causes of the First World War', 1 June 2001, http://www.historysite.org.uk/ww1/smith.htm, accessed 10 March 2006.

Aside from Web documents, there may be other online sources that you would want to cite. One mode of researching on the internet is through e-mail, which provides an easy way of accessing people with expertise whom you may want interview or ask for an opinion. Here, an in-text reference: (Jones, 2006), would lead to a bibliographical entry:

Jones, F. (2006) 'Some Ideas about Rembrandt', <FJones@artschool.ac.uk> 1 February 2006.

Here we have the author name, title of e-mail, e-mail address, and date sent.

One other kind of source you might want to cite could be a posting from an e-mail list or newsgroup. Here an in-text citation: (Harris, 2005), would lead to a bibliography entry:

Harris, S. (S.Harris@party.org.uk) 'Why we Lost the Election', sent 1 October 2005, Politics-L <listeserv@data.net>

Here we have the author, the author's e-mail address, title of the posting, date sent, the list name and the general list site.

One thing to note about entries of the latter sort is that, depending upon the nature of the research, you might not want to give out personal information such as individuals' names and contact details. This touches upon some of the ethical questions surrounding the conduct of research that are addressed in the chapter on ethics, and you should turn to this chapter first (Chapter 5) before considering how and what you can and should cite in these contexts. In general, however, sticking carefully to your chosen citation method will help you to avoid many of pitfalls of plagiarism. Finally, if you do choose to use the internet as a source, ensure that it is a valid and good one, of academic merit and produced by someone who knows what they are writing about.

Exercise 1: Copyright – whose idea is it anyway?

Discuss the core principles of copyright and then go online and find five pieces of material that are copyrighted and five that are not. For each piece used discuss why it is or is not copyrighted and how, if it is, you would go about getting permission to use it.

Exercise 2: Collusion – what to avoid

In a brief statement discuss what collusion is and how you can avoid it if you are involved in a group project or exercise, particularly if you are actively involved in a regular study group or set group within a class.

Exercise 3: Proper citation techniques

Each type of resource you utilise will require you to use different citation techniques. Because of this, you should practise. Find eight different types of sources (e.g., book, book chapter, journal article by one author, an online article without an identifiable author, etc.) that you have used in your research (or that are available to you both online and offline) and write up a citation for the source. Check with one of the major citation indexes to see if you have followed the correct procedure.

● References and Resources

Gibaldi, J. (2003), *MLA Handbook for Writers of Research Papers* (New York: MLA).

Indiana University (April 2004), *Writing Tutorial Services*, 'Plagiarism: What it is and How to Recognize and Avoid It', http://www.indiana.edu/~wts/pamphlets/plagiarism.shtml, accessed 23/06/2007.

Lipson, C. (2004), *Doing Honest Work in College: How to Prepare Citations, Avoid Plagiarism, and Achieve Real Academic Success* (Chicago: Chicago University Press). This text offers an accessible introduction to the issues associated with academic honesty. It does so not only in relation to academic writing but also in relation to classroom assignments and the information gathered in, and supplied to, study groups. Overall, the key to its use by students will probably be its extensive tips and advice on how to avoid plagiarism.

Southoe, M. (2001), 'Plagiarism on the Internet: Is Someone Plagiarizing Your Work?,   http://www.freesticky.com/stickyWeb/articles/plagiarism.asp, accessed 01/03/2007.

University of Purdue (September 2006), *The Owl at Purdue*, 'Avoiding Plagiarism', http://owl.english.purdue.edu/owl/resource/589/01, accessed 26/06/2006.

12 Conclusion

The internet represents one of the key advances in communication that has occurred in recent years. The increasing ubiquity of home computers with internet connections and networked workplaces has meant that for many the internet is a core component of their everyday lives. It provides information, entertainment, a mode of communication and a way of organising and arranging personal and professional needs – flights, hotels, video conferences, e-mail.

For those operating in an academic environment, the internet presents particular opportunities and particular challenges. The vast range of information available online means that information literacy in online technology is something no serious researcher can hope, or afford, to do without. From basic searches of the library catalogue of your home institution, to accessing online archives and specific databases in parts of the Invisible Web, the internet provides an unprecedented amount of information about, as well as a route to, previously difficult- or impossible-to-access material.

In order to be able to function within the academic environment, then, even at the most basic level of finding out on which shelf of the library to find a particular book, you need to develop specific information literacy skills. When undertaking research projects, whether involving writing an essay from a series of set questions that accompany a taught academic module within your degree program, or conducting independent research for a dissertation or thesis, you need to be fully familiar with the internet as both a search and a research tool. Historians need to know how to find out what archive material exists, whether it is possible, and how, to access it online. Political scientists, sociologists and anyone else interested in officially compiled statistics, surveys or reports will need the same skills. Regardless of the discipline in which you work, in order to access relevant secondary material – in other words, the scholarship available in the field with which you will need to thoroughly familiarise yourself in order to undertake your research project and engage meaningfully with the topic – you will need to conduct well-organised and clearly focused searches of specialised databases.

Beyond the now indispensable uses of the internet as a tool of access, its increasing social and cultural importance means that it is fast becoming the object of study for researchers interested in topics as diverse as e-activism, electronic art, and the anthropology of online communities. For this reason, as you begin to consider the topic of research you may wish to adopt, the internet itself may form part of your deliberations. It may be the main focus, form a separate section or provide you with an online comparison with what you are studying. For social scientists in particular, even if your focus of study is not directly linked to the virtual world the internet represents, it will inevitably form part of your methodological deliberations. The facility with which questionnaires and interviews can be applied, and the ease with which online observations can be made, mean that at least the possibility of using the internet as a research tool needs to be considered. If and when you do decide to mould your research techniques to include online as well as more traditional techniques of data collection, there will be knock-on effects in terms of the kind of methodological and ethical questions posed. In short, it is now practically impossible to conduct independent research in an academic environment without well-established internet skills and often a wider knowledge of the risks and opportunities of the virtual environment.

We have tried in this book to cover the practicalities of strategic incorporation of the internet into the research process. How you go about something inevitably determines what you can find out, and, properly used, the internet can enrich the quality and depth of the research you undertake. Although online research occupies a place of increasing importance in academic research, if you are to use it strategically it should be to augment rather than displace traditional practices. You can gather as much information as you like, and accumulate the definitive bibliography around any particular topic but, ultimately, your research output will only be as good as the hard work and focused thinking you have put into it. There is no substitute for sitting down and actually reading a book or article, whether online or in hard copy. No amount of surfing, scanning, cutting or pasting can replace this. Your goal in any research project is to increase your own, and possibly others', knowledge or understanding of a topic, as well as to develop and apply your own reasoning, deductive and even creative capacities. There is pleasure as well as pain to be gained from academic endeavour, and your returns will usually be in direct proportion to your efforts. The internet is often seen as a short-cut, something that helps researchers avoid some of the hard graft of research. While it can help with the logistics of researching a given subject, you should recognise that the final research paper, good or bad, will be determined by the quality of the practices you have used, the information you have gathered, and the self-discipline and thoroughness with which you have approached your work.

The omnipresence of the online environment does, of course, have an impact on us all – on what we can know and how we come to know it. It has often been blamed for a crisis in academic standards and the decline of rigorous research practices in the student body in particular. It is easy to do poor research, and improper use of the internet makes it even easier. Properly used, however, the internet can be a platform from which serious study can be conducted. Just as importantly, emphasis on its proper use, combined with competency in the requisite skills and knowledge about the discrete characteristics of the internet as a research medium, can help to ensure the quality of the research produced while using it, and to enrich some research practices which the Net's unregulated and uninformed use seem to be eroding.

Appendix A: Internet Country Codes

ad	Andorra	bv	Bouvet Island
ae	United Arab Emirates	bw	Botswana
af	Afghanistan	by	Belarus
ag	Antigua and Barbuda	bz	Belize
ai	Anguilla	ca	Canada
al	Albania	cc	Cocos (Keeling) Islands
am	Armenia	cf	Central African Republic
an	Netherlands Antilles	cd	Congo, the Democratic
ao	Angola		Republic of the
aq	Antarctica	cg	Congo
ar	Argentina	ch	Switzerland
as	American Samoa	ci	Ivory Coast
at	Austria	ck	Cook Islands
au	Australia	cl	Chile
aw	Aruba	cm	Cameroon
az	Azerbaidjan	cn	China
ba	Bosnia-Herzegovina	co	Colombia
bb	Barbados	cr	Costa Rica
bd	Bangladesh	cu	Cuba
be	Belgium	cv	Cape Verde
bf	Burkina Faso	cx	Christmas Island
bg	Bulgaria	cy	Cyprus
bh	Bahrain	cz	Czech Republic
bi	Burundi	de	Germany
bj	Benin	dj	Djibouti
bm	Bermuda	dk	Denmark
bn	Brunei (Darussalam)	dm	Dominica
bo	Bolivia	do	Dominican Republic
br	Brazil	dz	Algeria
bs	Bahamas	ec	Ecuador
bt	Bhutan	ee	Estonia

eg	Egypt	io	British Indian Ocean Territory
eh	Western Sahara	iq	Iraq
er	Eritrea	ir	Iran
es	Spain	is	Iceland
et	Ethiopia	it	Italy
fi	Finland	jm	Jamaica
fj	Fiji	jo	Jordan
fk	Falkland Islands	jp	Japan
fm	Micronesia	ke	Kenya
fo	Faroe Islands	kg	Kyrgyzstan
fr	France	kh	Cambodia
fx	France (European Territory)	ki	Kiribati
ga	Gabon	km	Comoros
gb	Great Britain	kn	Saint Kitts & Nevis Anguilla
gd	Grenada	kp	North Korea
ge	Georgia	kr	South Korea
gf	French Guyana	kw	Kuwait
gh	Ghana	ky	Cayman Islands
gi	Gibraltar	kz	Kazakhstan
gl	Greenland	la	Laos
gm	Gambia	lb	Lebanon
gn	Guinea	lc	Saint Lucia
gp	Guadeloupe (French)	li	Liechtenstein
gq	Equatorial Guinea	lk	Sri Lanka
gr	Greece	lr	Liberia
gs	S. Georgia & S. Sandwich Islands	ls	Lesotho
		lt	Lithuania
gt	Guatemala	lu	Luxembourg
gu	Guam (USA)	lv	Latvia
gw	Guinea Bissau	ly	Libya
gy	Guyana	ma	Morocco
hk	Hong Kong	mc	Monaco
hm	Heard and McDonald Islands	md	Moldavia
hn	Honduras	mg	Madagascar
hr	Croatia	mh	Marshall Islands
ht	Haiti	mk	Macedonia
hu	Hungary	ml	Mali
id	Indonesia	mm	Myanmar
ie	Ireland	mn	Mongolia
il	Israel	mo	Macau
in	India	mp	Northern Mariana Islands

mq	Martinique (French)	rw	Rwanda
mr	Mauritania	sa	Saudi Arabia
ms	Montserrat	sb	Solomon Islands
mt	Malta	sc	Seychelles
mu	Mauritius	sd	Sudan
mv	Maldives	se	Sweden
mw	Malawi	sg	Singapore
mx	Mexico	sh	Saint Helena
my	Malaysia	si	Slovenia
mz	Mozambique	sj	Svalbard and Jan Mayen
na	Namibia		Islands
nc	New Caledonia (French)	sk	Slovak Republic
ne	Niger	sl	Sierra Leone
nf	Norfolk Island	sm	San Marino
ng	Nigeria	sn	Senegal
ni	Nicaragua	so	Somalia
nl	Netherlands	sr	Suriname
no	Norway	st	Saint Tome (Sâo Tome) and
np	Nepal		Principe
nr	Nauru	sv	El Salvador
nt	Neutral Zone	sy	Syria
nu	Niue	sz	Swaziland
nz	New Zealand	tc	Turks and Caicos Islands
om	Oman	td	Chad
pa	Panama	tf	French Southern Territories
pe	Peru	tg	Togo
pf	Polynesia (French)	th	Thailand
pg	Papua New Guinea	tj	Tadjikistan
ph	Philippines	tk	Tokelau
pk	Pakistan	tm	Turkmenistan
pl	Poland	tn	Tunisia
pm	Saint Pierre and Miquelon	to	Tonga
pn	Pitcairn Island	tp	East Timor
pr	Puerto Rico	tr	Turkey
pt	Portugal	tt	Trinidad and Tobago
pw	Palau	tv	Tuvalu
py	Paraguay	tw	Taiwan
qa	Qatar	tz	Tanzania
re	Réunion (French)	ua	Ukraine
ro	Romania	ug	Uganda
ru	Russian Federation	uk	United Kingdom

um	USA Minor Outlying Islands	vu	Vanuatu
us	United States	wf	Wallis and Futuna Islands
uy	Uruguay	ws	Samoa
uz	Uzbekistan	ye	Yemen
va	The Vatican	yt	Mayotte
vc	Saint Vincent & Grenadines	yu	Yugoslavia
ve	Venezuela	za	South Africa
vg	Virgin Islands (British)	zm	Zambia
vi	Virgin Islands (USA)	zr	Zaire
vn	Vietnam	zw	Zimbabwe

Appendix B: Top-level Domain Organisational Codes

.aero   indicates an air transport industry site

.biz   tends to indicate a business site

.cat   indicates sites dedicated to the Catalan language/culture

.com   tends to indicate a commercial organisation, though the .com ending is not restricted to commercial organisations

.coop   is reserved for cooperatives

.edu   indicates post-secondary educational establishments

.gov   indicates a government site

.info   indicates informational sites, but the .info ending is not restricted to these sites

.int   indicates the site is operated by an international organisation – or an organisation that has been established by a treaty

.jobs   indicates employment-related sites

.mil   reserved for military sites

.mobi   indicates sites catering for mobile devices

.museum   for museums

.name   reserved for sites operated by families and individuals

.net   tends to indicate sites dedicated to network infrastructures

.org   tends to indicate organisations not falling within the other categories

.pro   indicates sites operated by certain professions

.tel   indicates sites dedicated to services involving connections between the telephone network and the internet

.travel   reserved for sites associated with travel such as: travel agents, airlines, hoteliers, tourism bureaus, etc.

The following are in the process of being approved

.post –   postal services

.asia –   Asian community

.geo –   geographically related sites

Appendix C: Domain Codes for Individual US State

State name	Corresponding Domain Code	Example of code as applied to a state government agency in general
Alabama	AL	state.al.us
Alaska	AK	state.ak.us
Arizona	AZ	state.az.us
Arkansas	AR	state.ar.us
California	CA	ca.gov
Colorado	CO	state.co.us
Connecticut	CT	ct.gov
Delaware	DE	state.de.us
Florida	FL	state.fl.us
Georgia	GA	state.ga.us
Hawaii	HI	hawaii.gov
Idaho	ID	idaho.gov
Illinois	IL	ilga.gov
Indiana	IN	state.in.us
Iowa	IA	state.ia.us
Kansas	KS	ks.org
Kentucky	KY	state.ky.us
Louisiana	LA	state.la.us
Maine	ME	me.us
Maryland	MD	mlis.state.md.us
Massachusetts	MA	mass.gov
Michigan	MI	mi.gov
Minnesota	MN	mn.us
Mississippi	MS	state.ms.us
Missouri	MO	state.mo.us
Montana	MT	state.mt.us
Nebraska	NE	ne.gov
Nevada	NV	state.nv.us

State name	Corresponding Domain Code	Example of code as applied to a state government agency in general
New Hampshire	NH	state.nh.us
New Jersey	NJ	state.nj.us
New Mexico	NM	nm.us
New York	NY	state.ny.us
North Carolina	NC	nc.net
North Dakota	ND	nd.gov
Ohio	OH	state.oh.us
Oklahoma	OK	state.ok.us
Oregon	OR	state.or.us
Pennsylvania	PA	state.pa.us
Rhode Island	RI	tate.ri.us
South Carolina	SC	sc.govt
South Dakota	SD	state.sd.us
Tennessee	TN	state.tn.us
Texas	TX	state.tx.us
Utah	UT	state.ut.us
Vermont	VT	state.vt.us
Virginia	VA	state.va.us
Washington	WA	wa.gov
West Virginia	WV	state.wv.us
Wisconsin	WI	state.wi.us
Wyoming	WY	state.wy.us

Appendix D: Writing Tips

These queues should help you to start out on a paragraph or sentence.

1. Cues that lead the reader forward:

To show addition:

Again,	Finally,	Next,
Moreover,	Further,	First, second, etc.
Besides . . . ,	Furthermore,	Lastly,
Equally important	Nor	In addition,
By inference	The implication is	A reasonable conjecture

To show time:

At length,	Finally,	Formerly,
Immediately thereafter,	Then	Next
Soon	Later	Before
Afterwards,	Previously	Initially

2. Cues that make the reader stop and compare:

But	Notwithstanding	Although
Yet	On the other hand,	While this is true
The former/latter	On the contrary,	After all
However,	Despite this,	Conversely,
Still,	For all that,	Simultaneously,
Never/nonetheless,	In contrast,	Meanwhile,
Actually,	At the same time,	If . . . . then,

3. Cues that develop and summarise:

Providing examples:

For instance,	To demonstrate	As an illustration
For example,	To illustrate	A case in point
As the figures/diagram/chart indicates . . .		

To emphasise:

Obviously	Indeed	That is (to say)
In fact,	In any case,	Clearly,
As a matter of fact,	In any event,	Necessarily,
Evidently	Undoubtedly	Certainly

To repeat:

In brief,	In other words,	As noted,
In short,	As discussed,	

To introduce conclusions:

Hence,	Accordingly,	Thus,
Therefore,	Consequently,	As a result,
Basically,	Essentially,	In effect,
So,	For that reason	In view of this,
We may infer	Inevitably,	Of course,

To summarise:

In brief,	In summary,	To conclude,
On the whole,	In conclusion,	To recap,

Make a copy of these and post them up beside your computer screen so you can refer to them easily when you are writing. They can help you out when you are stuck for something to say, or searching for a way to proceed.

Appendix E: Generating Diagrams and Charts:

For Diagrams:

1. Click on the *Drawing* toolbar, then select *Diagram or Organisational Chart* (or select diagram from the *Insert* menu).
2. Choose one of the available diagram types.
3. Click OK.
4. Do one or more of the following:
   (a) If you want to add text to an element in the diagram, right-click the element, click *Edit Text*, and then type in the text.
   (b) If you want to add an element, click *Insert Shape* on the *Diagram* toolbar.
   (c) If you want to add a preset design scheme, click *AutoFormat* on the *Diagram* toolbar, and select a style from the Diagram Style Gallery.
5. Click outside the drawing when you are finished.

You should note that when working with Cycle Diagrams you can only add text to the text placeholders that appear when you insert the diagram or diagram element.

For Charts:

1. On the *Insert* menu, click *Object*, and then click the *Create New* tab. This will list all the programs and types of illustration you can use in your document.
2. In the Object type box, click *Microsoft Graph Chart*, and then click OK. This will produce a bar chart and an associated datasheet containing sample data.
3. To generate your own graph, you can replace the sample data with your own. Click a cell on the datasheet (which automatically opens when you choose to insert as graph), and then type in new text or numbers. If your dataset is large, it is also possible to import the dataset (and a completed graph) from another file or program, including Lotus 1-2-3 or Microsoft Excel.
4. To return to Microsoft Word, click the Word document.

Appendix F: Selected Online Resources:

Sites for finding newsgroups and listservers:
http://www.liszt.com
http://www.ForumOne.com
http://www.well.com

Sites for finding databases and people:
http://dir.yahoo.com/Education/Higher_Education/Colleges_and_
    Universities/By_Region/Countries
http://www.bigfoot.com
http://www.worldE-mail.com

Sites dedicated to evaluating Web-based information:
http://www2.widener.edu/Wolfgram-Memorial-Library/Webevaluation/
    Webeval.htm
http://www.lib.sfu.ca/researchtools/internetsearch/Webevaluation.htm
http://www.sosig.ac.uk/desire/internet-detective.html

Sites dedicated to netiquette:
http://www.fau.edu/netiquette/net/index.html
 http://www.virtualsalt.com/evalu8it.htm
http://www.albion.com/netiquette/index.html

Sites dedicated to understanding and avoiding internet plagiarism:
http://www.lib.duke.edu/libguide/plagiarism.htm
http://www.lib.monash.edu.au/vl/sociol/soc17.htm
http://www.lib.monash.edu.au/vl/cite/citecon.htm

Sites dedicated to internet citation:
http://www.bedfordstmartins.com/online/citex.html
http://www.lib.duke.edu/libguide/bib_Webpage.htm
http://www.lib.vt.edu/eresources/eref/citation.html

Sites dedicated to finding sources on the 'undiscovered', 'hidden' or 'gated' internet:
http://www.invisible-Web.net
http://www.invisibleWeb.com
http://www.virtualsalt.com/search.htm

Sites for finding subject directories:
http://www.about.com
http://www.looksmart.com

General social science databases:
http://www.sosig.ac.uk
http://www.bubl.ac.uk
http://infomine.ucr.edu

Sites dedicated to finding media and reference outlets:
http://ajr.newslink.org
http://64.227.22.235/links/news
http://www.iTools.com/research-it/research-it.html
http://www.abyznewslinks.com

Sites dedicated to political information:
http://nationaljournal.com/misc/pusa_splash.htm
http://www.open.gov.uk/Home/HOHome/1,1031,~801b22~fs~en,00.html
http://www.policysite.org/
http://www.firstgov.gov/
http://library.albany.edu/subject/polsci.htm
http://www.sosig.ac.uk/politics/
http://www.betterworldlinks.org/politik.htm
http://userpage.chemie.fu-berlin.de/adressen/eu.html

Glossary

Academic legitimacy: means that the techniques you use to underpin your research, and the sources you use, provide information or data that conforms to the recognised standard of reliability and validity governing your academic discipline.

Bias: the introduction of an error into an analysis due to inclinations that brings in impartial judgement to the analysis or collection of data. Statistically, bias is the introduction of an error due to the inadvertent (or deliberate) favouring some results over others.

Blog: see Weblog

Blogging: process of creating, updating and posting a blog.

Browser: a software package that allows you to access the internet. It is normally used to access the World Wide Web. The most common browsers are Internet Explorer, Netscape and, increasingly, Firefox.

Categorical data: data that can be separated into specific mutually exclusive categories based upon some common characteristic.

Charts: illustrate the relationship between groups, individuals and variables within datasets.

Chat room: a Website (or part of a site) which provides a virtual space for individuals to discuss issues of common interest in real time. Most chat rooms can be accessed and used without the use of a special dedicated software program.

Closed-ended questions: research questions that have predefined response categories. Often used when the researcher is interested in coding the results for statistical analysis.

Coding: the process of labelling (or tagging) your data. The labels you use to separate pieces of data are known as the **codes** (or tags). Codes can be anything from a single word to a complex idea incorporating a range of related concepts.

Collusion: act of collaboration in which two or more individuals work on the same project without acknowledging their interactive efforts.

Computer-mediated-communications (CMC): the act of interacting with other individuals one-to-one, one-to-a-group or group-to-group, through computers.

Confidentiality: guarantees that only the individuals who are supposed to have access to the information you collect are granted access to it, particularly the identity of any study participants, or answers that they do not explicitly allow you to use in your write-up.

Constant variable: a variable that can take on only one value or category.

Continuous data: data that can take on an almost limitless number of values and can be meaningfully subdivided into continually smaller increments.

Copyright: the ownership of an idea, product, expression or information. If something is copyrighted you must obtain permission before you can use it in your own work and properly cite it.

Dependent variable: within experimental methods the dependent variable is what the researcher is interested in observing or measuring. It is the variable that is hypothesised to alter in relation to changes in the independent variable.

Descriptive statistics: numerical summaries of data. Descriptive statistics are not designed to explain or test a hypothesis. The most common descriptive statistics are probably the mean, median, mode and standard deviation.

Diagrams: illustrate the relationship between concepts, groups or individuals, but are not numerically based.

Dichotomous variable: a variable that can have one of two values or categories attached to it.

Discussion group: See newsgroups

Document: a written, printed, photographed, painted or recorded material that can be used to provide information or evidence.

Domain: the unique name or address assigned to every internet site. All domain names have at least two parts separated by dots (.) and forward slashes (/).

E-mail: short name for electronic mail. E-mail is a program that allows users to send messages from one computer to another over the internet. E-mail messages are stored in an electronic mailbox (an area of memory on the host server) until checked and deleted by the recipient.

Epistemology: the study of knowledge.

Face-to-face communications (FTF): the process of talking to or communicating with another individual or group in person, where you can both see each other.

File Transfer Protocol (FTP): the protocol governing the transfer of text or binary files between computers. Because FTP uses the TCP/IP it can be used to download everything from a simple text-based Webpage all the way to complete computer programs.

Focus group: a type of interview technique that involves bringing together a small group of individuals to pose questions to or to direct in discussion in order to gauge their attitudes and opinions.

Generalisability: when the findings of an individual study can be applied to other studies or samples. In quantitative studies generalisability generally refers to whether the sample population was drawn in such a way as to ensure that the results of the study can be applied to the entire population from which the sample was drawn.

Gopher: an online information distribution and retrieval protocol that predated the WWW. Gopher files brought together text-based files and then arranged them into hierarchically organised lists. With the rise of the WWW most gopher sites have been converted into HTML files.

Hawthorne effect: when a subject alters his/her behaviour as a result of their knowledge that they are being observed.

Hidden web: see Invisible web.

Homepage: the top or main page of a Website. Typically, it is the first page you visit when entering a site and it serves as a site index to the information available on the remainder of the site (or to information that the site links to).

Hypertext Markup Language (HTML): the language of the internet. It is the language Web pages are written in and indicates to your Web browser how to display information contained on the page.

Hypertext Transfer Protocol (**HTTP**): the underling protocol used by the World Wide Web. The protocol defines how messages are formatted and transmitted between computers. HTTP is also the protocol used by servers and Web browsers to interpret the actions they should take in response to inputed commands.

Hypothesis: a proposition as to why a particular phenomenon occurs or a statement as to how two or more variables relate to one another.

Inferential statistics: numerical summaries, drawn from a sample, that are designed to help you make judgements about a larger population or test a specific hypothesis.

Information gateway: a Website consisting of a collection of evaluated and categorised Websites that has been specifically designed to link you to subject specific resources and networks.

Information literacy: full competency in the processes and technologies of sourcing and accessing information, including the use of online information and techniques.

Informed consent: the concept that when conducting research involving human beings, participants are made fully aware that they *are* participants; that they are properly informed as to the nature and purpose of the research; and that they are given the opportunity to refuse to participate or to withdraw from the project.

Independent variable: within experimental methods the independent variable is the variable that the researcher manipulates, or changes on purpose in order to measure its impact on the dependent variable.

Instant messaging (IM): a software program that allows for real-time typed communication between two or more people operating on their computers at the same time.

Internet (Net): a worldwide system of computer networks connected through TCP/IP protocol which allows users at one computer to access information from any other computer in the network (if they have permission).

Internet Protocol (IP): the computer protocol responsible for regulating the 'data packets' sent from one computer to another through phone lines, optical cables and satellites. The Internet Protocol works in conjunction with the Transmission Control Protocol (TCP) to regulate the transmission of information from one computer to another.

Internet Service Provider (ISP): a business or organisation that an individual can subscribe to in order to gain access to the internet.

Interval data: data that can be used to establish measurements of statistical similarities and differences.

Interview: a type of survey used to collect data from an individual through a directed conversation. Most often used in qualitative studies in order to gather in-depth information.

Invisible Web: name given to internet sites that are not catalogued by standard search engines or that have not been added to a standard subject catalogue.

Keyword: the term, or combination of terms, that is entered into a search engine or directory.

Link: an embedded element on a Web page that takes you from your current location to that specified in the link. Links are typically underlined and blue (until used, when they turn a shade of purple)

Listserv (mailing list): a software program that allows the owner of the list to automatically distribute e-mail to everyone who subscribes to the list.

Lurking: the process of following discussions occurring on message boards, in newsgroups, chatrooms, or any other interactive system, without actively contributing to, or participating, in the discussion itself.

Mean: arithmetic average.

Median: middle value.

Message board: similar to a chat toom but uses online software technology in order to facilitate asynchronous (instead of real-time) discussions.

Mode: most common value.

Multipurpose Internet Mail Extensions (MIME): a standard for defining the types of files attached to mail messages. By communicating what kind of file is being sent the standard enables the receiving computer to automatically recognise and display of the information contained in the file.

Net: abbreviated form of internet.

Netiquette: conventions that govern online communications.

Newsgroups: forums used for the discussion of a specific topic. They work like e-mail, but instead of receiving individual mail participants read and post messages to a bulletin board accessible to anyone participating in the discussion.

Non-probabilistic: a sampling technique that does not attempt to randomise the sample. As such, it is not possible to engage in generalisation based on the study's findings.

Non-random sample: a sampling technique that cannot ensure each item has an equal chance of being selected. Cases are selected based on non-random criteria such as previous cases, the availability of the cases (opportunistic sampling), or expert knowledge.

Observations: involve the collection of data by watching, listening, touching or tasting something. Observational data can be left in its qualitative form or coded for quantification and statistical analysis.

Ontology: concerned with what constitutes reality or what kinds of things exist. As such, it helps us determine what we believe constitutes objective and subjective existence and thus what is an acceptable type of research design.

Open-ended questions: research questions that have no predefined response categories. Used when the researcher wants respondents to provide feedback in their own words in order to create a rich understanding of the situation as understood by the research participant.

Opportunistic sampling: drawing a sample based on its ready availability.

Ordinal data: data that can be placed in different orders.

Plagiarism: using, relying on or directly integrating someone else's work into your own without acknowledging that work. Treating someone else's ideas, or work, as if it were your own.

Polytomous variable: a variable that can be divided into a number of different categories.

Population: the entire collection of individuals, items or data from which a sample can be drawn.

Portal: a Website that acts as a gateway to a range of different online services and tools on a single page.

Primary sources: a primary source is an original work. It represents original thinking, observations, interviews, activities, accomplishments, reports on discoveries or events, or shares new information.

Probabilistic: a sampling technique that uses random sampling procedures to help ensure that its findings can be generalised beyond the study itself.

Qualitative: measurements of qualities, which tend to be expressed in words.

Quantitative: a measurement of amount or quantity expressed numerically.

Questionnaire: a survey relying on a specifically designed form containing a set of questions intended to gather information. Generally questionnaires are used to collect data that can be coded, quantified, and used in a statistical analysis.

Random sample: a sample in which every member of a population has an equal chance of being included.

Relevance: the way a search engine ranks and displays returns, or how close these returns are to what you are actually looking for.

Reliability: refers to how accurate your data gathering methods are. A reliable technique allows you to repeat the measurement using the same technique (in identical circumstances) and get the same results each time.

Representativeness: indicates how accurately the individuals or observations used in your study (the sample) speak for all the people you could have interviewed or sites you could have observed (the population).

Research: the process of systematically gathering information in an attempt to answer a specific question in order to solve a problem.

Research process: the systematic steps that are employed to gather, analyse and write-up information that has been collected in order to answer a specific question or problem.

Sample: a 'small' selection used to represent the whole population.

Search engine: computer program which uses electronic spiders to roam the internet compiling addresses that are then placed into the engine's database of sites. It is this database of sites that you then access when using the engine – not the Web itself.

Search tools: programs that have been designed to help you search the Web. The two most common forms of search tools are search engines and subject directories.

Secondary sources: consist of an analysis, interpretation or a restatement of primary sources. They reinterpret or discuss the meaning and context of primary sources.

Spam: an unsolicited bulk message sent generally to your e-mail (though it is increasingly appearing on blogs and in Wikis).

Spread: the distance between the highest and lowest observed value of your dataset.

Standard deviation: a measurement of the spread of values around the mean.

Subject directories: are catalogues of resources that you can search via the site's hierarchy. These sites have been developed by humans and the resources contained in their catalogues have been selected, often by subject specialists, for their quality and relevance to the subject.

Surfing: a process of going from Website to Website using hypertext links in an almost blind attempt to find 'something'.

Survey: the process of gathering information through interviews or questionnaires in an attempt to comprehensively understand or scrutinise a situation, event or issue.

TCP/IP protocol: the combined Transmission Control Protocol/Internet Protocol. TCP/IP is the basic language used to connect host computers to the internet.

Telnet: used to indicate terminal emulation or the process of using your computer to access and use the programs housed on a different computer. As such, you are using your computer to direct and use the programs and files on a host server. To start a Telnet session, you must log in to a server by knowing its internet address and having a proper login name and password. For information on the commands that you will need to use to operate a Telnet link see: http://www.microsoft.com/resources/documentation/ windows/xp/all/proddocs/en-us/telnet_ commands.mspx?mfr=true

Tertiary sources: consist of materials in which the information from secondary sources has been selected, condensed and reproduced in a convenient, easy-to-read form.

Transmission Control Protocol (TCP): the protocol responsible for managing the flow of information packets comprising the internet, and ensuring that the information packets arrive at their destination computers without errors.

Triangulation: the use of multiple data sources or techniques to check the accuracy and reliability of your findings. It is particularly useful in qualitative studies.

Universal Resource Locator (URL): the URL address is the address that Web browsers use for locating files and other resources located on the internet.

Usenet: an internet-based discussion network. This network is comprised of a range of subject-specific newsgroups in which members can read and post messages.

Validity: refers to whether your data collection tools are measuring what you think they are. A perfectly valid tool will have a one-to-one correlation between what you say it is measuring and what it measures.

Web: see World Wide Web

Web browser: a software program that is capable of reading and displaying Web pages, allowing its user to interact with the resources available throughout the internet.

Web ring (Webring): a way of organising sites in such a way that you are linked from one site to another, so that if you continue visiting the next link you will eventually go back to the first site.

Weblog: a personal online journal. They can be comprised of as little as a list of personal postings appearing in reverse chronological order all the way to journals with graphics, links and interactive zones.

Wiki: a Website that can be accessed and edited by anyone at any time. A Wiki site is best viewed as a collaborative or group project.

World Wide Web (WWW): the largest single part of the internet. The Web consists of a range of linked text, image, sound and video documents, which are accessible via a Web browser based on a simple point-and-click graphical interface.

WYSIWYG: 'What You See Is What You Get'. Commonly used to describe software programs that allow you to develop Web pages without having to know or even examine the underling HTML tags.

Index